Readers of the Book of Life

Readers of the Book of Life

Contextualizing Developmental Evolutionary Biology

Anton Markoš

OXFORD
UNIVERSITY PRESS

2002

OXFORD

UNIVERSITY PRESS

Oxford   New York
Auckland   Bangkok   Buenos Aires   Cape Town   Chennai
Dar es Salaam   Delhi   Hong Kong   Istanbul   Karachi   Kolkata
Kuala Lumpur   Madrid   Melbourne   Mexico City   Mumbai   Nairobi
São Paulo   Shanghai   Singapore   Taipei   Tokyo   Toronto

and an associated company in Berlin

Published by Oxford University Press, Inc
198 Madison Avenue, New York, New York 10016

www.oup.com

Oxford is a registered trademark of Oxford University Press

Library of Congress Cataloging-in-Publication Data
Markoš, Anton, 1949–
Readers of the book of life : contextualizing developmental
evolutionary biology / by Anton Markoš.
     p.   cm.
Includes bibliographical references.
ISBN 0-19-514948-3
1. Biology—Philosophy.   I. Title.
QH331 .M315 2002
570'.1—dc21   2001051352

9 8 7 6 5 4 3 2 1

Printed in the United States of America
on acid-free paper

To Fatima and Zdeněk

ACKNOWLEDGMENTS

This work was supported in part by the Grant Agency of the Czech Republic (401/97/0283), by the Grant Agency of the Charles University Prague (117/1998), and by the Ministry of Education of the Czech Republic (110000001).

I thank my colleagues from the Charles University in Prague for stimulating comments. I am particularly indebted to Zdeněk Neubauer, Alexandr Matoušek, Pavel Kouba, and Ivan M. Havel. My wife, Fatima Cvrčková, was always prepared to read my gibberish and pinpoint a concise solution. She is also the author of all figures appearing in this book. Ms. April Retter and Ms. Jennifer Bew provided invaluable help with the English translation. My thanks also to the editorial staff at Oxford University Press — specifically, Kirk Jensen and Robin Miura — and to the copyeditor, Patricia J. Watson.

Finally, my warm thanks for invaluable comments from reviewers of the first draft of the manuscript. Two of them — Scott F. Gilbert and Stuart Kauffman — have revealed themselves; I can only guess the identity of the other three. They helped to improve the text enormously; what the reader still finds disappointing is my responsibility alone.

CONTENTS

Readers of the Book of Life

It is said that when public dissections first began, the bodies used to be ordered from the executioner, who drowned a selected condemned man. It happened one day that in course of one such dissection an only partly drowned man woke up and opened his eyes. A wave of dismay swept the square. Novalis takes this horrific episode as an example: we are dissecting not only the damned, but also almost everything in the world. We dissect the world, which we have drowned so deftly that nobody has even noticed the fact. What a horror if this partly drowned world should wake up; what will we read in its face? And how much greater will our horror be if we have drowned it properly!

Zdeněk Kratochvíl

INTRODUCTION

Why should I, a busy man, read this book;
and what may I gain therefrom?

Anonymous referee

Primarily, this book is not epistemology, despite its focus in part I. As a biologist, I try above all to contemplate what living beings are and how sciences have reflected their nature in the course of the last hundred years. My basic point here is that life is a hermeneutic category. But, then, who in natural sciences knows what hermeneutics is? Isn't it—God forbid!—a version of "postmodern," or even New Age gobbledygook? I needed to start by introducing this method of interpretation, of unfolding meaning, which is widely used in the humanities. I chose to do so against the background of "objectivist" science, which is much more familiar to natural scientists. But in contrast to objectivism, hermeneutics might appear too "mystical" and incomprehensible for an untrained eye, thereby strengthening prejudices against humanities that exist in the scientific community. I therefore include a demonstration of a version of contemporary gnosis, as a true and opposite extreme to objectivism, simply to set the scene. What came out are chapters of the first, epistemological, part of this book: chapter 2 on hermeneutics is framed by chapter 1 characterizing objectivist science and by chapter 3 on contemporary philosophical gnosis.

Part II is devoted to the analysis of some currents of thought in twentieth-century biology, often half-forgotten, distorted, or discarded. Today, they often persist only as anecdotal shortcuts, despite years of experimental and theoretical work of the highest quality. Information about such currents, even if their representatives may still live among us, will almost never reach the textbooks. This is the fate of, for example, epigenetics (though it has currently resurfaced), biological structuralism, teleological explanations in evolutionary biology, views of the organism and superorganism, vitalism, and so forth.

Part III presents my attempt to comprehend living beings, a view that I call hermeneutic. My final goal is to show a parallel between a biological species and human culture. To avoid misunderstanding, I take my material mainly from publications that have appeared in recent years. Throughout the entire book, I have opted, perhaps more often than usual, for verbatim quotations from original authors, which I use as cues for the proper reading of my own text.

My goal is that my text should be readable and understandable for both biologists and those working in the humanities, for people concerned in different contexts with *physis*, life, knowledge. Maybe I should have written two different introductions directed toward these two different kinds of reader, to explain my intentions. But two introductions would raise the question of which should be put first. Maybe the solution would lie in a hypertext form. After all, the topic itself is of such a nature: culture, history, organisms, ontogeny, evolution, and so on, refer to each other and to many other things in a genuine "hypertext" way.

Finally, I would like to dissipate suspicions that I am calling for a paradigm shift that would completely reformulate contemporary biology. I do feel quite happy in the framework of biology as it is. What I am trying to grasp is to what extent "biology" covers all facets of the domain of "life." My opinion is that there is no one-to-one correspondence between both, and that life has aspects that are not—and cannot be—captured by contemporary biology. Call such conviction vitalism if you wish, but don't stop simply at calling names—try to understand what the word has meant in different historical contexts.

The reviewer who provided the epigraph for this preface also said: "I had the feeling, at the end, of coming out by the same door where in I went." I wish all readers to have the same feeling after reading this book. After all, the hermeneutic task for the reader is not to know what the author of the text intended, but to extract the meaning that is personally relevant.

Part I

Readers of the Book of the Universe

ATTACCTGGAT
CCGCCAGTACG
TAG:AACT.ACAT
CGAA & TTGTTAC
TGAT
CCGCCAC
T.AAAC
A GGTA
TACCAGA
CCGCTAG:
TTGTTA
GAAATACT
TCCAGAT
CCGTCA:
TTGCCCA
TCGA:AACGTACCGA

Part I

READERS OF THE BOOK
OF THE UNIVERSE

> Philosophy is written in this grand book of the universe,
> which stands continually open to our gaze. But the book
> cannot be understood unless one first learns to comprehend
> the language and to read the alphabet in which it is
> composed. It is written in the language of mathematics,
> and its characters are triangles, circles, and other geometric
> figures, without which it is humanly impossible to understand
> a single word of it; without these one wanders about in a
> dark labyrinth.
>
> Galileo

Both natural and cultural sciences may claim to be heirs of these famous words by the founder of modern science. Natural scientists will call for a literal reading of Galileo's words: Nature gives herself unambiguously, and language and its symbols are also unambiguous. What we need to do is to decipher or, better, to decode gradually, step by step, all the letters of Nature's alphabet, the words and their (unambiguous) meaning, and by so doing we shall finally understand the whole message. If our methods are adequate, then what has once been deciphered will remain so forever and may, at best, be refined. This belief lies in the background of the mechanistic worldview.

Philosophers, however, will point to the fact that in performing the above-mentioned activities, a great many natural scientists have somehow forgotten that their models of the world are metaphors based on man-made machines. They have simply reified the metaphor and then claim that nature is in very deed mechanistic. Could it even be that scientists themselves are the authors of the Book and that they force Nature to behave according to it? Such is the critique offered by Friedrich Nietzsche of the mechanists of his time:

> While you rapturously pose as deriving the canon of your law from nature, you want something quite the reverse from that, you strange actors and self-deceivers! Your pride wants to prescribe your morality, your ideal, to nature, yes to nature itself, and incorporate them in it; you . . . would like to make all existence exist only after your own image. All your love of truth notwithstanding, you have compelled yourselves for so long and with such persistence and hypnotic rigidity to view nature falsely, . . . you are no longer capable of viewing it in any other way—and some abysmal arrogance infects you at last with the Bedlamite hope that, because you know how to tyrannize over yourselves, . . . nature too can be tyrannized over. (Nietzsche, 1984, p. 21)

In the metaphor of the Book of the Universe, we could also stress the idea of a "book" that is open for "reading"—not simply "decoding" according to some unambiguous clue, but genuine reading! The reader moves in a circle of never-ending confrontation of her own experience, she herself constantly changing during the reading. A single unambiguous interpretation valid for all epochs, readers, and situations is only a limiting case never encountered in the real world—such cases may exist only as special constructs (e.g., computer languages, mathematical theories). For Hans-Georg Gadamer, the task of hermeneutics lies in confronting the polarity between the intimately known and the alien, in uncovering conditions that make understanding possible despite linguistic, temporal, or contextual distances. Interpretation is always a process, a creative discovering of new meanings. What, then, happens if we view Galileo's Book through Gadamer's (1996) prism?

> Of course the reader before whose eyes the great book of world history simply lies open does not exist. But neither does the reader exist who, when he has his text before him, simply reads what is there. Rather, all reading involves application, so that a person reading a text is himself a part of the meaning he apprehends. He belongs to the text that he is reading. The line of meaning that the text manifests to him as he reads it always and necessarily breaks off in an open indeterminacy. He can, indeed he must, accept the fact that future generations will understand differently what he has read in the text. (p. 340)

In his book, Gadamer describes the long journey of hermeneutics, starting with the early interpretation of the biblical text and ending with the modern method. This method is used by all cultural sciences in cases where the historical nature of knowledge plays a primary role, or where a meaning has to be deciphered, that is, wherever we encounter an internal indication of context (history, linguistics, exegesis of texts, aesthetics). Many thinkers point to the fact that the very nature of the world is also hermeneutic. Only in our Euro-American civilization was this view, over the last few centuries, somehow restricted to the subconscious. We never start from zero—we always own the reality and shape *our* world from what has already existed before.

But the task may not end even with hermeneutics. The human spirit can push even harder and end in some version of gnosis or panpsychism, for example, the following radical interpretation of the Book of Nature by Raymond Ruyer (1974):

> The Universe, in its all-embracing unity, is a language to be spoken. It is not a text to be read, emanating from a speaker or an Author who should be understood and the message thus transmitted exactly decoded. It is not a text, but an endless potential for creating texts. God (or the Great Mother) is a universal participable. He/She is not a Speaker, but a universal language—the foundation of all languages. A tongue indeed universal, motherly, live and life providing, spoken not by imitation, but by participant invention. The Universe is a culture, not a nature, it is an active enactment, and not something that has been constructed. (pp. 201–203)

Three interpretation frames—those of physicalism, hermeneutics, and gnosis—are the subject of chapters 1–3. Why do I include this "epistemological" part in a biology book? When I started this project, I often encountered situations where my scientific colleagues had no idea about the very existence of hermeneutics. Often they took it as just another of the plethora of superstitious beliefs that belong to boxes labeled "philosophy," "metaphysics," "postmodernism," or even "New Age." I therefore found it necessary to write an introductory chapter devoted to hermeneutics. Then, just to highlight the differences and to increase the sensitivity threshold for distinguishing different branches of human knowledge, I decided to frame that chapter between two others. It is therefore preceded by chapter 1, dealing with a scientific or "objectivist" worldview so often encountered in practicing natural scientists. To distinguish it from mythological part of human experience, chapter 2 on hermeneutics is followed by chapter 3 illustrating a radical gnostic worldview.

Despite their apparent irreconcilability, our three selected approaches—objectivist, hermeneutic, and gnostic—refer to and condition each other. They may be viewed as three points on a scale or, even better, vertices of a triangle. All three contexts are cosmological, and it is only too easy to become trapped in endless speculations in either of them. I do not wish to succumb to such temptations, and therefore I limit myself in parts II and III to the area bounded by the metaphysical realism typical of natural science on the one hand, and by hermeneutics on the other. My ambition is to show the hermeneutic nature of *all* living beings (i.e., all those beings that are the subject of biology).

Unification of Knowledge — Possible, Wanted, Necessary?

These days we often hear calls for the unification of human knowledge. Paradoxically, the final end of such attempts at unification would depend heavily on the point of departure; that is, several different forms of "unified" knowledge could be attained. If we start from the triune scheme as set out above, we get three different results.

First, one of the main streams of unification may derive from the extreme metaphysical view that the world is identical to objective reality, and that the reductionist method is the most appropriate (or maybe the only) tool for understanding this reality. It follows that such an effort is driven by the aim to include all knowledge in the realm of the natural ("objective") sciences. It is made legitimate by a conviction that knowledge can be based on a small number of simple axioms: the existence of objective reality, strict causality, and a limited set of basic and unchanging laws. A necessary precondition of science based on such a foundation is therefore the suspension of historical exegesis, an a priori assumption of constancy, of the stability of the objects under consideration. This is usually expressed in some variant of the following statement: "The natural sciences and their core — physics — have in principle discovered how nature works; now it is sufficient to rigorously apply the scientific methods of reduction and synthesis to all other realms of knowledge in order to reveal basic truths and laws even there." The best candidate for such a transformation at the present time is, of course, biology, followed by history and by psychology, sociology, and other sciences concerned with the human mind. Problems such as these are dealt with in chapter 1.

Second, the struggle for unification could also emerge from the ontology of the hermeneutic circle, which will accentuate the historic nature of all knowledge and consider experimental science as merely another branch of knowledge. This view would stress the fact that our worldview is dependent on context and experience. In the preceding paragraph it was tacitly assumed that all aspects of reality lie *in front* of the observer; that is, they are not part of him. The task of the observer, then, is simply to decipher what is important and exclude what is accidental. During the process of observation, the observer must suppress any change in his thinking and suspend any speculation or exegesis. Such a skill can be attained only by special training. The hermeneutic approach, in contrast, recognizes the fact that knowing the world is the task of the consciousness, which itself is embedded in that same world in which it participates. This recognition opens up a space for hermeneutics, the science of explanation. If our search starts from this point, living beings will come out as entities that are able to take care of themselves. Chapter 2 is an introduction to hermeneutics as an alternative to an objectivist view.

Third, attempts at unification could also start from a cosmological assumption that the whole world is alive, that it is endowed not only with spontaneity (described as, e.g., energy potentials) but also with intentionality, that it is characterized by constant meaningful transformations. From such a standpoint, we ourselves become only one of countless demonstrations (expressions) of the creative potency of the self-conscious universe. In contrast to the preceding point, the ability to reflect (and co-construct) the world is not specifically human—it also includes, for example, molecules and galaxies. Chapter 3 is an illustration of such a gnostic attempt. It is meant as a kind of warning: an approach that is intuitively very attractive, seemingly more vital than any, but obviously not science.

The Method

What is the *method* of science, understood so broadly as to encompass both natural sciences and humanities? Whereas the natural sciences rely on observation and experiment, the humanities prefer explanatory, hermeneutic approaches. Each methodology defines an area, a context where it is meaningful to pose only certain questions, and that limits the view to certain selected aspects of the world, necessarily setting aside other, equally legitimate ones. As a result, natural sciences and humanities also get different answers, and there is a gulf between them—they do not understand and therefore largely ignore each other. Does such a situation reflect only our imperfect nature, or rather the internal nature of the world? If it is a reflection of the real nature of the world, then an integrated knowledge devoid of antagonisms and paradoxes, of complementary truths and ambiguities could be found only in God. This is why the ethos of modern science is so attractive: it has the ambition to set human beings in the "God-like" position of an external unbiased observer who will be able to know the world free of all the paradoxes produced by mutually exclusive interpretations. If a search for unambiguous truth fails, it is because of faulty logic or methods, or lack of data, and so forth. The idea that a human being, or even *every* living being, is constantly negotiating his/her/its truth is unpalatable to most scientists.

We can also stay with the opposite view, that our explanations of the world are nothing but models that mirror our conceptions of the world, whereas the true nature of the world ("physis") will remain hidden forever. That is, our world is artificial, whereas physis is alive but hidden. In this case, the path to knowledge would require contemplation, a concentrated effort of reason, and initiation, an approach that is typical of the humanities and even more typical of religion.

We can also start with the fact that we ourselves are alive and then draw analogies with our own experience to negotiate an understanding of the world. But what should be understood by "living reality," and what methods are available for studying it? All these questions have been posed many times and in endless variations, and the quest for an answer has led to a deep split in our knowledge.

I believe that two or more complementary views are necessary. We can never end with an unequivocal description of a world that is at the same time repeatable and historical. We should realize that an experimental approach is fully applicable only in cases where the degree of interpretive freedom can be reduced to a minimum and where only attributes of the world enacted by the community are studied. Sometimes the very nature of the object studied does not require much interpretation. Sometimes interpretation needs to be suppressed artificially—by introducing special experimental conditions, clones of organisms, and so on. Even then, we often cannot avoid paradoxes originating in antinomies between the constant and the historical, the "objective" and the artificial, and so forth.

The position of the life sciences reveals all the paradoxes mentioned above. Biology, psychology, and sociology all straddle the gulf between the experimental and historical sciences, often balancing or being tugged to one or the other shore. Mixing of the genres can lead to many misunderstandings and pointless conflicts. In the twentieth century, biology established itself largely as an experimental science. Biologists focused their attention on phenomena that could be described as *functioning* and explained by mechanical models. Such an approach was successful, but biology paid for it by minimizing the historicity and spontaneity, even the intentionality of living beings. It is now time to assess the gains and losses of such an approach.

1

AN OBJECTIVIST PROPOSAL FOR THE UNIFICATION OF KNOWLEDGE

Nevertheless, if our methods only were sufficient, an analytical mechanics of the general life process would be possible. The conviction rests on the insight . . . that all changes in the material world . . . reduce to motion. Therefore even the life process cannot be anything but motion. But again, all motions may ultimately be divided into those which occur in one direction or another along the straight line connecting two hypothetical particles. Therefore, even the process within the organic state must ultimately be reducible to such simple motions. This reduction would indeed initiate an analytical mechanics of those processes. One sees, therefore, that if the difficulty of analysis does not exceed our ability, analytical mechanics fundamentally would reach even to the problem of freedom of the will.

Emil du Bois-Raymond

In this chapter I discuss scientism, a worldview that holds that the natural sciences possess a monopoly on deciphering reality. *Any* worldview is a very peculiar construct: the world is replaced by its image. The scientistic worldview does not acknowledge any plurality of views and presents instead an illusion that we have found the only possible means to grasp the reality, an illusion that things are at hand as objects and that it is possible to materialize, reify the structure of the world. To "possess" a worldview means to avoid responsibility for how the world is being understood—seemingly, all that is required is to choose the single correct worldview. Adherents of a worldview do not permit any doubts; should some appear, they will eliminate them at the very beginning. The worldview is an expansion of banality into the realm of things distinct and profound, resulting in the devastation of the world and the fragmentation even of the banal. The difference between the worldview and ideology is imperceptible.

Reality, for scientism, is identical to objective reality. The natural sciences develop methods to reveal its nature. Atkins (1992), for example, states: "Scientism . . . refers . . . to the sufficiency of established [natural] sciences as providers of explanations for all phenomena" (p. 32). The society should rely exclusively on knowledge gained by the (natural) sciences and take this as the single reliable anchor in the world, because "[h]istorically, the unstopped flow of science gives us reason to believe that it is omnicompetent" (p. 33).

We often encounter open or hidden scientism in discussions about the capacity of the sciences and/or the knowability of the world. As an illustration, I discuss here two books written by distinguished scientists—*Consilience* by Wilson (1998) and *The Unnatural Nature of Science* by Wolpert (1992). It should be stressed that the views of these authors are by no means extreme.

The Heritage of the Enlightenment

In most textbooks, the principal theses of the Enlightenment can be summarized as follows: (1) the confidence that all problems can be solved by reason; (2) the rejection of all superstitions, prejudices, and preconceptions; (3) the belief in progress and in the supremacy of a current level of knowledge above all previous ones; and (4) the belief in the need for an aristocracy of the Spirit, that is, in the dissemination of rationality.

In *Consilience*, Wilson aligns himself with these ideals. He considers the Enlightenment to be the only complex program of consistent application of rationality to all areas of human life and regrets that this splendid program was never brought to a climax. This is partly, says Wilson, because it became discredited by drastic attempts to apply it during the French Revolution, but especially because the humanities abandoned it, slipping toward romanticism and never returning to rationalism. He pinpoints here the main cause of the schism that has lasted for the last two centuries: whereas natural sciences have consequently stuck to the ideals of Enlightenment, humanities have not respected and have even opposed them.

Wilson's view of these affairs, however, does not need to be taken for granted. The problem starts with the very meanings of key words in our definition (reason, superstition, progress, rationality, etc.): they may differ substantially in different contexts. For example, in contrast to Wilson, Gadamer (1996) holds that the very fulfillment of the Enlightenment in the humanities came as late as the romantic period. Romanticism further interpreted the rationalist perspective as an antipode to reigning historicism: a proper historical science willing to stop judging the past according to present criteria has emerged only as a reaction to historicism and its negation (p. 276)—in short, only *after* the *prejudices* of the Enlightenment itself had been overcome! Here is the beginning of the historical hermeneutics that will recognize tradition and respect it as an indispensable limit for "absolute reason." "Prejudices" of the Enlightenment to be "overcome"? readers might ask—I return to this point in chapter 2.

Not only philosophers and historians, but even the "scientific" rationalists of the time did not present a homogeneous group. Prigogine and Stengers (1977) call attention to a fact that may be hard for many scientists to digest: that even among the most radical rationalists of the eighteenth century (e.g., Diderot), we can observe outbursts of vitalism. It emerged in protest to the dehumanization caused by an uncritical application of Newtonian mechanics:

> Seventeenth-century man is on the outer edge of the world, a material body, a Cartesian automaton, a soul created in God's image: by eluding the natural order, he occupies an intermediate position from which he can question nature, reduce it to a blind interplay of forces and to an indifferent movement of atoms without throwing doubt on his human specificity. In the eighteenth century, this is no longer true for those atheists who, like Diderot, question Newtonian science. They want and consider themselves to belong to nature; it is thus necessary for nature to be able to produce them, and to organize itself spontaneously into increasingly complex forms, until the level of the thinking animal is reached. (p. 321)

To end this illustration of possible interpretations of the Enlightenment period, I must mention that Webster and Goodwin (1982) take even the rational morphology of the nineteenth century as a successor to the Enlightenment (i.e., not as its abandonment, as Wilson suggests):

> The rational morphologists subscribed entirely or partially to the Enlightenment ideal of a mathematical natural science whose philosopher was Kant and in which the exemplary achievement was Newtonian mechanics. They were primarily, though not exclusively, concerned with "Being" or "Order," with the universals hidden in diversity and the permanence behind change—which does not exclude consideration of change. The empirical "laws" they were concerned to discover were formal laws which would enable the multiplicity of "given" forms to be reduced to, that is, to be described in terms of, a small number of general relational statements. . . . Thus, although this science was not mathematical, in other respects it conformed to the Enlightenment ideal. (p. 19)

Certainly, neither vitalism nor rational morphology is a model for contemporary biology—indeed, they are far more likely to be suspected of mysticism. What, then, is driving Wilson when he expresses his admiration of the Enlightenment? It seems that he takes as a prototype of the Enlightenment the situation in science 100 years later, at the end of the nineteenth century. By that time the exponents of the Newtonian form of reification of the world could easily do without vitalism, rational morphology, and historicism (though at the expense of overlooking certain phenomena).

From this short exposition, the reader should bear in mind that even the simplest statements that seem to be beyond any doubt can be heavily context dependent. This message recurs throughout this book.

World Maps, Common Sense, and Objective Reality

Scientism is based on conviction, or *belief,* in the unity of knowledge, in the orderliness of the world, which can be described by a small number of laws. Wilson has no problems with the statement that the whole edifice of science has been built on such a belief (which, as he stresses, is more than a working assumption; see Wilson, 1998, pp. 4–5). As a sociobiologist, he recognizes that processes in our brain must function in the way in which they were formed and inscribed with our instincts in the course of evolution. Among other things, we have also inherited a faculty he calls "religious instinct." Because of the architecture of our brains, it is not possible for us to sense the world differently than we actually do. But despite this, he can see a way how to liberate our religious instinct from religion and common experience and center it in science: "Science is religion liberated and writ large. . . . Preferring a search for objective reality over revelation is another way of satisfying religious hunger" (Wilson, 1998, p. 5). Only by strict application of a rigorous scientific method will we be able to perceive the world as it really, objectively *is.* Our way of thinking is not very well suited to such a task. After all, it was optimized for the survival of a primitive group of hunter-gatherers who did not need to solve tasks too remote from everyday practical life.

Let us look at the problem more closely. Accepting the notion that we see the world through the filters present in our brain means accepting that we are continuously creating maps of the world. Any map, directory, language, culture, and so forth, provides examples of filters for our consciousness. These represent not only tools but also projections onto certain new dimensions of reality, which will enable us to perceive the given aspect of reality and to orient ourselves within it. Obviously, science is a very effective filter, but only one of many. Wilson obviously claims (as, indeed, do many thinkers who have developed a consistent system of thought) that science finally succeeded in separating grain from chaff: we finally came upon a filter that, in contrast to all others developed so far, is the only correct one.

The second of our scientist authors, Wolpert (1992), does not go so far as to declare science to be the religion of modern times, but he, too, points out that the very nature of science is alien to our way of thinking: "I would almost contend that if something fits in with common sense it almost certainly is not science" (p. 11). Apparently, this is why science has appeared in human history only once: all cultures, with the exception of Judeo-Christian civilization, can do without it. Scientific truths are counterintuitive, have little relation to everyday life, and as such can be accommodated today only after highly specialized training. Hence, scientific knowledge seems alien, incomprehensible, even fictional to those who lack this special initiation. "Science does not fit with our natural expectations" (p. 1): it is an acquired taste.

Both Wilson and Wolpert remind us that it is necessary to overcome the drawbacks of human nature. Are we, then, the elect who have finally discovered how nature works? Let us have a closer look.

The natural sciences as we know them today have also emerged as a result of a very special context and tradition. Monotheism played an important role because it implied a belief that a world created by God would behave rationally and follow simple and discernible laws. Furthermore, this tradition gave birth to two other tricks. First, it invented a letter alphabet where the signs (letters) as such bear no meaning except that they differ from other signs. Second, it confined the world into three-dimensional geometric space. Science came into existence when these two areas became linked in analytical geometry: the whole "flesh" of the world became transformed into linear strings of signs, and mathematics thus became instructions of how to "construct" the world. After this transformation, the signs attained their own life, and science, suddenly emancipated from the world of imagination and the world of the flesh, could limit itself to the study of logical relations between the signs.

Undoubtedly, mathematical operations reveal a new kind of human imagination, opening entirely new and incredibly rich realms to it. Maybe we *are* indeed heirs of a line of thinking that enables us to see *directly* how the world *is*. But we should stay alert and avoid transforming such a belief into blind faith. Some ambitions of scientism make me suspicious. Take, for example, the ambition to bring all realms of human knowledge — even philosophy — into the temple of science (e.g., Wilson, 1998, p. 12). Philosophers should finally understand and help the project from their part. When we succeed, the whole culture will become a science of a new quality, encompassing all branches of human knowledge.

Wilson claims that the unwillingness of the humanities to participate in the pansophic program is the only serious impediment to *consilience*. The natural sciences represent discovery, whereas those working in the humanities just deal endlessly with the same problems (Wilson, 1998, p. 56). In addition, postmodern thinking comes up with a monstrous heresy when stating that reality is but a state constructed by the mind, with no external objective truths: "In general scientific culture is viewed as just another way of knowing, and, moreover, contrived mostly by European and American white males" (pp. 40–42).

Wilson (1998) characterizes science as "organized, systematic enterprise that gathers knowledge about the world and condenses the knowledge into testable laws and principles" (p. 53). Repeatability, economy, mensuration, heuristics, and finally consilience—internal coherence and the absence of discords—should distinguish it from pseudoscience. Such a definition could, of course, easily apply also to the humanities. From the context, however, we can understand that, in addition, "true science" must encompass the basic method of contemporary natural sciences—reductionism—and this apparently makes it difficult for the humanities to enter the club. But even in humanities and philosophy, it is often argued that what cannot be absorbed by the reduction is a superstition. I suspect that even this criterium is not the way to distinguish both streams of human effort. Wilson's worldview ends with this statement: "No one should suppose that objective truth is impossible to attain, even when the most committed philosophers urge us to acknowledge that incapacity. In particular, it is too early for scientists, the foot soldiers of epistemology, to yield ground so vital to their mission" (pp. 60–61).

Behind such words one almost feels materializing committees deciding what is objective truth and what is not, and perhaps common agreement of the learned (*communis opinio doctorum*) is indeed the only way to settle the quarrel. Then, however, it is not easy to speak of "objective truths." I shall not follow this line of thinking further. It should be acknowledged, however, that physicists, undoubtedly "foot soldiers" of the front line of science, have already retreated, and I doubt that they did so under fire from philosophers or anyone else. Four decades before *Consilience*, Heisenberg wrote his *Physics and Philosophy* (1959) and included the following statement (he was writing about quantum physics, but the conclusion has a general validity):

> It may be said that classical physics is just that idealization in which we can speak about parts of the world without any reference to ourselves. Its success has led to the general ideal of an objective description of the world. Objectivity has become the first criterion for the value of any scientific result. Does the Copenhagen interpretation of quantum theory still comply with this ideal? One may perhaps say that quantum theory corresponds to this ideal as far as possible. Certainly quantum theory does not contain genuine subjective features, it does not introduce the mind of the physicist as a part of the atomic event. But it starts from the division of the world into the "object" and the rest of the world, and from the fact that at least for the rest of the world we use the classical concepts in our description. This division is

arbitrary and historically a direct consequence of our scientific method; the use of the classical concepts is finally a consequence of the general human way of thinking. But this is already a reference to ourselves and in so far our description is not completely objective. (p. 55)

"As far as possible" puts the scientific effort into quite a different context.

Kantian and Aristotelian Barriers

Another proposal for the unification of human knowledge, in many respects similar to that of Wilson, was put forward by Kováč (1999/2000). For him, too, the starting point is the rationalism of the Enlightenment. He introduces the concept of four "Kantian barriers," which isolate humans, dwellers in the macroworld, from the macro-, mega-, psycho-, and socioworlds. These worlds are not available to us directly, and we tend to interpret their phenomena through conceptions and terms borrowed from the macroworld. For ages, he says, the best way to do this was by a continuous narrative or myth, which becomes implanted in all members of a cultural group in their early childhood. Only the Hellenic Greeks made the very important discovery that mythological truths can be both doubted and complementary. By falsification of hypotheses, they found a means to definitively escape the power of myth. After 2,000 years of further cultivation, the empirical sciences were born from this ingenious discovery. Knowledge of the world ceased to be a random mixture of complementary truths and became cumulative; it was accompanied by instrumentation, which led to technology. Cultural sciences, in contrast, have not yet found a means to cumulate facts. They still dwell behind another—Aristotelian—barrier, which defines the limit of knowledge accessible by pure reasoning. There is only one way to surmount the Aristotelian barrier and start to cumulate knowledge—by introducing experimental testing of hypotheses:

> No vestiges of Aristotelian ideas have remained in the natural sciences by now. The reality constructed by these sciences is very remote from the world of our experience and intuition. It cannot be otherwise: natural sciences now penetrate even to worlds behind the Kantian barriers. Aristotle is not cited in the reference lists of publications in the natural sciences, and his name is rare in the citation indexes. In cultural sciences and humanities the situation is different: Aristotle is cited often and in citation indexes he remains well established. Could it be that Aristotle was completely wrong in his ideas on nature, but was able to discover crucial truths on man and society? I doubt it. In the cultural and human sciences, the Aristotelian hypotheses and theories survive. They are close to our intuitive understanding, self-evident, but alas—untrue. Simply nobody has yet been around to falsify them. (p. 48)

As no method of falsification is at hand, argues Kováč, humankind undertakes massive "testing" of its hypotheses not in the laboratory but in the real world—with disastrous results, such as Nazism or communism. In the wake of such catastrophes, unification becomes the imperative of the day. This is not in order for the two branches of human knowledge to understand each other. Quite the opposite: once the cultural sciences have developed their own methods, they will become as counterintuitive as the natural sciences are. Despite (or perhaps because of) this, we will learn something about the human nature. Kováč suggests a recipe for attaining such a goal: to accept the reductionist method, which has proved itself in the natural sciences, at the same time discarding all those intuitively attractive but untrue explanations and, above all, to avoid postmodernism, which is an expression of resignation and an acceptance of pluralistic views: "What mankind needs is not postmodernism, but neomodernism: a learned return to the Enlightenment with its casting out of myths, preconceptions and falsified theories. The scientific community is a home not for shapeless postmodern resignation, but for Monod's imperative: 'The scientist should be modest but not at the expense of his convictions, which he must defend'" (Kováč, 1999/2000, p. 107). Kováč's proposal for obliterating the backwardness of cultural sciences is to shift the pendulum of research away from the natural sciences toward the realm of culture, but by using all of the armory developed by natural sciences.

An Alternative in a Hermeneutic Approach?

All discussions referred to above more or less deny the possibility of any complementary layouts outside the realm of experimental science. Yet such complementary views do exist, and one of them is that provided by hermeneutics. The difference between the scientific and hermeneutic approach was well summarized by Heelan (1998): "The hermeneutic orientation is contrasted with the explanatory tradition which in the English-speaking world is simply called 'science.' Explanatory method aims at the construction of a mathematical model comprising measurable (theoretical) variables, to be accepted or rejected by reason of its ability under laboratory circumstances to predict and control the causal outcomes of assigned initial conditions" (p. 274). The interface between the natural and cultural sciences is, of course, not too well defined, but Heelan agrees with Kováč that they can hardly be reconciled: "The story they tell about the natural sciences can hardly be reconciled with the noble ideas of knowledge and reality stemming from the philosophical tradition. . . . Whence comes an embarrassing dilemma: either natural science is not worth the name of 'knowledge' and deserves no more than to be called 'useful' opinion, or the philosophical analysis of knowledge and reality needs to be revisited and reviewed" (p. 275).

Heelan (1998) then analyses sciences from a Heideggerian position, and concludes with the statement that "[w]e scientists are today Galileans in a way in which Galileo himself was not a Galilean (pp. 276–277). Of course, such a characteristic holds for all "founding fathers," but if we accept this banal truth, we should also ask to what extent natural sciences can be characterized as mere accumulations of new findings. I return to hermeneutics in more detail in chapter 2; here I shall introduce only one idea of Gadamer (1985). He, like other authors cited above, understands that with the arrival of experimental sciences we relinquished the "anthropomorphic worldview." However, he also knows that, despite that,

> the heritage of classical philosophy endures—in the very understandable fact that we want and must take our world as understandable and not only manipulatable. In contrast to the constructivism of modern science, which takes as known and understood only what can be reproduced, the Greek concept of science is characterized by physis, the horizon of the order of being of things ordered in itself and self-expressing. The question is to what extent the Greek heritage holds some truth which remains hidden under special conditions of modern epistemology. (p. 4)

Gadamer thus maintains that certain fields of human experience will resist objectivization forever. These include especially the phenomenon of language and also of logos, "the world itself evoked by speaking, and, due to language, disposible and communicable" (p. 7). The "second half of truth," which according to the scientistic view calls for objectivization, is still here and has remained actual, and only through it can the experience of science become an experience of an individual or a group. I return to these problems in chapter 2.

Reductionism, Basic Level of Description, and the Scientific Truth

The most successful method of natural sciences is undoubtedly reductionism. Again, I take an example from Wilson (1998), who illustrates the importance of the reductive method by comparing medicine and the social sciences—two spheres of knowledge that should, intuitively, be very close to each other. Yet there exists a deep difference. In medicine, success depends on a systematic effort to unify the observed phenomena "across all levels of biological organization, from the whole organism down, step by step, to the molecule" (p. 182). In social sciences, despite a comparable wealth of methods and levels of description, only chaos and a lack of vision reign. This is because "social scientists by and large spurn the idea of the hierarchical ordering of knowledge that unites and drives natural sciences" (p. 182). His criticism culminates: "Each of these enterprises has contributed something to understanding the human condition. . . . But never—I do not think that too strong a word— have social scientists been able to embed their narratives in the physical real- ities of human biology and psychology, even though it is surely there and not some astral plane from which culture has arisen. . . . Consequently, too many social-science textbooks are a scandal of banality" (p. 193).

Those working in the social sciences, according to Wilson, have no chance to predict or understand anything because they despise the natural sciences and rely instead on folk psychology. He demonstrates this view by several ex- amples of the scandalous collapse of social sciences (e.g., their inability to predict the disintegration of the U.S.S.R.). In defense of psychologists against such hard condemnations, I would suggest again the complementary view of Heisenberg (1959):

> [T]he whole tendency of biology of our time is to explain biological phe- nomena on the basis of the known physical and chemical laws. Again the question arises, whether this hope is justified or not. . . . One of the argu- ments frequently used in favor of this theory emphasizes that whenever the laws of physics and chemistry have been checked in living organisms they have always been found to be correct. . . . [I]t is just this argument that has lost much of its weight through quantum theory. Since the concepts of physics and chemistry form a closed and coherent set, namely, that of quantum theory, it is necessary that whenever these concepts can be used to describe phenomena the laws connected with the concepts must be valid too. Therefore, whenever one treats living organisms as physicochemical systems, they must necessarily act as such. . . . We would never doubt that the brain acts as a physicochemical mechanism if treated as such, but for an understanding of psychic phenomena we would start from the fact that the human mind enters as object and subject into the scientific process of psychology. (pp. 92–95)

Wilson's call for the integration of natural and cultural sciences (i.e., the engulfing of the second by the first) is almost identical to that in his previous book *On Human Nature* (1978). In some respect he goes even further there, saying that science even has the ability to "devise laws of history that can foretell something of the future of mankind" (p. 215). Why not, if mental processes "represent a programmed predisposition whose self-sufficient components were incorporated into the neural apparatus of the brain by thousands of generations of genetic evolution" (p. 214).[1] If we accept such

---

1. A hundred years before him, Nietzsche ridiculed the effort in the following words: "[A]s things are they had to be, as men now are they were bound to become, none may resist this in- evitability" (Nietzsche, 1997, p. 107).

a shortcut from genes to psychology (but see possible alternatives, e.g., Michel and Moore, 1995), it follows that biology should have the final word even on moral questions. We could strive toward a new biology of ethics (Wilson, 1982, pp. 203–204) and explain traditional religion by the mechanistic models of evolutionary biology (p. 208). We may consider Wilson's views to be extreme, but he is not alone and his opinions are widely accepted.

Wolpert's (1992) stance is somewhat different. He does not approve of a possible merge of science and spiritual knowledge; rather, he views their relationship from the point of a Galilean Book of Nature: "A work of art is capable of many readings, of multiple interpretations, whereas scientific discoveries have a strictly defined meaning. . . . Whatever the scientists' feelings, or style, while working, these are purged from the final work."[2] There exist objective and shared criteria for judging scientific work, whereas there are numerous interpretations for artistic creations and no sure way of judging them (p. 57).

This is why in contrast to the arts, the natural sciences can do well even in the absence of geniuses: it would, in any case, be the foot soldiers of science who would finally seize the peak (compare this with Heisenberg's statement above on the importance of historical context in the evolution of knowledge). Wolpert is more radical than Wilson (or Kováč). Wilson, however convinced of the supremacy of natural sciences over other realms of human knowledge, makes an offer to all of them. He suggests they join the "true" sciences and participate in the great work toward understanding human nature, that is, the evolution and biology of human beings. Wolpert (1992), on the other hand, would easily do without such an attempt, and one even gets an impression that he may be afraid of it:

> For scientists, defining the nature of science is of only marginal interest, for it has no impact on their day-to-day activities. For philosophers of science, and for some sociologists, by contrast, the nature of science and the validity of scientific knowledge are central problems. These observers have found the nature of science puzzling, and some have even come to doubt whether science is, after all, a special and privileged form of knowledge— "privileged" in that it provides the most reliable means of understanding how the world works. While providing no real threat to science they have become an increasingly vocal group, with an unfortunate influence on the study of science and its history. (p. 101)

---

2. This is a first part of the well-known phrase, which continues "whereas an artist lets his emotions come up." It is a matter of discussion whether either part of this sentence is true. See, for example, Stent (1972).

The incompatibility of philosophical views concerning the nature of the world is thus the problem of philosophers.[3] After having shown that science is alien to natural experience, Wolpert dismisses philosophy on similar grounds. Surprisingly, however, at the very end of his analysis he returns to the common sense, which he had declared at the beginning of his book to be unreliable: "My own position, philosophically, is that of a common sense realist: I believe there is an external world which I share with others and which can be studied. I know that philosophically my position may be indefensible, but—and this is crucial—holding my position will have made no iota of difference to the nature of scientific investigation or scientific theories. It is irrelevant" (p. 106). Is it really so? Is it not, above all, necessary to understand what our conceptions, facts, entities, and so forth, mean and what the relationships between them are? Again, I turn to Heisenberg (1959)—in connection with the Copenhagen interpretation of quantum theory, he says:

> It has sometimes been suggested that one should depart from the classical concepts altogether and that a radical change in the concepts used for describing the experiments might possibly lead back to a nonstatistical, completely objective description of nature. This suggestion, however, rests upon a misunderstanding. The concepts of classical physics are just a refinement of the language which forms the basis of all natural science. Our actual situation in science is that we do use the classical concepts for the description of the experiments, and it was the problem of quantum theory to find a theoretical interpretation of the experiments on this basis. There is no use in discussing what could be done if we were other being than we are. (p. 55)

This already goes beyond our discussion of objectivist (scientistic) outcomes of natural sciences, and a problem arises of how we can understand each other (and the world) by using inaccurate concepts. I turn to this field in chapter 2.

The Philosophical Roots of "Objectivism"

Can we in our time, when the ambitions of the positivists have been more or less abandoned, find a philosophical trend that would cultivate the ideas presented above? Scientists lacking a deeper philosophical background may obviously have presented their views in a relatively crude form. At first sight, it would seem that suspicions toward philosophers held by scientists are amply

---

3. Here Wolpert (1992) refers to Wittgenstein's alleged assertion that philosophy is in fact a synopsis of trivialities (p. 106). Compare with Gadamer's (1996) statement that science "leads through mathematics and reason to an insight into what is intelligible in itself" (p. 182).

returned from their side. For example, in their *Foundations of Biophilosophy* (1997), Mahner and Bunge state the following:

> Some scientists . . . may still be somewhat suspicious about the relevance of metaphysics to their discipline. After all, it is still popular to equate metaphysics with religion, wild speculation, or some unintelligible discourse about Being, Nothingness, *Dasein*, deconstruction, and the like. Thus, understandably, there are still antimetaphysicians among scientists, and even the odd philosopher expresses doubts as to whether ontology can be helpful for biology at all. . . . Yet the fact that some ontologies are wrong or useless does not render all metaphysics objectionable: after all, every human belief and action involves some metaphysical presuppositions. For example, most of our actions presuppose that there is, in fact, a world external to the knowing or acting subject. Thus, as has been remarked many times, and rightly so, an antimetaphysician is just one who holds primitive and unexamined metaphysical beliefs. (p. 3)

We should, then, ask whether what was discussed above was not some primitive metaphysical belief of philosophically naive scientists who do not deserve attention. I believe not. To prove this, I return to the end of the nineteenth century, because the worldviews of scientists such as Wolpert or Wilson and many other biologists reflect this period. At that time, Newtonian mechanics was so commonplace that nobody questioned the conditions that allowed it to emerge. For Helmholtz, one of the last great spirits who encompassed both philosophy and science, Newtonian physics represented the ideal of modern natural science. He saw natural laws as independent of our conceptions or desires, these objectively valid principles asymptotically approached by our research efforts. Nature as a whole simply *must* follow such laws—otherwise scientific knowledge would have no legitimacy. Helmholtz (1896) insists on strong causality and the a priori nature of natural law—no randomness is accepted:

> The only alternative on our horizon would be randomness; but it is in fact only an expression of the limitation of our knowledge and the clumsiness of our combinatory abilities. Even in the wildest vagaries of weather, a spirit equipped with a precise knowledge of reality, whose mind worked so rapidly and precisely that it could outrun events, would see what we can only suppose and feel: the harmonic reign of eternal laws, as in the paths of stars. (pp. 162–163)
>
> The role of theoretical natural science will be complete when phenomena are transformed into simple forces and, at the same time, it is proved that this transformation is the only one possible with the phenomena in question. Such transformation would appear as a necessary conceptual form of understanding nature, and would acquire the status of objective truth. (Helmholtz, 1982, p. 18)

A similar passage by du Bois-Reymond, a friend of Helmholtz, is cited as an epigraph at the beginning of this chapter. According to Gould (1977), the evolutionist Ernst Haeckel transfers even the Darwinian phylogeny into such frameworks: everything can be reduced to simple physical and chemical processes.

However, it should be said that even among contemporaries there were many opponents of such blind determinism. Nietzsche, for example, openly ridiculed such opinions. Similarly, the dialectical materialism of Engels may have also been a reaction to the blindly applied mechanicism then reigning. Engels's *Dialectics of Nature* (1972) contains a passage that is a mirror image of Helmholtzian determinism:

> Among natural scientists motion is always as a matter of course taken to mean mechanical motion, change of place. This has been handed down from the pre-chemical eighteenth century and makes a clear conception of the processes much more difficult. Motion, as applied to matter, is *change in general*. From the same misunderstanding is derived also the craze to reduce everything to mechanical motion, . . . which obliterates the specific character of the other forms of motion. This is not to say that each of the higher forms of motion is not always necessarily connected with some real (external or molecular) motion. . . . But the presence of these subsidiary forms does not exhaust the essence of the main form in each case. One day we shall certainly "reduce" thought experimentally to molecular and chemical motions in the brain; but does that exhaust the essence of thought? (pp. 247–248)

Finally, it is worth mentioning the view of Helmholtz and du Bois-Reymond as expressed by the Czech biologist and philosopher Rádl (1909), who was a strong opponent of efforts to introduce physics into biology, because, in his opinion, such an activity would strip biology of its own subject:

> They introduced physical methods into biology and thus transformed physiology from a life science into a discipline of delicate electrical, optical, acoustical etc., tools. They had the advantage of precision, but they paid for it by limitations in problems. They sought to formulate their theories in mathematical terms and ended with a science devoid of life. For them life was nothing but an electric current in a nerve, the flip of a muscle removed from the body, the refraction of light in an eye. . . . They called such a science physiology only because in their circuits there was a nerve instead of a piece of wire, because they saw light as absorbed by an eye instead of a photographic plate, and sound by an ear instead of tuners and resonators. As they did not forget to add, all these tools were far from perfect if compared to physical instruments. (p. 94)

By all these, possibly annoying, quotations, I wish to remind the reader that the development of biology to its contemporary state was by no means a straight trajectory that could have been predicted in advance. At the beginning of the twentieth century, biology offered many alternatives to that which eventually prevailed. At that time, it was still balancing at the interface between natural and historical science. In part II of this book, I list some of these alternatives.

A very expressive comment on the nineteenth-century mechanicism comes from Max Delbrück, a quantum physicist who became one of the founders of molecular biology. In a famous lecture in 1949, he revealed the roots of objectivist sciences in a change in perception of Newtonian physics:

> Some of the contemporaries of Newton took quite a different view of the Newtonian principles. To describe motions in terms of forces acting at a distance seemed to them like introducing magic. Moreover, to correlate forces with acceleration . . . seemed to them the height of abstraction, going beyond what should be permitted to occur in any science, and threatening to remove it from the realm of rational pursuit. Between the times of Newton and Helmholtz, then, a strange inversion took place. What had seemed magical and extravagant at the earlier period, after a century of success had become the *only* way in which one could hope to account rationally and visualizably for the phenomena of nature. Actually, most branches of biology manage to flourish without any recourse to this ideal. (p. 17)

The "strange inversion" mentioned by Delbrück was, I suppose, reification. Newton was well aware that, in his time, action at a distance meant magic. To reduce the tension, Newton entitled his opus magnum *Philosophiae Naturalis Principia Mathematica*: in mathematical (i.e., purely abstract) constructions even such effects were allowed. Newton's followers, however, committed the sin of reification and replaced a mathematical symbol for gravitation by a physical magnitude. Two hundred years later nobody was any longer aware of this operation.[4]

To return to mechanicism: in the second half of the twentieth century the Darwinist Monod (1979) could hardly deny the role of chance in evolution, but the organisms themselves remain for him the same kinds of machines as for Helmholtz and colleagues. Monod's understanding of the cell deserves quotation: "The entire system is totally, intensely conservative, locked into itself, utterly impervious to any 'hints' from the outside world. By its properties, by the microscopic clockwork function that establishes be-

---

4. For a plethora of examples of biological reifications ending up in caricature see, for example, Gould (1996).

tween DNA and protein, as between organism and medium, an entirely one-way relationship, this system obviously defies 'dialectical' description. It is not Hegelian at all, but thoroughly Cartesian: the cell is indeed a machine" (p. 108). And when describing the cellular hierarchy of functions, he says: "The determining cause of the entire phenomenon, its source, is finally the genetic information represented by the sum of the polypeptide sequences, interpreted (or more exactly, screened [orig. *filtrées*]) by the initial conditions" (p. 94).

What, however, are the "initial conditions," and why should it be demanded to narrow the interpretation to an unambiguous "filtrate"?

The Strengths and Weaknesses of the Reductionist Method

Reductionism is a key term to understand developments in the twentieth century. First, it is necessary to distinguish between methodical and ontological reductionism. The former is a commonplace part of the methodological armory of science. The latter is a matter of our attitude toward the world driven by a conviction that a given thing can or even must be described at a single, *basic*, level, and if we do so, the thing becomes clear and apparent. From this comes an optimistic conviction that, after breaking down the "Kantian barriers," we should be able to derive phenomena on one level of description from our knowledge of phenomena at different level(s). Moreover, the levels should be ranked on a scale of complexity; that is, such a scale should have a bottom level. According to Mahner and Bunge (1997), such a worldview is indeed grounded in the philosophy of ontological realism (known also as metaphysical materialism):

> *Reductionism* or, rather, *microreductionsm* is a research strategy, namely, the adoption of the methodological principle according to which (micro)reduction is in all cases necessary and sufficient to account for wholes and their properties. The ontological partners of microreductionism are physicalism and atomism (or individualism). According to physicalism, things differ only in their complexity, so that wholes can be understood entirely in terms of their parts. Therefore, all the sciences are thought to be reducible to physics, and such reduction to physics would result in the unity of science—one of the illusory programs of logical positivism. . . . The dual of microreductionism is macroreductionism which is often called "antireductionism." . . . [Its] ontological counterpart . . . is holism. The microreductionist thesis is that we know a thing, if we find out, what it is "made" of, while the macroreductionist thesis is that we know it if we figure out its place in "the scheme of things" (i.e., the larger system). Yet to explain how systems of any kind work, we need to combine *microreduction* with *macrore-*

duction. The reason is that a system is characterized not only by its composition, but also by its environment and structure. (p. 116)

Mahner and Bunge propose a mildly reductionist approach, descending whenever possible to lower levels of description, but at the same time not disregarding the diversity of things and their emergent properties. This version of metaphysical realism is termed "emergent materialism" or "emergentism." It is also a search for the unity of all knowledge. However, in contrast to radical, fundamental reductionism, it tries to unify different branches of sciences by looking for a common language—that is, *not* by the reduction of all branches of knowledge to a common denominator (e.g., physics).

Havel (1996) further corroborates the argument as to why we should not move further than to mild emergentism: the more we dare to proceed on the hierarchic scales, the more metaphors we bring there from the scale we feel at home in. Instead of discerning foreign worlds, we end up transforming them into things we know from our experience: we bring them to "our side of the horizon." Havel instead puts forward the views of some physicists who perceive the world as a system of (quasi)autonomous domains, stable and to a great extent insensitive to what is going on in other domains (in chapter 3 I discuss similar views held by Ruyer). I feel that a related approach should be adopted even in the realm of living beings. Here, different "levels" of organization are emancipated from the others, in ontogeny as well in evolution. Although intertwined, they have their own dynamics, on different time scales. It seems to me that at each "level" there can be a most "economical" description of phenomena. If we try to describe the same phenomena from other levels, the image becomes more and more complicated and its contours tend to become blurred.

Phyllotaxis (the arrangement of leaves on a plant stem) may serve as an example. It can be easily grasped and described at the level of the entire plant: the description requires a simple geometrical algorithm (see, e.g., Prusinkiewicz and Lindenmeyer, 1990). It is much more difficult to describe the same thing in terms of cell lines branching away from the primordia. It is perhaps possible to describe the whole phenomenon even at a molecular level, but it would be an immense task due to the scale shift: there is no phyllotaxis at the molecular level, so it is no trivial task to "articulate" it from there. Now, phyllotaxis, cell divisions in the meristeme, and the movement of molecules are all undoubtedly expressions of life, but none can stand for life itself. Life proceeds synchronously on innumerable space, time, and organizational levels. Nothing on any single level can reveal its essence. For this reason, many authors strive for a view coherent across all dimensions, which would be neither atomism nor holism. I return to these views in part II of this book.

Whereas biology is still divided over the question of whether it is possible to reduce life to physics, the physicists themselves, paradoxically, abandoned the quest for some basic level of description long ago as fruitless and vain. The standpoint of quantum physics is shown above in the quotations from Heisenberg. The school of physical chemistry founded by Prigogine (see, e.g., Prigogine, 1980; Prigogine and Stengers, 1977, 1985) has taken a similar stand. Here, too, they stress the basic impossibility of canonical transformation of descriptions gained on one level to another level (e.g., between molecular and macroscopic). Each such transition between levels of organization will be accompanied by gains and losses and also by changes in the very meaning of concepts. If, however, there is an incompatibility of descriptions *in principle*, all radical reductionist efforts are a dead end:

> The point where the trajectories cease to be determined, where the *foedera fati* governing the ordered and monotonous world of deterministic change break down, marks the beginning of nature. It also marks the beginning of a new science that describes the birth, proliferation, and death of natural beings. "The physics of falling, of repetition, of rigorous concatenation is replaced by the creative science of change and circumstances" [A quotation by M. Serres]. The *foedera fati* are replaced by the *foedera naturae*, which ... denote both "laws" of nature—local, singular, historical relations— and an "alliance," a form of contract with nature. (Prigogine and Stengers, 1985, p. 304)

But is not all this but a kind of poetry? I think not. The interpretation of the world should be based on a hermeneutic effort to tune often-incompatible (scientific) descriptions with the experience of the world. That, of course, takes us out of the realm of strict natural science, with its declared logic and metaphysics, into the realm of narratives, myths. (It is, in fact, questionable whether mythical experience has ever been totally expelled from the natural sciences—it is often concealed beneath the euphemism "cultural context.") To stress this point, I conclude here with an analysis of the reductionist view published by Schweber (1993), who again stresses the quasi autonomy of emancipated hierarchical levels in physics. This, together with the regular appearance of emergent phenomena, leads to a situation in which physics itself is a *creator* of systems that have *never occurred before* in the whole history of the universe! Reductionism is, of course, impossible in such a universe. Schweber refers to an earlier article by Anderson (1972), who states:

> The reductionist hypothesis does not by any means imply the "constructionist" one: The ability to reduce everything to simple fundamental laws does not imply the ability to start from those laws and reconstruct the universe. In fact, the more the elementary-particle physicists tell us about the nature of fundamental laws, the less relevance they seem to have to the

very real problems of the rest of science, much less to those of society. The constructionist hypothesis breaks down when confronted with the twin difficulties of scale and complexity. (p. 393)

Both authors see the basic cause of such a situation as the fact that basic equations do not describe the world itself: the world is described by their *solutions*. Emergent phenomena result from solutions that are not deducible from equations alone. Because complexity and emergent phenomena cannot be deciphered from another level of description, the famous formula "Science X is nothing but application of the science Y" is pure nonsense. "Biology is nothing but physics and chemistry" is therefore untrue.

2

IN THE QUEST FOR THE MEANING

There is a story that when a neo-grammarian was asked about the content of an old Lithuanian manuscript which he had studied in great detail, he answered: "The content? Oh, I didn't bother with the content." They studied sounds, phones of the language as such, faithful to the demands of empiricism and naturalism.

Jiří Fiala

It would be to completely mistake the nature of the things with which our science is occupied, if one thought it had to do with objective facts. Objective facts in their reality never emerge in our research.

Johann Gustav Droysen

Immediately after the invention of writing, problems arose with the interpretation of texts—religious, political, and legal. Even if the texts were written by contemporaries and addressed to their fellows, ambiguous interpretations were common. Texts that spoke from the past or translations from foreign languages made the problem even harder.

Even in cases where entire texts are available, they place special demands on the reader/interpreter because they come to contain passages that become incomprehensible, conflicting, or even offensive. Unless readers are unwilling to cast the blame for such anomalies on the author, they must somehow deal with them. If the text can be dated, it may be possible to find out more by studying that era and its cultural, linguistic, religious, and so forth, contexts. The reader can also consult other texts by the same authors and by their contemporaries and critics. Much greater demands are placed on the reader in the case of canonical (e.g., religious) texts, as well as those distorted by errors in copying or translation or by fragmentation. *Consilience* must be constantly renegotiated.

The problem of the interpretation of old texts was already well known in ancient Greece, whereas for Christian civilization it became acute in the times of the early Church Fathers, who wrestled with the task of achieving an unequivocal interpretation of the Holy Writ and its translations. Throughout the centuries, the hermeneutic method has been consciously cultivated, and since the nineteenth century it has become commonly used for interpreting any text. (For a comprehensive history of hermeneutics, see Grondin [1994] and Eden [1997].)

Interpretation of history faces similar problems. Moreover, the time frames of historical events are very fuzzy, especially regarding their beginnings: there always was some "before." Historical events must therefore automatically be considered fragmentary. Thus, tensions between the contexts of the interpreted and the interpreter will play a crucial role in the interpretation of both texts and historical events.

Because this chapter is a prolegomenon to the biological parts of this book, I encourage the reader to look in parallel for analogies that can be encountered in living beings. I myself make such digressions throughout the text. Throughout this and the following chapters the reader should bear in mind two basic analogies: (1) the string of nucleotides in the genome can be understood as a text that requires interpretation, not simply decoding; (2) living beings, that is, interpreters of genetic information, are historical beings, molded by the contingencies of four billion years of evolution.

How to Extract the Meaning

One of the main concerns of this book is the interpretation of "biological texts" inscribed in DNA or elsewhere. Interpretation processes in living beings can be understood as signatures of what living beings are, what they were, and what they might be in future. We can speak of "biological utterances" in the form of proteins, structures, morphologies, and morphogenesis, and so forth, all based on understanding the message coming from the past and inscribed in both strings of genetic texts and bodily structures. How to analyze written texts is therefore of the utmost importance, and I take this as a starting point to help in further analysis.

Again, let me start with a longer quotation:

> The written word and what partakes of it—literature—is the intelligibility
> of mind transferred to the most alien medium. Nothing is so purely the trace
> of the mind as writing, but nothing is so dependent on the understanding
> mind either. In deciphering and interpreting it, a miracle takes place: the
> transformation of something alien and dead into total contemporaneity and
> familiarity. This is like nothing else that comes down to us from the past. The
> remnants of past life—what is left of buildings, tools, the contents of
> graves—are weather-beaten by the storms of time that have swept over
> them, whereas a written tradition, once deciphered and read, is to such an
> extent pure mind that it speaks to us as if in the present. That is why the ca-
> pacity to read, to understand what is written, is like a secret art, even
> a magic that frees and binds us. In it time and space seem to be superseded.
> People who can read what has been handed down in writing produce and
> achieve the sheer presence of the past. (Gadamer, 1996, pp. 163–164)

Keep this inspiring analogy in mind when we come to deal with species-
specific interpretation of genetic messages (e.g., in chapters 4 and 12).

Before I try to show the promise that hermeneutics holds for biology, it is necessary to provide a short description of contemporary hermeneutics. What
follows is based mostly on Gadamer's work *Truth and Method* (1996), which is
considered a climax of the twentieth century's hermeneutic effort.

Hermeneutics was for a long time—up to the time of romanticism—considered only as an ancillary, exegetical method of historical research, especially in theology, philology, and law. It was considered useful for the redis-
covery of things that were themselves known but that had ceased to be
directly accessible, without mediation, owing to the passage of time. In contrast to this, during the Reformation, Scripture was understood as a self-contained text (*sui ipsius interpres*), that is, requiring neither tradition nor the four
levels of understanding coined by the church fathers (literal, allegorical,
moral, and anagogic). All that was necessary to understand was a literal
reading, the *sensus literalis*.

In biology, the genome is often taken for such a *sui ipsius interpres*. According
to this, the "interpretation" of a genetic script should mean simply decoding
according to a known key.

It was from such a foundation that the universal hermeneutics was to appear
in the nineteenth century, no longer just as a method for other branches of
sciences, but as a framework for historical and textual research. Hermeneutics grew out of the knowledge that a possibility of misunderstanding and
a feeling of alienation are universally present in any conscious act. Any text
will therefore be approached as a priori not understood, and hermeneutics
represents the art of understanding. From this moment on, difficulties ceased

to be taken as occasional drawbacks and became an indispensable part of the task that had to be faced from the very beginning. In other words, understanding (or mutual understanding between different subjects) should always be negotiated.

Remember this when the relationship phenotype-genetic information is discussed.

But how to overcome the alienation? Gadamer illustrates this with two extreme attempts of nineteenth-century hermeneutics. One pole is represented by Schleiermacher, who presented a project of reconstructing the meaning of the work in the context of its own time. On the second pole, we see Hegel pointing out how vain such efforts were and insisting that we should adopt the past in our own context. Nietzsche (see, e.g., 1984, 1997) ridiculed such attempts to turn history into a science—the illusion that it is possible, by whatever method, to gain an objective image of time past. He stressed that the present is symmetrical to the past and the future, and that the whole projection of future events depends on how we have integrated the past to the present: "When the past speaks it always speaks as an oracle: only if you are an architect of the future and know the present will you understand it. The extraordinary degree and extent of the influence exercised by Delphi is nowadays explained principally by the fact that the Delphic priests had an exact knowledge of the past" (Nietzsche, 1997, p. 94).

For Gadamer (1996), in contrast to his forebears, hermeneutics is not a mere *method* of deciphering meaning, as such a method would simply reveal what *has existed* from the very beginning. Rather, hermeneutics is the very act of *acquiring* knowledge, understanding, becoming acquainted with a given thing, that is, *creating meaning*. Knowledge and understanding will *arise* in the very process of study:

> [The hermeneutic phenomenon] is not concerned primarily with amassing verified knowledge, such as would satisfy the methodological ideal of science—yet it too is concerned with knowledge and with truth. In understanding tradition not only are texts understood, but insights are acquired and truths known. But what kind of knowledge and what kind of truth? Given the dominance of modern science in the philosophical elucidation and justification of knowledge and the concept of truth, this question does not appear legitimate. Yet it is unavoidable, even within the sciences. The phenomenon of understanding . . . also has an independent validity within science, and it resists any attempt to reinterpret it in terms of scientific method. (pp. xxi–xxii)

According to Gadamer, the cause of repeated failures to find "consilience" between the human sciences (*Geisteswissenschaften*) and the natural sciences was, and is, often seen as the lack or low accuracy of data (as, e.g., in meteorology), rather than in the inherent impossibility of the task. In the first case, the maxims for the human sciences should be identical with those of inductive natural sciences: even if causes for particular effects cannot be ascertained, it should be possible to establish regularities. However, we shall immediately agree that induction as a tool to gain a universal rule or a law is impossible in human sciences:

> The experience of the sociohistorical world cannot be raised to science by the inductive procedure of the natural sciences. . . . Historical research does not endeavor to grasp the concrete phenomenon as an instance of a universal rule. . . . The aim is not to confirm and extend these universalized experiences in order to attain knowledge of a law—for example how men, peoples, and states evolve—but to understand how this man, this people, or this state is what it has become or more generally, how it happened that it is so. (pp. 4–5)

There is no such thing as an objective interpretation of texts, let alone objective history or mandatory criteria for aesthetics or value. There is no positivist "this and no other way," but only a narrative reference to all possibilities. To create a background for his own narrative, Gadamer refers to Helmholtz (see chapter 1), with his unlimited credit in the natural sciences. He points to the fact that, despite his positivism, even Helmholtz understood that the methods of natural sciences cannot be applied to all branches of knowledge. He therefore distinguished two types of induction, logical and artistic-instinctive, and also suggested that "the practice of induction in the human sciences is tied to particular psychological conditions" (Gadamer, 1996, p. 5). Gadamer comments:

> [O]ne might well ask, with Helmholtz, to what extent method is significant in this case and whether the other logical presuppositions of the human sciences are not perhaps far more important than inductive logic. Helmholtz had indicated this correctly when, in order to do justice to the human sciences, he emphasized memory and authority, and spoke of the psychological tact that here replaced the conscious drawing of inferences. What is the basis of this tact? How is it acquired? Does not what is scientific about the human sciences lie rather here than in their methodology? (pp. 7–8)

Our task is to assess what of this could be useful in biology. Clearly, it is not necessary to start with psychological tact, but questions concerning relations to possibilities, of choices between given possibilities, memory, trends, a higher level of internal relations (which can be denoted by the term "teleology") are highly legitimate. It is in this area that the tension between the

hermeneutic (interpretational) tradition of the humanities and the explanatory tradition of the empirical sciences lies (see, e.g., Heelan, 1998).

Natural Sciences and Two Branches of Humanities

Here I present an outline that is complementary to that of E. O. Wilson, who
saw the natural sciences as a model for understanding reality (see chapter 1).
Gadamer states that the natural sciences of the nineteenth century do not belong to either history or reality—they drifted apart from both and *created an
artificial world for themselves*. They studied phenomena beyond time and context, *objectively*. The situation in human sciences was not that simple. One
current also tried to grasp reality in objective terms, in an attempt to bring the
humanities into the mainstream of the mechanistic world of the natural sciences. This effort culminated in the works of Wilhelm Dilthey, of Hegel, and of
Marx.

At the same time, however, another current was emerging, one that rejected any attempts at an abstract historical knowledge. This current began
with Nietzsche and culminated in the twentieth century with Heidegger.
Here, as in the theory of arts, in text interpretation, or in history, there is a
recognition that *seeing* requires classifying, dissecting, distinguishing ("seeing
means articulating"—Gadamer, 1996, p. 91). No abstract, bare impression
or seeing can be assumed: it is always bound to an effort to identify meaning.
"Pure seeing and pure hearing are dogmatic abstractions that artificially reduce phenomena. Perception always includes meaning" (p. 92). This current
of thought therefore sought to return to images, allegories, and symbols, so
common before but abandoned by the Enlightenment, and to point out the in-
adequacy of a mechanistic worldview. The play can serve as good allegory for
the aims of the proponents of this school: "The movement of playing has no
goal that brings it to an end; rather, it renews itself in constant repetition" (p.
103). "Play is really limited to presenting itself. Thus its mode of being is self-
presentation. But self-presentation is a universal ontological characteristic of
nature" (p. 108).

Authors and actors do not exist as such: only what is being played is important. Here something will emerge into the limelight that would otherwise
remain hidden or withdrawn forever. The same holds for seasonal feasts and
celebrations. In what sense do we speak of the *same* holiday? Gadamer (1996)
then applies the allegory of a play to reality, and states: " 'Reality' always
stands in a horizon of desired or feared or, at any rate, still undecided future
possibilities. Hence it is always the case that mutually exclusive expectations
are aroused, not all of which can be fulfilled. The undecidedness of the future
permits such a superfluity of expectations that reality necessarily lags behind

them" (p. 112). Understanding emerges—or better, reemerges—in the course of a play (here Gadamer refers to Plato's *anamnesis*). It would be senseless to search for a single or optimal (objective) performance of a play (or a feast). And "to be present means to participate" (p. 124; see similar statements by Ruyer in chapter 3).

With reference to biology, the play, the rerun of a performance in a current context, is what is going on in both ontogeny and phylogeny: the "same" is attempted again and again.

Participation in the world is the most important question if we want to understand life. It is even more important to realize that a model of life as a play, as self-representation, as participation, is as justifiable as that of living beings as three-dimensional mechanical constructs. We are simply accustomed to seeing them according to the second model. It is often claimed that the mechanical model has been legitimized by successful applications (in medicine, animal husbandry, etc.), but I do not think that such a claim is justified. First, a successful application by no means mirrors the ontological credibility of our model of the world. Second, the domination of the mechanical model is based on its decades-long acceptance when alternatives were only rarely taken into consideration. All practical achievements, then, were interpreted as proofs of the model.

Understanding

Every interpretation is a problem of understanding. Three very important factors are bound up with this rather banal statement. First, someone who understands never starts from point zero: we are always part of the world's context. As far as memory can reach, we always have been participants in cultural interactions, and, of course, also a co-former of such interactions. Moreover, as a living being, the interpreter is a product of evolution and part of a biological context.

As Ruyer (chapter 3) would say, we have never been dead; we are the heirs of four billions years of biological evolution. Through *this* network of interactions, we are also participants and co-creators of history: we carry our history along with us.

Second, we are confronted, as cultural and at the same time biological beings (from the point of understanding, this is essentially the same), with the existence of texts (written or genetic) that themselves represent only dead strings of characters. They enter the network of interaction and "speak" only through us.

The cell reading a genetic text is in a similar situation. In this case, moreover, the cell itself represents both the story and the interpretation of the text. In both cases the achievement depends on the situation of the "reader" in the network.

Third, the properties of natural language come to the fore, and with them also the question of how a written text can be a bearer of "information"—or better, how information can emerge through the text. Hermeneutics, therefore, has its roots in a common experience of the world, in the fact that there never is a "beginning" to start from, that some prior understanding must always be supposed. The slogan "the aim is to understand the author better than he would understand himself" is a legacy of the nineteenth century. Later, this situation was to give rise to Heidegger's ontology of the hermeneutic circle.

Ontology of the Hermeneutic Circle

In his *Time and Being* (1927), Heidegger decisively changed the development of hermeneutics by introducing his ontology of the hermeneutic circle:

> This circle of understanding is not a circle in which any random kind of knowledge operates, but it is rather the expression of the existential *fore-structure* of Dasein itself. The circle must not be degraded to a *vitiosum*, not even to a tolerated one. A positive possibility of the most primordial knowledge is hidden in it which, however, is only grasped in a genuine way when interpretation has understood that its first, constant, and last task is not to let fore-having, fore-sight, and fore-conception be given to it by chance ideas and popular conceptions, but to guarantee the scientific theme by developing these in terms of the things themselves. (Heidegger, 1996, §32, p 143)

By introducing the concept of *Dasein*, Heidegger created an alternative to a hitherto accepted view of the world as an opposition of subject and object. It enabled him to get rid of archetypes and other ready-made constructions previously used to constitute our relations with the world. The essence of *Dasein* is concern, involvement in one's own life. *Dasein* has been thrown into the world, but not as a tabula rasa. It always *understands* the world in one way or another; its "thrownness" is fore-understanding. The understanding of the present situation is negotiated through this fore-understanding. In this way, hermeneutics became not merely one of a number of possible model approaches, but experience with reality itself. Due to fore-understanding, *Dasein* is able to orient itself in the world. Understanding becomes the true way of its existence: to be is to understand. Everyday understanding, the way of existence, the things and events we manipulate, all of this is already *fore-interpreted* by the fore-understanding. A true understanding, then, supposes an explanation as a process of clearing up what was already present in the fore-understanding. The self-explanation of *Dasein* should be considered as the original form of language; statements as logical constructs are only derived. The goal of hermeneutics is no longer a theory of explanation, but explanation as such. Hermeneutics is thus raised from a mere method to an ontology.

I see all of this as a challenge for biology. I dare even to say that we should accept the task of seeking a status of *Dasein* for *all* living beings. I must admit, however, that most philosophers whom I consulted are very skeptical about such a project. For them, the existence of the *Dasein* will suppose the presence of understanding, of language, and of disposition. The main objection, then, is the absence of language in beings different from humans. Here, either I am struggling with a lack of my understanding, or the topic is simply not clear enough. As far as I understand the problem, analogies of the kind "if I as a living being, then *any* living being" are apparently not allowed. The ontology of the hermeneutic cycle is therefore confined to beings who are able to communicate in language (children do not fulfill the requirements either). From the point of view of a biologist, I see the relation "*Dasein* = any living being" as fully legitimate. I have, of course, no ambitions to provoke philosophers into giving new meanings to well-established concepts. It is for biology to overcome their reservations one day. One way would be to take the stance that understanding itself is a form of self-understanding of *Dasein*, even when understanding is bound not to a language, but to signs and symbols. Thus, biosemiotics can do much to solve the problem. The second way should be to show that all living beings relate themselves to the world through "languageness." I return to this second position in part III of this book.

Gadamer (1996), Heidegger's main successor in the domain of hermeneutics, described Heidegger's contribution to hermeneutics as follows:

> What Heidegger is working out here is not primarily a prescription for the practice of understanding, but a description of the way interpreting understanding is achieved. The point of Heidegger's hermeneutic reflections not so much to prove that there is a circle as to show that this circle possesses an ontologically positive significance. . . . For it is necessary to keep one's gaze fixed on the thing throughout all the constant distractions that originate in the interpreter himself. A person who is trying to understand a text is always projecting. He projects a meaning for the text as a whole as soon as some initial meaning emerges in the text. Again, the initial meaning emerges only because he is reading the text with particular expectations with regard to a certain meaning. Working out this fore-perception,

which is constantly revised in terms of what emerges as he penetrates into the meaning, is understanding what is there. (pp. 266–267)

The ontology of the hermeneutic circle may—if understood by a philosopher with a biological background—become a starting point for our understanding of how all living beings understand themselves in the world. From here, a better understanding of phenomena such as adaptation, morphogenesis, evolution, and so forth, could emerge.

On Prejudices

Hand in hand with the interpretation of texts and the ontology of the hermeneutic circle, and of course with life, comes the question of prejudices. Gadamer made a substantial contribution to hermeneutics by pointing out that prejudices are a form of fore-understanding. He showed that prejudices have only come into dishonor since the Enlightenment; in earlier times they were a fully legitimate part of knowledge. Until the Enlightenment, no member of Christian civilization had come across the idea of interpreting the Holy Writ from the position of an atheistic, rationally reasoning spirit. The authorities were a natural part of the interpretation framework. If, however, we have an ambition to interpret the Script or any other text "without prejudice," we are automatically confronted by the fact that any work that exists in a community of readers already has an authority of sorts. Therefore, for Gadamer (1996) the main goal of the Enlightenment can be expressed as follows: "True prejudices must still finally be justified by rational knowledge, even though the task can never be fully completed" (p. 273). Such an aim is of course burdened by its own load of prejudices, the principal one being the "prejudice against prejudices." The Enlightenment submitted authority to reason, but authority becomes an authority just because it *knows*! Authority legitimizes the prejudices implanted in our minds: "The recognition that all understanding inevitably involves some prejudice gives the hermeneutic problem its real thrust" (p. 270). From this point of view, Wilson's claim (see chapter 1) that the humanities betrayed the ideal of the Enlightenment because they shifted toward romanticism may not be true. If we accept Gadamer's position, the very paradox of tradition and rationality will, of course, disappear. Tradition inevitably enters any interpretation through our prejudices: it is a part of the fore-understanding:

> The anticipation of meaning that governs our understanding of a text is not an act of subjectivity, but proceeds from a commonality that binds us to the tradition. But this commonality is constantly being formed in our relation to tradition. Tradition is not simply a permanent precondition; rather,

we produce it ourselves inasmuch as we understand, participate in the evolution of tradition, and hence further determine it ourselves. Thus, the circle of understanding . . . describes an element of the ontological structure
of understanding. (p. 293)

If we understand this point, we should become more sympathetic to Kuhnian
or even "postmodern" thinkers who maintain that *all* knowledge, including
that residing in scientific paradigms, is *also* a matter of tacit knowledge, en-
actment, of peers who mark out what belongs to this or that body of knowledge.

Lineage as an Analogy to a Culture

Many different cultures are known that have developed from common roots
and are based on identical or very similar generic, canonic texts. How many
cultures have arisen based on different interpretations of a single canonical
text—the Bible? We will find no difficulties here, because, along with the
text, *people* (or peoples) also transmit the way to interpret it. But who is the
interpreter in a biological species? In addition to the canonical text—two
versions of genome inherited from our parents—we also inherit a small but
very important piece of body: the egg cell itself. This is the agent that reads
the dead text of genetic inscription and transforms it into information, technical documentation that can be consulted according to situation. And this
arrangement is the clue to the species-specific interpretation, that is, recognition of the text and of signals from outside on the basis of the history, experience of the cell, cell lineage, and species. The fertilized egg manipulates
the genetic text according to rules inherited from countless generations of
its predecessors. Driven by this tradition, it builds the specific morphology.
I maintain that a species can be understood as a culture; it follows that the
emergence of new species may equally be a matter of the mutation of the
text (DNA) and/or changes in the rules for manipulating it. The species (lineage) as a cultural phenomenon is a common theme in biosemiotics (see,
e.g., Deely, 2001).

Structuralism

If I here interrupt the discussion of hermeneutics by an structuralist inter-
mezzo, it is for two reasons. First, since the 1980s, a discipline of biological
structuralism has emerged. Its proponents wish to create an alternative to the
reigning molecular biology and neo-Darwinism (see chapters 4 and 5). Before
discussing this, it is necessary to say something of structuralism proper. Sec-

ond, here is the most natural place for the antinomy between structuralism and hermeneutics to surface.

Structuralism has played a considerable role in some branches of linguistics, mathematics, psychology, and cultural anthropology. It stresses the relationship between the whole and its parts. A thing is to be understood not as a conglomerate of its parts, but as a totality, and only as such does it have any meaning. Parts gain their meaning only from their position in the whole structure. This is, of course, in no way revolutionary, but in structuralism it is supposed that a *structure* is a system of relationships that always has existed. Transformation of the structure proceeds according to fixed rules (though this does not mean that transformations themselves are given in advance—the *rules* are conservative, but not the *outcomes*). A structural analysis will not consider the meaning of the phenomenon in question, only analyze the order of formations of the thing, provided that the rules of formation were known in advance. Meaning is not an initial hypothesis, but can be discovered or produced. If we succeed in deciphering the nature of the relationships between the parts and the whole, we get a model of a given structure that becomes a formal analogue of all models organized by that structure. Piaget (1971), one of the founders of the movement, states that structuralism, by identifying isomorphisms, makes it possible to unify even domains that, at first sight, have nothing in common (e.g., various mathematical theories).

In science, I understand the structuralist approach as an attempt to overcome—or better, to complement or correct—attempts to explain the world from the molecular level. Each level of description becomes the basic level with its own structural laws.

The parts of a structure are not determined from outside, and nor do they carry any meaning: what counts is the meaning given by the *position* of a particular element in the structure (compare this to the alternative approach of Ricoeur discussed below). The structure itself, in fact, is not present: what is present is its incarnation. The structure is real even if not present, and ideal even if not abstract. Even such an encyclopedic survey suggests that structuralism is, to a great extent, in opposition to the hermeneutic approach, which works with tradition, archetypes, and the semantic fields of particular symbols.

A structure is characterized by *wholeness, transformations,* and *self-regulation.* Wholeness reflects the subordination of elements to rules that characterize the whole system, rules that cannot be reduced to cumulative associations. Transformations assume that there is bipolarity (or dialectics) in all properties of elements. The elements form the structure and are formed by it. Self-regulation assumes rhythms, feedback loops—that is, dynamics characteristic of cybernetic networks. It also means that transformations inherent to a given structure will never lead to transgression of that structure. They generate only such elements as always belong to that structure and conserve its laws (Piaget, 1971).

The last point is extremely important: the system of transformation is *closed*; it develops and becomes enriched because of inherent rules that are independent of outside influences, and at the same time it does not allow the structure to transgress its own limits. Novelties have always been virtually present as potentials of the structure. Historical events, that is, trajectories of the system in time, cannot change the rules—otherwise no structured space would exist, only a kind of eternal flow akin to the Heraclitean River. From the postulate of self-sufficiency of a structure, it follows that a structure can be totally known in itself, without any need to refer to elements outside the structure. Neubauer et al. (1989) characterized the difference between structuralist belief and hermeneutics as follows: "The structuralist analysis of a text aims to understand it from its fabric. It does not refer to historical or social aspects, to the intentions, status or beliefs of the author, to the anamnesis or conditions accompanying the generation of texts. The text exists as such, and what is not a part of it does not belong to it" (p. 61). If we project this theoretical background onto a real world, the problem arises of the relations between logical-mathematical structures used for causal explanations of laws and proposed real structures in the flesh. From this broad outline, the linguistic, mathematical, and social structures took over. Biological structuralism, discussed in chapter 5, is only a latecomer.

Structuralism also has a thematic bearing on positivism's task of creating a contrast-free language based on formal logic. Heisenberg (1959) commented on such a task as follows:

> [Modern positivism] expresses criticism against the naive use of certain terms like "thing," "perception," "existence" by the general postulate that the question whether a given sentence has any meaning at all should always be thoroughly and critically examined. This postulate and its underlying attitude are derived from mathematical logic. The procedure of natural science is pictured as an attachment of symbols to the phenomena. The symbols can, as in mathematics, be combined according to certain rules and in this way statements about the phenomena can be represented by combinations of symbols. However, a combination of symbols that does not comply with the rules is not wrong but conveys no meaning. The obvious difficulty in this argument is the lack of any general criterion as to when a sentence should be considered as meaningless. A definite decision is possible only when the sentence belongs to a closed system of concepts and axioms, which in the development of natural science will be rather the exception than the rule. In some cases the conjecture that a certain sentence is meaningless has historically led to important progress, for it opened the way for the establishment of new connections which would

have been impossible if the sentence had a meaning. . . . Insistence on the postulate of complete logical clarification would make science impossible. (pp. 77–79)

The concepts are not sharply defined in their relation to nature, in spite of the sharp definition of their possible connections. The limitations will therefore be found from experience, from the fact that concepts do not allow a complete description of the observed phenomena. (p. 91)

So some degree of "softness," some ambiguity of concepts, is a precondition of knowledge. Only in this way can language (speech) escape a tautological cycle of noncontradictory sentences. If so, then knowledge, orientation in the world, will become a truly hermeneutic feat, and the area for structuralism to operate will become limited.

Structuralism in Linguistics

In linguistics, structuralism created a new conception of language by disregarding the diachronic approach and concentrating on discovering what all isolated, synchronous phenomena have in common. Saussure (1959; originally published in 1916), a French linguist and one of the founders of structuralism, divided language into two planes: synchronic and diachronic. The first is represented by language in the strict sense—*langue* (words, vocabulary, grammatical rules)—and the diachronic part by utterances, speech—*parole*. The *langue* is not a function of the speaker but exists passively and synchronously for many speakers, whereas *parole* is an individual act of will and consciousness—the message. It was the synchronous part of the language (i.e., *langue*) that was the main focus of Saussure's interest. It represents an autonomous system of transformations without any reference to the content of spoken accounts. This orientation in a synchronous code (its structure, system, logic) subsequently prevailed at the expense of *parole*, which is not so easy to grasp for analysis. Researchers tended to believe in universal variations and permutations that would lead to the generation of all statements possible in a given language; the meaning of a statement would appear only secondarily, when it is actually realized.

Ricoeur (1976) questioned this outline. He, like Saussure, takes the code of a given language as collective, synchronous, and anonymous. This part of a language is neither intended nor conscious. On the other hand, discourse always has its speaker, is "diachronous" in time. Whereas the code is systematic and obligatory for the whole community of speakers, the communication act is arbitrary and contingent. Ricoeur, however, contends that *parole*—discourse—cannot be reduced to a system of combinatorial possibilities. Ricoeur directs his criticism toward the four basic postulates of Saussurian semiotics: (1) a synchronous approach must precede the diachronic, (2) the set of discrete entities (phonemes, vocabularies) is finite, (3) no entity is endowed with a meaning—there are only *differences* between them, and (4) all relations between the signs are immanent to the system; that is, there is no relation to the external, nonsemiotic, reality. The sign is not defined by the relationship between it and the thing it describes, but through two aspects, the "signifier" (a sound, a written word) and the "signified" (e.g., an entry in a dictionary). The signs therefore refer to each other.

A language thus defined, argues Ricoeur, ceases to function as a communicator between subjects and things; it is no longer alive and creates its own closed world with elements referring to other elements of the system. The language becomes self-contained and the discourse disappears, and we end in a sort of mathematics (see also Heisenberg above).

For discourse to reenter the language, Ricoeur (1976) suggests a two-dimensional approach based on entities as well as sentences, the first being the subject of semiotics, the second of semantics. The system of signs (codes) is only virtual: the true existence of the language is dependent on discrete and singular acts of discourse, which will actualize the code. What, however, follows from the ontological priority of the discourse?

> [I]f the "instance of discourse" . . . were merely this vanishing event [then] science would be justified in discarding it, and the ontological priority of discourse would be insignificant and without consequence. An act of discourse is not merely transitory and vanishing, however. It may be identified and reidentified as the same so that we may say it again or in other words. We may even say it in another language or translate it from one language into another. Through all these transformations it preserves an identity of its own which can be called the propositional content, the "said as such." (p. 9)

For this "said as such," for the meaning of the expression, Neubauer (2001) coins the term *eidos* and broadens it to encompass the whole realm of living beings (this point will be discussed in the introduction to part II). The enunciation of a discourse (and in a broader conception, of all living nature) is a one-off event, but it is endowed with a meaning that becomes transformed into a piece of communication. Only in enunciated sentences does the language cease to be a mere system of signs and become an entity that, by means of grammatical rules referring to each other, refers *beyond* its own frame.

In chapters 12 and 13, I introduce a biological analogy for this explanation, identifying *langue* with the genetic text inscribed in DNA: it represents a code, a message written in a synchronous language. *Parole*, then, is the reading of the message—genetic regulation, gene expression, and "body building."

A Written Word and Its Reading

I have shown that the timeless system of the language (i.e., its structure, *langue*) neither appears nor becomes lost—it simply lasts. It exists before the events. On the other hand, an utterance is an *event*: it becomes extinct at the very moment that it is pronounced. There is often, therefore, a need to fix it in some medium that is separate from the memories of the participants in a discourse. But whenever a discourse is written in the form of a text, the manifestations of language attain new and unsuspected dimensions.

Again, parallels for the system "DNA–protein" or "genetic inscription–body" come to mind and call for elaboration.

In structuralism, events represent nothing more than an epiphenomenon, a self-justification of the structure itself. However, when we try to fix the discourse into a lasting medium, we seek to capture this or that discourse, not a timeless *langue*. We do, of course, use the grammar and the vocabulary, but they merely represent a means for fixing the discourse (or for deciphering what has been fixed). And now a strange transformation occurs: the script suddenly represents much more than simply a trace, a fixation of the discourse. *Littera* takes over from *vox* in the discourse, and the text becomes semantically autonomous, *separate from the speaker.* It escapes beyond the horizon of its author, and suddenly the meaning of the text for the reader is much more important than its author's intentions. The person receiving the message is autonomous of its author, and everybody who can read can become an interpreter. (The same holds for translations from one language into another: the very fact that the message is translatable means that the pattern is not *part* of the structure but is *implemented* into it.)

Hermeneutics is a product of this distance: the possibility of manifold readings is a dialectical counterpart of the semantic autonomy of the text. Hermeneutics begins where dialogue ends, in the dynamics of interpretation, says Gadamer (1996). The text gains in importance by the fact that it is accessible to an unlimited audience. This fact means that *human beings*, and only they, have the world at their disposal in more than one way—not only through present situation and/or memory.

If we take the genetic script as a genuine text, we can substitute, in the sentence above, "living being" for "human being." Of course, some questions may arise as to who is the "author" of the genetic text. In the first place, let us assume that it is the parents who, together with the text, also communicate the framework for the *usual* interpretations.

Working from an analogy with the visual arts, Ricoeur (1976) introduced for this situation the concept of *iconic augmentation*, by which he means that the painting is never the same as the painted. The painting *amplifies* the meaning of the world by fixing it to a network of abbreviating signs. The written text is also simply a particular example of iconicity. The *inscription* of a discourse is a *transcription* of the world, but this transcription presents not a duplication but a metamorphosis of the world. Because of this very fact, reading becomes a hermeneutic problem. This is the place of the dialectics of the distance and ownness: by reading, "the meaning of the text is 'rescued' from the estrangement of distanciation and put in a new proximity, a proximity which suppresses and preserves the cultural distance and includes the otherness within the ownness" (pp. 43–44). This brings us to what Ricoeur calls the *surplus of meaning*: there will always be a semantic overlap from the inscription to the metaphor.

> Only for an interpretation are there two levels of signification since it is the recognition of the literal meaning that allows us to see that a symbol still contains more meaning. This surplus of meaning is the residue of literal interpretation. Yet for the one who participates in the symbolic signification there are really not two significations, one literal and the other symbolic, but rather a single movement, which transfers him from one level to the other and which assimilates him to the second signification by means of, or through, the literal one. (p. 55)

If, however, we cannot simply return to the supposed situation of the author, what is the "right" meaning of the text? To interpret the verbal meaning of the text, according to Ricoeur, means to judge. I return to this problem in part III in connection with the analysis of two interfaces: genetic texts–organism, and environment–organism. At this point, it may again be interesting to call again on Heisenberg (1959). He points to the fact that, in sciences, attention was paid especially to simple patterns of logical reasoning, whereas other language structures were neglected. But meaning can often arise especially through the secondary meanings of words instead of through logical patterns. After all, we do not wish to speak of the facts represented, for example, by black spots on a screen, but about atoms and their properties. At the same time, it is impossible to speak about atoms in ordinary language—therefore, physicists accepted the use of speech, which is prone to associations and metaphors:

> I believe that the language actually used by physicists when they speak about atomic events produces in their minds similar notions as the [Aristotelian] concept "potentia." So the physicists have gradually become accustomed to considering electronic orbits, etc., not as reality but rather as a kind of "potentia." The language has already adjusted itself, at least to

some extent, to this true situation. But it is not a precise language in which one could use the normal logical patterns; it is a language that produces pictures in our mind, but together with them the notion that the pictures have only a vague connection with reality, that they represent only a tendency toward reality. (pp. 154–156)

As already mentioned above, history is also closely involved with the problems of reading, of interpretation. A historian is in a more precarious position than is a philologist. His subject is history, and for him an individual text is simply one source, a single point, but it also constitutes the *potentia* of Heisenberg. Moreover, as the "Book of History" will always remain a mere fragment whose beginning is lost in the tumults of the past, it lacks the overall consistency and integrity so typical of texts. Two further complications face the historian: first, history has not yet come to an end; second, we ourselves are part of history—and with our personal history we are never in the role of mere readers of a text.

These complications produce a tension in the human sciences that is never surmounted. On one hand, they follow in the scientistic struggle to gain firm, "objective" support, and on the other hand, they understand the historicity of human life. The second condition means that the first goal can never be achieved and the hope of finding an Archimedean fixed point must be relinquished. The idea of a universal history, even of a concise history of the recent past, should be abandoned: the past is a source of a great variety of singular facts that cannot be glued together into an unequivocal, objective whole. Above all, this is because we do not know the end of the quest (if there is one).

But despite all this, the primary task of a historian is to write a "biography." History, however, offers many different possibilities of meaningful understanding, which is why each generation writes its history anew. Gadamer (1996, p. 226) refers to Dilthey's statement that one precondition of a historical science is the very fact that humans themselves are historical beings— they study history and at the same time they participate in it; they are both subjects and objects of history.

I should add that the same undoubtedly holds for other living beings: they participate in the interpretation of the past and have their share in the ongoing evolution. Gadamer's (1996) conclusion has particular relevance for the later stages of this discussion: "[For Dilthey,] significance is not a logical concept, but is to be understood as an expression of life. Life itself, flowing temporality, is ordered toward the formation of enduring units of significance. Life interprets itself. Life itself has a hermeneutic structure. Thus life constitutes the real ground of the human sciences" (pp. 225–226)

I have shown in this chapter that a plethora of outlines exist in the humanities that may serve as tools of reconciliation between blind universe on one side and meaningful world on the other. Because of the fragmentation of knowledge, however, natural sciences are not merely unaware for the most part of such methodological hardware; they do not feel the need to pose certain kind of questions at all.

In my analysis of scientific approaches to the world, I have moved from the ontology of metaphysical realism to that of the hermeneutic circle, and I have indicated that I proceed in this direction in this biological investigation. Before doing so, however, chapter 3 is a brief pause at another branch of knowledge, which I believe has a bearing on our topic and should not be ignored. It also will put these hermeneutic efforts into their proper place on the imaginary scale of readers–interpreters.

3

LIVING NATURE—A GNOSTIC APPROACH

Verbally scientists dismiss all mythology. They treat the myth
with a disdain of boors, just to accept another myth, which
can be called the Myth of Absolute Blind. The Universe as
a unity does not see and does not know itself. It is an
emporium of bodies, which meet without sensing the
encounters; where mechanical "information" becomes blindly
applied; where the senders and receivers of "messages"
experience the contents in a way the telephone cable does;
where the postmen are illiterate and blind; where the post
connects beings incapable of speaking or writing and for who
the transmitted and exchanged messages do not make any
sense. The myth of Absolute Blind is absurd. It is a myth,
because it is repeating endlessly as in a mirror just several
phenomena of our everyday experience that happen to be
blind indeed. All phenomena of classical physics are blind.
If a myth is necessary, the gnosis will at least choose one
that is not that absurd.

Raymond Ruyer

In chapter 1 I addressed the mechanistic worldview as one limit to understanding the world. I now address the second limit of our scale of approaching the world. Readers may ask what can be gained by taking the whole Universe as a living being. I take as companion the French philosopher and
mathematician Raymond Ruyer, who interviewed leading world scientists
(mainly physicists) who worked at Princeton University in the 1960s and embedded their views in *The Princeton Gnosis* (1974). The world according to this

modern gnosis[1] is characterized by a hierarchy of domains, which represent different levels of spirit and are conscious. Any entity that can say "I" is regarded as conscious. Ruyer is even more radical than classical gnostics in that, to him, spirit and matter are no longer in opposition. The spirit constitutes matter, gives it substance (*étoffe*). The universe is conscious and consists of conscious domains and their interactions, that is, in the exchange of information (as opposed to the empty, spiritless, mechanical interactions of bodies in classical physics or of molecules in chemistry). Ruyer (1974) exposes the image of the "right" and "reverse" sides of all beings; the reverse is what can be observed from outside, whereas their right side is their inwardness:

> The gnosis is the antipode of materialist scientism. All beings are conscious, embodying, or better, full of sense, informing and receiving information. Not only is their body nothing but a superficial aspect for an external "observer": *they do not have a body, they are not bodies.* They are the "right" side; only for others do they appear as a "reverse," as a body. They perceive themselves, and in the process of seeing they mutually transform into visible things. The Cosmos is a tapestry, and science describes it faithfully, but from the reverse. The gnosis goes behind and beyond what science can observe, toward the knowledge of real life of beings. We all are "gnostics" and not only "scientists" whenever we try to become intimately acquainted with someone, when we understand a message or read a letter, when we sense the meaning behind symbols, or an expression behind aesthetic forms. (p. 63)

The gnostic views, therefore, are not richer than are those of science; they simply take a different approach, from a different angle. Ruyer explains the difference by the analogy of a live flower compared with a scientific description of the same flower: despite all the details contained in the scientific report, something of what constitutes a living flower is still lacking. *The Princeton Gnosis* aims to reveal the soul of beings, which Ruyer compares with drawings on the face of a tapestry (whereas science also describes it in considerable detail, but from the reverse). By doing so, the gnosis generalizes over the whole universe what we spontaneously perform in our hearts. Con-

---

1. It is by no means my aim to enter the fascinating world of ancient gnostic teachings with their sophisticated theology. What they had in common was a belief that the world has been created and is reigned by a Spirit (Highest consciousness, *nous*). The world is strictly divided into hierarchies with corresponding levels of spirituality. On its own level, the human soul is a reflection of the highest spirit, but the image has become distorted, imperfect, "noncanonical" due to the many intermediate levels. The same holds for all levels lower than the highest. Gnosis is a teaching on how barriers can be overcome to attain perfection through concentrated spiritual effort and initiation. The principal drawback to such an effort is an absence of automatic translation.

sciousness is a form of information, but directed inward, to the right side, and the universe is therefore self-conscious. It is not simply "composed" of physical bodies, of "things." Mere physical forces cannot explain its activity, and its body of information is not blind: "The 'observer' cannot, by definition, see anything other than an object where, in fact, a subjective consciousness resides. He cannot, by definition, observe a consciousness. He can, however, reveal it or participate in it" (p. 58).

Ruyer also has an answer to the question of why our belief in materialist physics is so strong: most objects in our everyday experience (a house, a river) are composites not endowed with any inwardness, any right side. Yet, from an analogy with similar aggregates, we extrapolate to the whole world. But the molecules contained in such objects know very well what they are doing, much better, in fact, than the physicists claim (p. 70). I do not feel competent to judge whether molecules have a consciousness or whether the universe can think. Even if answers to these questions exist, they are irrelevant to the discussion here. I have introduced Ruyer's ideas because they may enrich our view of living beings. First of all, Ruyer (1974) states—and here recall Gadamer's analysis—that any "I" cannot think otherwise than "here and now" (*ici-maintenant*). This here-and-now encompasses the whole memory of the past:

> Each "I" can claim that it has always lived, that it is the site of the creation of the Universe, its eternal center, the Spirit. It can do so because, like a physicist, it can define its own immobile system of coordinates in space. It is true that it cannot halt time, but it is what makes time by participating in subordinate and superior consciousness, and it cannot evade this creation as long as it is alive. The world of space and time is constructed from inside, like a snail molding its shell. It is a product of all the "Is" that are active there. (p. 72)

We have been here from the very beginning of the world, claims Ruyer; we never have been dead. The death of any "I" is something absolutely unprecedented. This idea resonates with Heideggerian and Gadamerian fore-understanding and fore-projection. Ruyer, however, eliminated the friction concerning the definition of *Dasein* (see chapter 2); his concept of "I" is much broader than that of the founders of the ontology of the hermeneutic circle.

A second metaphor in connection with every "I" is that of "tree of life." Ruyer gives a new dimension to the classical genealogical trees of biology when he claims that we, twigs on the ends of the tree's branches, are linked not only through the time axis. We also cohere through our here-and-now, we participate in the existence of the Tree, and we give it a pattern communicated through an invisible trunk. The trunk, for him, is a higher order spirit, God. This is the only God whom we can experience directly, because we participate in him, and he sees himself only by virtue of our existence. We are responsible to this tree of life *alias* God (*alias* culture?) and at the same time participate in it. As long as "I" live, I am participating and behave hermeneutically. After I die, I leave an incision on the trunk.

Participation is, I think, one of the most important of Ruyer's (1974) concepts and is particularly appropriate for biology. All entities that can be reflected by a consciousness can be divided into "observables" and "participables":

> Each conscious and surviving individuality—domain has two modes how to become informed: by observation or by participation. It can observe other domains in space, and can also participate in topics that reach beyond space, and topics from its own past. Because the past (since what is living has never been dead) extends long before the instant of individual birth, it reaches back to the very origins of life and the Universe. (p. 181)

To participate does not mean to merge, coalesce, and amalgamate with the participated; similarly, to participate in one's past does not mean to return to the past.

The mother tongue is an example of participation. When we speak, our consciousness does not run through a database of dictionaries and grammar in the way a computer word processor does. When we speak, we participate in the language: it sustains our speech on advisable trajectories. Instincts, morphogenesis, and, according to some biologists, even evolution are similar cases of participation. In general, Ruyer distinguished four groups of participables: the memory of an individual, the biological (genetic) memory, cultural memory, and supra-individual and supraspecies memory. Living beings do not exist, let alone understand, except through participation in a thesaurus that cannot be observed but can be participated in, that can be compared to a mother tongue. This thesaurus is not constituted, but constituting, and it can be steered by the actions of individual "speakers." What relation do these two categories stand in to science? I maintain that, despite differences in terminology, Ruyer's (1974) stance is very close to those of Gadamer and Heisenberg:

> Science claims that there is nothing but "observables," objects radiating or reflecting various waves or producing effects that can be observed. It ignores the "participable" or claims that they are in fact observables. It is therefore condemned to never understand the thematized epigenesis, morphogenesis in the true sense, the invention of forms. It will never understand beings participating in their own past that can say "I." This ignorance is serious and limits the extent of scientific knowledge. It is the participables, themselves nontemporal (or devoid of time in the memory), that el-

evate time to something more than a mere condition of the functioning of spatial structure: they endow it with *meaning*. (pp. 187–188)

Why do I consider participables so important for understanding our world? It is because of the impermeability of hierarchical levels, of the unimaginability or even impossibility of the unequivocal transfer of information from one level of description to another. Each domain communicates easily on its own level—horizontally—but it always has problems with vertical communication. Meanings, speech, images flow from one level to another, but they are "grammatically void."[2] Participation is an art of living, inhabiting and exerting experience and tact—in short, of behaving hermeneutically. The more removed the levels are, the more precarious the understanding. That is why gnostics aspiring for the highest level require long, painful, patient training and initiation. These ideas, however, go far beyond our topic.

---

2. Havel (1996) introduced a concept of "causal domain" for an area with which all causal relations appear apparent, understandable, and mutually coherent—at least more apparent, more understandable, and more coherent than the relations *between* different domains.

Part II

Biology from the Mechanistic to the Eidetic

I II   III

TEL   TEL

XĪS   ILŪ

         cenii

ce   ce

NI   Rˊ

         iii

abe   ūRa

hīs   coc

met   ste

TEL   TEL

Part II

BIOLOGY FROM THE MECHANISTIC
TO THE EIDETIC

DNA characters are copied with an accuracy that rivals
anything modern engineers can do. . . . We — and that means
all living things — are survival machines programmed to
propagate the digital database that did the programming.
Darwinism is now seen to be the survival of the survivors at
the level of pure, digital code.

Richard Dawkins

We should really understand that *esse intentionale*, that is,
the being of a thing which arises from the soul in the
cognitive process, is a "physical" being. We can then easily
grasp the view of modern epistemology that the thing to be
understood takes its shape in the very process of
understanding. Such a pretense may seem scandalous against
the background of "the prejudice of objectivity" which
reduces reality to *esse obiectivum*. If, however, the thing
being discerned is identical with the very process of arising,
that is, growing-into-known, then any reason for shock will
disappear. The content of a fact is not a "mere phenomenon."
In the act of genuine, true understanding, a "mere
phenomenon" will change into demonstration, in correlation
with a transformation of impression into a concept(ion).
The transformation is of the order of physis and belongs
to the reality of the thing being understood, to its
natural being.

Zdeněk Neubauer

In this part of the book I present a survey of some biological theories that profoundly influenced the development of biological science in the twentieth century. I maintain a scheme similar to that in part I, where we moved from objectivism to hermeneutics to gnosis. In this part, the ground will be delimited by two extremes. One is the postulate that the phenotypic characters (structure, physiology, and behavior) of the organism can be derived from a basic, digital level of description, that is, from information implemented in the molecule of DNA. Neo-Darwinism, the leading paradigm of contemporary biology, lies close to this end of the scale. The opposite extreme stresses the importance of bodily experience, history, and environmental contingencies and sees genetic makeup as a necessary but far from sufficient precondition. Close to this end of the scale belong the theories of biological field, epigenetics, and superorganism and what I call the language metaphor of life. Between lie biological structuralism, vitalism, and also the theoretical background of what became Lysenkoism. I follow the struggle to conciliate the contradictory demands of the "living state" with objectivist science.

Mechanism versus Organism

During the last 200 years, this topic has been treated ad nauseam by myriad works of theoretical biology. Whole careers have been devoted to various stands on the conflict, and elaborate philosophical systems have been developed, just to reach the conclusion that either (1) living beings are *nothing but machines* or (2) living beings *are not machines* and need some element in addition. Thus, the centuries-old dispute addresses the single question of whether the living (the "organic") can be identified with the mechanism. If not, how to characterize it? One of the greatest frustrations of biology lies in the fact that it is not able, despite incessant effort, to break through this "Aristotelian barrier" (see chapter 1 for this concept) and provide a clear resolution to this seemingly simple conflict.

The modern (Cartesian) tradition of thought, with its stress on strict causality, has of course resisted any attempts to support the existence of anything other than unequivocal causal chains and has instead proposed a machinelike conception of life. Despite this, the problem of organicity has tendency to resurface again and again. Abram (1996) has reflected it as follows:

> First, the "mechanical philosophy" suggests that matter, itself, is ultimately inert, without any life or creativity of its own. The great worth of the machine metaphor is that it implies that the material world is, at least in principle, entirely predictable. According to this metaphor, the material world operates like any machine according to fixed and unvarying rules; laws that have been built into the machine from the start. It has no creativity, no spontaneity of its own. (pp. 234–235)

A machine always implies someone who invented the machine, a builder, a maker. A machine cannot assemble itself. . . . If we view nature as machine, then we tacitly view it as something that has been built, something that has been made from outside. (p. 242)

Abram, of course, only restates a classic problem for our times. Almost identical formulations can be found in Kant's *Critique of Judgement* (1790). Also, for Kant, organic beings *should* be distinguished from mechanical devices. In contrast to machines, they possess one principal property: all their parts are at one and the same time the cause and the effect of their form.

On the part of mainstream biology, now as in the past, the whole mechanism versus organism problem has been declared a pseudoproblem or, in the milder form of rejection, put aside with a comment that it is beyond the powers of contemporary knowledge to solve it. In both cases, it is considered advisable to concentrate on more relevant problems (e.g., modern, successful, mechanistic science) instead of wasting time on metaphysical speculations. This advice has usually been followed—biologists do not protest against a mechanistic understanding of their subject. The prerequisite for understanding life in this framework is a linear and unidirectional (i.e., mechanical) relationship between the genetic text as the cause and the phenotype pattern as the effect of the process. The absence, in recent decades, of any alternative approaches has been balanced by the rocketing progress of mechanistic theory, which is most often called modern or neo-Darwinian synthesis (chapter 4).

The Reproduction of the "Living Machine"

Suppose that a device exists that is executing a program in a constant environment. This device has two functions: writing a copy of the program and building a copy of itself. This is the essence of so-called von Neumann interstellar automaton; here on Earth the cells of asexual microorganisms grown in a chemostat may be close to such a scenario. Both functions are carried out by metabolic subroutines, which serve both the production of construction parts and their compilation into an identical copy of the interpreter. A machine functioning in this manner could build a copy of itself in one of three ways (or a combination thereof):

1. By building the new machine *de novo* from construction parts it has produced: either they will self-assemble, or the mother machine will help to do this
2. By dividing into two nonidentical parts and completing them from the store of construction parts (modules) synthesized in advance (semiconservative reproduction)

3. By growth and subsequent division into two identical copies of the original machine

The task is, in the strict sense, fulfilled only in the first case — in other cases, the original phenotype in fact goes through changes, and there must be a loop in its states that will reestablish the starting position. It is symptomatic that the first alternative is *not* present in living beings.[1]

Whatever the means of reproduction of our machine, two complications will inevitably arise even in the absence of disturbances from the environment: copy errors (owing to the fact that analogue magnitudes cannot be measured with absolute accuracy) and attrition. The parts — but also the sensors and standards for space, mass and other measures — will be subject to wear and tear, and consequently they will not be able to produce an ideal copy of themselves. It could be argued that one of the program's subroutines might detect and replace the damaged parts, but for this sensors are needed, which themselves are parts of the device. The demand can therefore be satisfied only to some extent — by the high turnover of all parts of the device, including those that execute the turnover. Replacement will become a stochastic process, which necessarily is also prone to error. There are two ways out of this vicious circle, both requiring an external source of information:

1. Invariant factor(s) in the environment that can serve as calibration standard(s): ontogeny and physiology provide many examples of "bootstrapping" in the background of life cycles. The surrounding world thus interferes with the functioning of the machine.
2. The number of replicas of the system is high: those differing from the norm (due to errors) will be incompatible with their environment and will be eliminated. In this case, there is no need for the environment to contain invariant factors. Even in a variable environment, some variants in the progeny *will* cope with the environmental demands.

If we compare both ways, we see that the first is more or less applied in ontogeny; the second is at the core of the Darwinian evolutionary paradigm. In both cases, even a simple hypothetical system, with a constant genetic program and in a constant environment, will necessarily produce variations. The whole developmental loop will therefore require corrections from the environment (external or internal). Again, is an organism a machine?

---

1. At this point, many readers may argue that viruses are such an example, but this argument could take us too far. First: is a virus alive? What is its phenotype during periods when the virus itself does not "exist," when it is reduced to a piece of viral nucleic acid incorporated into a host cell? What is the boundary of the viral organism? We could come to the conclusion that a virus is a very atypical machine that incorporates a large part of the biosphere. We can, of course, pretend that we "know" what a virus is, but the textbook definition does not fulfill the basic criterion of a self-reproducing machine, that is, self-reproduction.

Genotype and Phenotype

If the metaphor of organism as a machine is encountered frequently, it may be worth delineating the boundaries within which it has a heuristic value and beyond which it becomes a caricature. Every biology textbook begins with a statement that organisms have a timeless, enduring component. This is the one-dimensional genetic script, a digital code easily reproducible in a form implemented with nucleic acids and transposable into other media (i.e., magnetic disk or a sheet of paper). The nucleic acid can also be removed from the cell, stored, amplified in vitro, or inserted into cells of virtually any biological species. Copying is highly accurate, and for all practical reasons copies can be considered identical to the original. Mutations—changes in the script—may occur either because the maintenance machinery is not absolutely error-proof or because of external causes. Everything else, the story goes on, in a living cell or an organism is of a corporeal, phenotypic, and therefore ephemeral nature. Living beings embody a tension between an (eternal) genetic code and a (transitory) pattern, or, more precisely, it is we who feel such a tension.

With contemporary biological techniques, it is much easier to study the lasting genetic message than to study phenotypes. This is why the body of (scientific) information concerning the genetic message is much more voluminous than is that concerning phenotypes. It is no wonder, then, that there is a well-established theory that considers genetic script both a necessary and a sufficient *cause* of a phenotype. The theory is based mainly on the observation that a single, nondifferentiated cell (e.g., a zygote) can give rise to a plethora of cell phenotypes, and that these—in the case of multicellular organisms—will build the entire body. Such phenomena, of course, do not necessarily mean causality: causality enters the field only when an *assumption* is introduced that the totality of functioning, differentiation, and ontogeny is a function of the digital information in the form of a linear string of symbols (bases).

Proteins can be considered as connecting links between the genetic information and the body. The machinery of transcription and translation can, to a great extent, be considered as constant and indifferent to whichever part of the information is being read, what proteins are being built, and what proteins were built in the past. The development of the whole system can be seen as an analogue of a computer program: each step of the reading will modify the existing protein context, which will modify the next decision as to which subroutines will be switched on, and so forth. Differentiation and morphogenesis can then be understood as higher steps—reiterations on other levels—of this simple successive program of differential protein synthesis in different daughter cells arising from the zygote (see, e.g., Stubblefield, 1986).

If development always starts from a zygote (or a spore) with an identical

setup, the genome could be indeed considered a *cause* of the resulting phenotype. Such causality can be proved, for example, by mutations of the genetic
text. If everything remains the same, a change in the sequence of bases will
(or *may*) elicit a change in the function of a particular protein. This will or
may result in a change in the phenotype of a cell (organism), even up to the
activation of programs that are normally not in use or even forbidden. In similar cases, the direct causal relationship between the genetic text and the phenotype should be obvious. Hindrances to the construction of an artificial cell
able to realize developmental program(s) would then be technical only and
would not exist in principle. E. O. Wilson (1998, p. 91) compared the task
with the Moon mission in 1969: no new principal discoveries were necessary
for its accomplishment, only money and technical skill. The "Jurassic Park
Fallacy"—the conviction that the knowledge of the complete sequence of
DNA of an individual is wholly sufficient for its "production" (resurrection,
creation?)—reemerges periodically, not because of science fiction writers, but
from the proclamations of serious scientists (at least two such projects of resurrection were announced in 1999 for the Tasmanian wolf and the Siberian
mammoth).

But a strictly mechanistic approach may not be satisfactory. Even at the
level of transcription and translation, the above model will seem oversimpli-
fied. Genetic information is a necessary but not sufficient condition to assign shape, localization, and function to a protein that is synthesized. This fact
was proved when the first attempts were made to synthesize commercially or
medically important eukaryotic proteins in bacteria (genetically transformed
with the gene for the particular protein). Transcription or translation generally proceeded without problems, but outside the context of their "maternal"
cells, many proteins collapsed into nonfunctional denatured chunks. We are
now well aware of the fact that proper reading of the genetic text is a function
of a context constituted from hundreds of proteins and other structures. The
external and internal environments are sources not only of physical and
chemical "forcing" but also of signs, hints coming from other cells and organisms. The receiver will recognize such signals and interpret and evaluate
them in the context of other signals and its own experience. All this, together
with the high interspecies similarity of genetic texts (recall, e.g., the genetic
proximity of humans and chimpanzees), suggests that species-specific morphologies will depend not only on genetic but also on epigenetic interpretation processes. They are "cultural" achievements—results of a "tradition"
perpetuated in a given line, as well as of active care on the part of an individual. If we accept such a notion, then life in all its manifestations becomes
a hermeneutic achievement.

Where Is the Information Hidden?

Owing to its usage in many different connotations, the word "information" has become largely devoid of meaning. To avoid misunderstanding, I will try to describe how it is used here. First of all, I maintain, together with Hofstadter (1979), that information as such does not exist objectively. Anything that can become information will do so only if the interpreter can distinguish it from the background *as* a message and is able to interpret it. Hofstadter distinguished three levels of information:

(1) The *frame message* is a clue, a trigger signaling to the interpreter the need for a decoding device. Hofstadter gives the example of a sealed bottle washed up on the seashore, with a piece of paper in it. A learned interpreter will instantaneously recognize it among junk on the beach, as something to be decoded. Note the effort required even in such a simple example. Those able to receive the message as a message must know that a bottle is an artifact and not something commonly encountered on the beach. They must know the common use for bottles—they will not pay attention to an empty bottle or a bottle full of seawater. They should know something about the specific properties of bottles (that bottles will not dissolve in seawater, will float if sealed empty, etc.). They must know the use of paper and distinguish writing from simple dirt. They probably know that messages used to be sent in bottles. All this will arouse a receiver's willingness to focus attention on bottle and its message, and then a second level of deciphering can take place.

(2) To understand the *outer message* means to know how to get an adequate decoding mechanism to read the message proper. In Hofstadter's example, the message is in Japanese. The receivers, even if they cannot read Japanese, should be able to decipher that it *is* in Japanese and act accordingly to find a translator. The message itself cannot serve as a source of information for decoding—the *way of decoding* should be deciphered independently of what the message contains.

(3) The *inner message* is the message proper, which can reveal the meaning. This level is the closest to a receiver, but first the receiver must go through the first two levels of recognition, taking cues from outer characteristics of the information medium. The *experience of the receivers* plays a decisive role here —they must distinguish the message from the background and choose the adequate decoding procedure. Similarly, if genetic messages are to be the *cause* of anything, there must exist a receiver (mechanism, device, "subject") that is able to decipher them *as* such and interpret them. The outcome of such an effort can be, for example, the selection of a particular program and its execution.

But if we take the phenotype as a decoding mechanism, we immediately find ourselves in a difficulty, because the very act of reading the message may—and usually does—change the interpreting device itself. The execution of the developmental program means entering the physical world. This would lead to an endless expansion of new phenotypic variations, which are also subject to change owing to changes in their environment. An incompatibility of the phenotype with the environment would arise, quickly followed by the breakdown and death of our "device." As one of the key programs is the simple command "copy me," which ensures error-free copying of the message itself, we would very soon witness the collapse of the prerequisite of the whole process—the message.

The only way to avoid such a catastrophe is to provide a loop in the program after some steps of execution, leading to the reestablishment of the initial conditions, that is, a copy of the genetic message and of the original reading (interpreting) device—the phenotype. The loop may be reset in several ways. One of them is a limited choice of degrees of freedom—phenotypes—following one after another in an invariable sequence and ending up back in the starting position. One example of such a simple loop is the life cycle of a unicellular organism, for example, a bacterium, which switches periodically between a vegetative cell and a unicellular spore. Environmental factors act as triggers for switching between states, or the organism itself generates endogenous cues (rhythms). If cells of a common origin can cooperate, then cellular phenotypes can arise that do not return to the initial state and die without leaving descent. If there is at least one cell line that can close the loop, there is nothing to prevent the generation of many abortive specialized cell lines, which will help to ensure that the loop is closed by the single line that is able to do so.

In multicellular sexually reproducing organisms *all* cell lines are abortive, and the line of the *organism* can be saved only by fusing two gametes (which themselves are abortive). Hence, an individual comes into existence from a *newly formed* cell line equipped with a specific version of both genetic information and structures. A new generation starts not from a precisely recreated initial state, but with a mélange of genetic programs and construction elements: both the message and the interpreting device are unique. A species will be characterized by an endless number of variants (dialects) of the genetic message—genotypes—and with a similar plethora of interpreting devices. What, then, makes the whole process "species specific" in each individual?

Genidentity

Faced with the enormous variability of living beings, we are confronted with the question of what is that *sameness* that we can recognize in all manifestations of life, and what is the essence of their unity in time? Is it a precisely copied genetic message, a controlled network of relations, or genealogical lines? A very useful concept here might be that of *genidentity*, introduced in 1922 by Kurt Lewin. He posed a seemingly trivial question: How we can know that a thing in time t_1 is the same thing in time t_2? The stone on my desk, or a star in the skies, remains the same despite the possibility that it may undergo some change during the observation period. Surprisingly, says Lewin, it is not easy to explain how we recognize the identity of two objects *a* and *b* in two times (a_1, a_2, or b_1, b_2), and why we prefer the relation a_1-a_2 and not a_1-b_2. Even when an object remains relatively stable in shape and material (e.g., a stone, or test tubes in a rack), we often have to rely on a label put on the specimen. It is this identity in time (stone a_1 to stone a_2) that Lewin called "genidentity." The relation of genidentity is not a logical one: from the logical point of view, the object *could* have changed—acquired scrapes and cracks or changed its color, or grew from child to adult, and so forth. This means that the relation of simple identity (*Gleichheit*) does not hold here. Nor can genidentity be reduced to a mere sequence of changes to the object in time or of causal sequences (here the relationship is open: genidentity and causality may or may not mean the same). Genidentity is the very precondition for the existence of physics or chemistry.

In the case of living beings, determining genidentity is of course not an easy task: How can we assess the genidentity between a chicken and the hen it has grown into? Here, again, if we cannot be absolutely sure (e.g., by witnessing the development of *the* chicken into *the* hen), we have to rely only on labels—for example, a ring on the leg or a DNA fingerprint (and, of course, to believe in the genidentity of such labels).

But what is the essence of the genidentity of two texts, if one is a copy of another and may, moreover, contain typing errors or even word deletions? What is the genidentity of different descriptions of the same thing, landscape, or situation? Such questions become important in the reconstruction of genealogical lines where no label can be placed on the predecessors, and we are left with learned guesses based on paleontology and other traces. A similar situation is encountered in comparative biology. We must believe the experts who have been initiated into a given field, who are able to immerse themselves in the essence of the thing under investigation; that is, we need a hermeneutic task. What, then, connects "the same" in different times and situations? One answer comes from the concept of eidetic biology.

Eidetic Biology

A corollary to both biological structuralism and hermeneutics of the living is the "eidetic biology" developed and pursued by Neubauer (e.g., 1996, 1997, 2001). The central concept refers to the ancient Greek word *eidos*, which in the vernacular of that time meant something like semblance, likeness, shape, kind. (In Czech texts, Neubauer uses the word *podoba*.) *Eidos* refers to self-presentation or display of a living being to the surrounding world: what it looks like. We recognize a primrose, a lizard, a snowflake, a composition by Mozart, or a person by their *eidos*, the internal characters they communicate to the outside world. We do recognize them at repeated encounters, despite the fact that none of these "specimens" remains the same (see also genidentity, above, and chapter 3). No two absolutely identical snowflakes have ever been formed: an encounter with any snowflake is in fact different from that with any other. It is its *eidos* that makes us recognize something as *something* —not only by being the same but also by being different. *Eidos* also endows us to recognize—on the background of similarities—*differences*, individual features. Thus, eidetic biology refers to everyday experience (with perception and self-perception, knowledge, memory, etc.) to understand the nature of the living.

Eidos uplifts a mere thing to the realm of both being-like *and* being-different from other specimens of the kind. It allows us to see "the difference that makes the difference" (Bateson's definition of information, 1988) and— what is important—ignore irrelevant differences. Such knowledge concerns the very being of the entity in question (I would say, along with Ruyer, that it somehow invites us to participate in its being, instead of only observing what is *objectively* visible, measurable, classifiable from outside).

Eidos thus refers to the essence or identity of a thing, consisting of the unique way in which it is *related* to everything else. This general relatedness makes up both its being and its being-known by others. *Eidos* is what knowledge—and any kind experience—is about. It is the "format" in which the information is received, stored, and processed. This format is the prerequisite of the organic wholeness and any reasonable, meaningful behavior.

One might suspect that *eidos* is simply a disguised Platonic idea. Neubauer's background ontology, however, is somewhat different. The difference may be illustrated by the English usage of the term "idea." In sayings such as "I have no idea," "It is a good idea," and so forth, the word "idea" belongs to the natural, dynamic sort of being that eidetic biology ascribes to all living existence. The ideas of our everyday experience are being conceived and born *here*. They grow, differentiate, recombine, adapt, compete, survive with fertility, or become extinct. (It is in this sense Bateson speaks about the ecology of ideas.) And, most important, they are not inert rules to obey: they are the very process of self-imitation through inside formation—*in-formation* for short. That is exactly what *eidos*—the nature of living beings, forms, and processes—is like. Their likeness takes a form of relation of similarity, correspondence, analogy, complementarity. The relation of likeness rests on a reference: whenever we say that something is like something else, we must also state *in what respect*. To see the likeness among things requires us to *under-*

stand in what sense they are similar, correspondent, alike. In Neubauer's words, how they are fitted and oriented in the eidetic space. To *know* something means to understand its *eidos*, to enter its eidetic field, and to see in what respect diverse phenomena are related, are but different aspects, cases, versions of the same thing. The eidetic space, once understood, is open for exploration for new possibilities (eidetic variations), following known rules of transformation or discovering new ones.

Understanding, orientation, discovering of new possibilities is knowledge gained by interpretation—that is, a genuine hermeneutic feat. Eidetic biology understands life processes precisely in these terms. It views living beings as eidetic spaces or semantic fields of formative causation. Like knowledge and learning, development and evolution are based on the interpretation of the embodied living experience stored as *eidos*, that is, as a specific formative strategy, way of formation—information, interpreted by imitation within the current context.

At first glance, such an approach to living beings as mindlike existences might seem to be in sharp contrast to the traditional view, according to which the bodily existence is reducible to a particular composition of material parts filling the inert geometrical space. For eidetic biology, the elements of life are elements of meaning rather than chunks of Cartesian space; a mechanism is merely a projection of *eidos* into a geometrical space. But any mechanism is by definition an *eidos* (purpose, strategy, instruction) implemented in a special way of mechanistic causation (as an abacus is an implementation of numbers into strings of beads). To make use of a device—mechanical or not—means to understand it.

Is such a shift of perspective as preposterous as orthodox scholarship holds it to be? In the foreword written for the Czech version of this book (Markoš, 2000), Neubauer points out that such a switch of perspective had actually taken place within the womb of the most orthodox and prevailing stream of recent biology—in the neo-Darwinian theory of evolution. The spectacular and celebrated shift from organisms to genes (so-called genocentric revolution; see chapter 4) meant not just a shift in scale dimension from macroscopic bodies to the molecular level: unwittingly, it was accompanied by a deeper, *ontological* transition, from a material (geometrical, mechanical) existence to the informational one. From the gene's point of view, the competition that is the driving force of evolution takes place not among different living forms, but among different *instructions*, that is, formative strategies, ways of life. Information does not increase through multiplication (redundancy): it is the success to *prevail*—irrespective of the survival of its carriers (vehicles). Information *is* selfish. But its selfishness does not concern quantity, volume, or number of copies, but rather quality, meaning, semantic content.

What is really being selected through natural selection, then, is *eidos:* the form of evolutionary experience stored. *Eidos* is implemented not only in the genetic text, but also in the way the text is used, that is, how it is understood. It refers to its semantic context. The Darwinian struggle for survival corresponds to the "conflict of interpretations" (Ricoeur, 1976). A successful interpretation amounts to "fitness"—ability to fit into the given context of relations and communications, to make use of the polysemy of the *eidos*.

> The very nature of Life *as* Life cannot be "survival." A species (*eidos* in Greek, *species* in Latin; in both cases semblance, appearance, expression) is nothing but the "eidetic space" open for any individual to reveal its individuality and originality, in the way an artist, a poet, or a scientist does. Not only are most living beings equipped by a unique version of genetic information, they also represent a unique interpretation of their genetic thesaurus. Any given interpretation—a decision among possible readings —discloses novel possibilities of interpretation (a hermeneutic space), curtailing or excluding the others. Hence, an organism is not merely a passive result of the realization of its "genetic program," but an active expression, an incarnation, a manifestation of a certain interpretation (application) of a genetic recipe. The recipe, in its turn, has also arisen from the mutual competition of different variants of reading. (Neubauer, 1996, p. 21)

Neubauer's eidetic biology puts the established scientific tradition into a larger context of European thought. To disclose and select the link between mechanistic, structuralist, and informatic (syntactic) tradition in biology on the one hand, and the eidetic and semantic side of life on the other, it is necessary to recur to the concepts, notion, and terminology of hermeneutics.

4

NEO-DARWINISM

DNA can be regarded as a set of instructions how to make a body.

Life is just bytes and bytes and bytes of digital information. Genes are pure information—information that can be encoded, recoded and decoded, without any degradation or change of meaning. Pure information can be copied and, since it is a digital information, the fidelity of copying can be immense.

Richard Dawkins

When seen from outside, much of biology appears to be the building of data bases—making the "whole life catalog." Sometimes, in a pensive mood, I fancy that to biologists the living world is a vast set of book collections held in interconnected libraries. In this dream, the biologists are like competent librarians who devise the most intricate classification of every new library they discover but never read the books. They sense that something is missing from their lives, and this feeling intensifies as new collections of books grow hard to find. I see the biologists expressing an almost palpable sense of relief when joined by molecular biologists who dare to start the even greater task of classifying the words the book contains. It means that the search for the answer to the awesome question of what the books are about can be put off until the new and infinitely detailed molecular classification is complete.

James E. Lovelock

Life and creativity, as the antithesis of a mechanism, cannot easily be reconciled with standard natural science with its reproducible a priori laws of causal chains and mechanisms. If, despite this paradox, biology is to remain one of the standard natural sciences, it must be equipped with a theory that can explain away the paradoxes and to show that life and creativity are simply epiphenomena of mechanistic rules working in the background. The only success in meeting these requirements to date can be claimed by the neo-Darwinian theory of the emergence and evolution of life.

Mechanistic models are undoubtedly of great heuristic value. It is useful to have a view of a mechanical device whose behavior can be fully anticipated. It can convey very good experimental models. The only problem I can see is in extrapolation from the laboratory to the whole world, in the assertion that "if my models work, the world must follow them, too."

Abram (1996) advances an idea that mechanicism was a product of rational theology in a time when the territories of the church and the sciences were being marked out, with the Creator remaining the single link between them. With a care-taking constructor in the background, the mechanistic world was fully acceptable. It was only Darwin who found the courage to shatter this symmetry and discard the question of the Creator. He declared evolution to be inherent *even* to a mechanical world devoid of any creative powers.

If we speak of natural laws, it is not to utter some banal truth of the kind that, for example, the second principle of thermodynamics or some other truth of physics and chemistry "holds good even in living organisms." This route was taken, as I showed in chapter 1, by mechanistic biology of the end of nineteenth century, especially physiology. Even if relapses into such thinking can be found today, in the age of dissipative structures, deterministic chaos, neuronal networks, modern psychology, and so forth, they are not likely to prevail. Biology is not interested in the quivering of ordinary molecules, but rather focuses on a very particular kind of molecule: the replicator that is able to produce its own copies. Because of this property of self-replication, the molecule—through its copies—becomes more durable than a diamond. Kováč (1999/2000) aptly formulated the essence of neo-Darwinism as follows:

> Molecules do not compete, do not fight, do not adapt, they have no goals, they do not even survive. They simply exist. What they display is onticity (occurrence). A molecule of any substance will exist until it decays or changes into another molecule. Thus, the criterion of the onticity of a molecule is its stability. A molecule can exist as a single entity, or in an enormous number of identical copies. Its stability can be static—the molecule resists the destructive powers of its environment—or dynamic—either the damage can be repaired, or the molecule maintains its onticity by produc-

ing copies of itself. The more identical copies, possibly distributed exten- sively in space, the greater the chance that at least one of them will survive. If we mix molecules with different degrees of stability and follow their on- ticity in time, the more stable ones will be detected for longer whereas the less stable will gradually disappear. Molecules do not know anything of their fate, of their environment, of other molecules, or of their own exis- tence. It is we—the observers—who describe their onticity, their survival in time. (p. 646)

The onticity (presence, genidentity) of more stable molecules is realized in their copies. What is at stake is not the simple material identity of the copies, but their structure, the "in-formation" they carry. As the environ- ment is not infinite (in either space or resources), it does not permit geomet- rical propagation of replicators. It follows that replicators propagating at the highest speed will finally prevail in the population. The molecules can, in ad- dition, change their properties (mutate), and mutants may replicate at dif- ferent speeds: if a mutant appears whose fitness is greater than that of the mother molecule, it will itself gradually become the mother molecule for subsequent populations. The molecular progeny can, of course, accumulate further mutations. We—the observers—come to the conclusion that the occurrence of the prevailing molecule is the result of *natural selection*, and the property quantifying the frequency of its occurrence is its *fitness*. Greater fitness is therefore a criterion for the ability to fill the space with its own copies.

It should be realized that changes in fitness are not due to simple and re- versible switches in the conformation of the replicator (in the way that, e.g., a glucose molecule will change its conformation according to ambient condi- tions). Owing to the very high number of points on a molecule that can be subject to mutation, and to the low frequency of mutation, the probability of backward mutations at the same point is very low. Mutations of the replicator molecule thus become practically irreversible, and the transformation of replicators over time has—in retrospect—a direction. This, very briefly, is the essence of neo-Darwinist theory. Dawkins (1987), one of the leading theo- reticians of neo-Darwinism, states: "The theory of evolution by cumulative natural selection is the only theory we know of that is in principle *capable* of explaining the evolution of organized complexity. Even if the evidence did not favor it, it would still be the best theory available! In fact the evidence does favor it" (p. 317). For the uninitiated reader, I should add that evolution in this quotation means evolution of *life*. Life, however, means bodies, not strings of symbols implemented into linear polymers. How, then, has a shift from nonliving molecular replicators to living beings occurred?

Origins of Life

If we leave aside the question of how organic molecules came into existence (several plausible scenarios have been suggested), the most prominent problem is the same as that of the chicken and the egg: what came first — replicators or metabolism? Neubauer (in foreword to Markoš, 2000, p. 18) compares following two statements: (1) the cell (i.e., body) controls its own replication; (2) DNA controls its own replication. He continues: If we stick to the first statement, the whole cell becomes a replicator, ensuring the production or reproduction of *any molecule* it contains. Somehow, however, we feel that two daughter cells are not identical, their reference is not identity but similarity, semblance. In the case of the second statement, truly identical DNA copies *can* be made, but it requires a lot of armchair thinking to show how DNA "controls" its own replication and what is the difference between the copies of DNA and, say, of citric acid molecules.

With this difference in mind, our goal is to find a credible model of how the inorganic planet could give birth to either (1) a self-propagating metabolism lacking the possibility of digital inscription of its achievements, or (2) self-replicating molecules not dependent on metabolism, that is, molecules whose replication could be assured by the "inorganic" environment. Another goal is to show how either pathway, in the course of its evolution, could have invented the complementary part or, if they had developed in parallel, how their merger might have occurred. This last aspect is, I think, the neuralgic point of all existing theories of life's origin. It is beyond the scope of this volume to list them all; I chose two extreme approaches, each representing one of the alternatives mentioned above.

The "metabolism without code" scenario has been elaborated by Kauffman (2000). He argues that the "catalytic task space" comprising all the necessary reactions may be covered by some 10^8 different catalysts: however high the number is, it is not infinite. Provided that some kind of organization (matrices, membranes) endorsed the compartmentalization of such a system, it could have been able to establish two kinds of closures: that of metabolic reactions (catalytic closure) and that of necessary work cycles. From this point of view, life started as a collective property of complex systems of catalytic polymers and of molecules whose reactions are being catalyzed. Such a dynamic network does not require a genome to evolve: if conditions are favorable (e.g., providing a steady and sufficient supply of catalysts and substrates), it will maintain itself and become more and more complex. It may gradually develop both sophisticated control over its environment (homeostasis, well-defined metabolic pathways, and sets of optically active metabolites), and finally also a medium where information on the best catalytic molecules can be stored. Models developed so far are highly speculative but scientifically feasible.

The complementary "code without metabolism" scenario has been developed by Cairns-Smith (1985). He suggests that the first "organisms" were inorganic, self-replicating crystals. Organic compounds are irrelevant from the point of the appearance of a replicator—they may have entered the system later. Ever-present clay minerals seem to be the best candidates for a primitive replicator. They grow readily in aqueous environments, their crystal lattices can accommodate various inhomogeneities that will be perpetuated in subsequent layers as the crystal grows, and "progeny" can be generated simply by breaking the crystal. These nonliving "organisms" can be subject to natural selection; that is, with time, qualitative shifts can occur in the populations of crystals. For the inorganic scenario, the biggest challenge is to explain the transition, the takeover by organic molecules.

Whatever the initial steps and direction of the takeover might be, life emerged when dissipative catalytic structures became able to store information in a form that itself is not a dissipative structure and bring stored attributes to life again by a process of decoding. When, where, and how this relation became established is *the* real enigma of life's origin. It is often supposed that the first step *after* such a takeover was the so-called RNA world, with RNA performing both the information storage and the metabolic catalysis. Eigen and colleagues (see, for example, Eigen and Winkler-Oswatitsch, 1992) provided a model of a hypercycle that can explain how the evolution of replicators–catalyzers might have taken place (figure 4.1). If a set of replicators–catalyzers becomes confined in an enclosed space, they may share both metabolites and the efficacy of the replication. Such a team will evolve as a single unit toward higher efficiency and the specialization of replicators–catalysts in the team. Gradually, metabolic pathways become established, and the information storage will also be separated from the catalytic functions.

Note that a nested hierarchy of hypercycles can easily be obtained by recurrent use of the same principle. What is even more important is that such hypercycles can be explained *only* from their own hierarchical level—it is pointless to look for some basic level of description. This is the point further developed by Maynard Smith and Szathmáry (1995).

Replicators and Vehicles

In neo-Darwinian synthesis, however, a molecule of DNA is often understood as an utmost replicator, as a level to which all other levels can be reduced and from which they should be explainable. Different kinds of DNA molecules *may* differ in their physical and chemical properties (e.g., behavior at different temperatures), but these properties are irrelevant to our story here. What is important is the nonrandom sequence of four types of monomers–bases, ordered covalently into the linear string of the DNA molecule. The chain is very

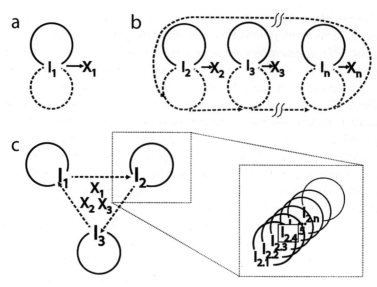

Figure 4.1. A hypercycle. (a) Replicators I_1 autonomously ensure their own repli-cation cycle. Besides this ability to replicate, each of them is endowed with some auxiliary function, for example, catalysis of reaction producing the metabolite X_1. (b) If a set of replicators becomes confined in common space (e.g., by a mem-brane), elementary catalytic reaction provided by one member of the set may help the replication of others, and vice versa. Such a team of replicators—the hyper-cycle—has an advantage compared to isolated replicators in an open space: the metabolites X_1–X_n are present in much higher concentrations than they are out-side and can be shared by all replicators. The probability of efficient propagation of all members of the team will increase. (c) At this point, Darwinian evolution can begin: multiple copies of any of the replicators can bear various mutations (here shown as successive variants of I_2). Those that—via increased ability of team cooperation—increase their own replication will finally prevail. Evolution will become a matter not of isolated replicators, but of a whole hypercycle. If the autonomy from environment is retained, evolution will lead to continuous spe-cialization of members of the set. Even the very process of replication will finally become the business of only certain specialized members of the team. Adapted from Eigen and Winkler-Oswatitsch (1992).

long, containing from thousands to hundreds of millions of bases, and can be very precisely copied. If a mutant appears, it will differ from the mother DNA molecule in the sequence of bases in the string (e.g., point mutations—the change of a single base to another one, or deletions, insertions, or inversions in the string). As stated above, if a mutated molecule improves its speed of copy production even infinitesimally, it will finally prevail in the population. The increase in the number of copies means being more efficient in exploiting the limited resources (building blocks, energy) provided by the environment, that is, outcompeting other molecules. And at this point life enters the scene.

DNA is not capable of self-replication—it needs a device able to perform the copying task. Let us call it a body or a phenotype or, in Dawkins's somewhat poetic term, a survival machine. In the logic of the theory, the body is *not* a replicator, however one might like to see it as such; it suffers decay and must periodically be built *de novo*. To close the cycle, DNA (to be replicated at all) must supply the body with information about how to build a new body. This information (genetic inscription, or simply gene) is encoded as the sequence of bases in the DNA molecule. The quality of the replicator is given by the sequence of bases, but this quality surfaces only when a new body is to be built. Mutations in DNA will change the phenotype of all its bearers—bodies—and it is these bodies that will decide the competition for resources in the process of natural selection and the occurrence of the mutant DNA in subsequent generations. The subject of natural selection, therefore, is not the replicator but the phenotype, the survival machine.

What remains is to ensure that phenotypes will work only on the replication of their own genetic text and avoid the replication of other replicators present in the environment. This is achieved by individuation, that is, the insulation of replicators and their phenotypes into higher order units—cells, multicellular organisms, or even superorganisms. Such units, then, can also be considered as replicators and be subject to natural selection. Proper analysis, however, will show that there is *always* a basic level made up of molecular replicators determining epigenetic events at other levels. Organisms (phenotypes built according to a genetic recipe) express hypotheses about their environment; if the hypotheses are not "falsified," their construction of the world becomes reality and they will transfer their replicators into the next generation. As a consequence of this pattern, evolution proceeds to ever more complex phenotypes, from body fabric, through behavior, to abstract thinking. All this will, however, remain a mere epiphenomenon of replicators endowed with a single "property"—their occurrence.

I do not go into the entire rich landscape of neo-Darwinian theory, which covers and explains a broad diversity of phenomena, such as the emergence and evolution of sexuality, the dynamics of populations, speciation, macroevolution, the behavior of animals and humans, including spirituality, and so forth—in short, all the aspects of life.[1]

Because of its inherent simplicity, the theory is able to produce new hypotheses and submit them to falsification. There is a general agreement that no falsification has occurred so far that could seriously jeopardize the theory. Such a peril could arise if, for example, an anomaly appeared that could be explained as Lamarckian evolution. Recent claims of this type were either re-

---

1. For further reading, see popular treatises (e.g., Dawkins, 1987, 1989, 1995; Ridley, 1994) and special monographs (e.g., Gillespie, 1991; Dawkins, 1982; Maynard Smith, 1996; Maynard Smith and Szathmáry, 1995; Li, 1997).

jected as irreproducible (see, e.g., Gorczynski and Steele, 1980) or flexibly accommodated (e.g., RNA editing, directed mutation, epigenetic heredity, etc.).

The theory is also relatively successful in explaining ontogeny, when a single genotype can yield multiple cell and/or body phenotypes (see the reaction norm, chapter 8): there can be a large number of "hypotheses" about the environment that can be fully compatible with survival. Multifinality is now an accepted fact, and neo-Darwinists often protest when they are presented as "genetic determinists" (though it should be admitted that the previous generation, e.g., Monod, 1979, did often cling to such a view). They do not deny the existence of emergent phenomena at "higher" levels of organization. Neo-Darwinists even introduced a concept of a new type of replicators—memes—which, especially through human civilization, substantially affect the dynamics of evolution. Despite all this, there is a tacit belief that a time will come when genetic determinism will be proved, that a detailed and sensitive study of genetic texts will provide a detailed knowledge of ontogeny and phylogeny. Some authors even trace causality on the physical level: "If the thread of connecting causal explanations has been well laid, it is nonetheless possible to follow any pathway quickly in reverse, back through the behavioral sciences to biology, chemistry, and finally physics" (Wilson, 1998, p. 67). Wilson, of course, immediately adds that the analysis works only in the given direction. The multifinality of developmental pathways and the extreme complexity of living beings hinder the reverse path. However, Wilson considers this a technical problem, not one of principle. Most people will not, of course, go that deep, that is, to the atomic level. But an intensive search for an unequivocal relationship between the genetic level and the phenotype is underway.

Why, Then, This Book?

The reader may now ask why, when the neo-Darwinian paradigm seems to be invincible, I wish to mention branches of biology that are in concealed or open conflict with it. Most such alternatives are without doubt "contaminated" by the humanities. Why not adopt the view of Kováč, who sees them as dwelling in the tenets of Aristotelian truths, eye-catching, intellectually extremely expressive but, alas, untrue? Why not reject all alternative views with a resignation similar to that in the following passage by Gould (1996) on Lamarckism?

> We deny our preferences all the time in acknowledging nature's factuality. I really do hate the fact of personal death, but will not base my biological views on such distaste. Less facetiously, I really do prefer the kinder La-

marckian mode of evolution to what Darwin called the miserable, low, bungling, and inefficient ways of his own natural selection—but nature does not give a damn about my preferences, and works in Darwin's mode, and I therefore chose to devote my professional life to this study. (p. 37)

The reason for my apparently foolish task is my conviction that the neo-Darwinian theory, like any other, reflects only a certain set of ideas and values. Those who have espoused these ideas and values have focused their attention on certain properties of living beings and generalized them into a viable theory. These undoubtedly truthful and very efficient filters help us to put our understanding of reality in order. I am, however, convinced that there may be other filters, other theories that would allow us to discover different aspects of living beings. I must confess to a "postmodern" heresy that it is *we* who construct truth in order to find an orientation in *our* world. Competition between several truths is more important than the hegemony of a single Truth, however invincible it might look to us and our contemporaries. I do not believe that knowledge elaborated by the natural sciences is different in principle from other forms of knowledge, just because science has found a way to cumulatively improve the truth, whereas the humanities have just wandered in an endless vicious circle for the last 2,500 years. I maintain that *any* knowledge is both cumulative *and* circular. The circle, however, is not an erratic whirling, but a hermeneutic activity. Because of this, it is useful also to retain knowledge of half-forgotten, abandoned alternatives, dead ends, and even frauds of the past—if for no other reason then simply as a corrective for the overly confident and pompous judgments of some protagonists of the theory reigning at a given time, as an antidote against ideology. Neo-Darwinism is a beautiful edifice of the human spirit, and heuristically it is invaluable. However, we should venture into different regimes of thought and seek for phenomena that are ignored, neglected, or even rejected by the leading theory. I see a hermeneutic approach as a good alternative in biology. If there are calls for the unification of knowledge, why not undertake the enterprise "democratically," from different angles and by different methods? Life on Earth arose as a result of certain chemical and physical conditions in force on the virgin planet. Such conditions opened—or better, created—new realms that had never been present before. Because of this, life is, and at the same time is not, explicable by chemistry, thermodynamics, and physics. The existence of replicators enabled one particular kind of evolution. New realms came into existence because of that very fact, and they, too, both are and are not explicable in terms of the "selfish" replicator.

Chapters 5 and 6 may seem like a deviation from the mainstream narrative, as they are devoted to two streams opposed to neo-Darwinism: biological structuralism and Lysenkoism. My intention, of course, is not to equate them. Whereas biological structuralism is a serious attempt to find an alternative to neo-Darwinism, Lysenkoism was a prophetic vision implemented by very harsh political methods. Certain characteristics, however, point to a common background for both movements.

5

BIOLOGICAL STRUCTURALISM

The only general principle that can be applied is position, the relations, and the dependence of the parts, that is to say by what I name and include under the term connections.

Geoffroy St. Hillaire

Structuralism endorses a renewed interest in the generation and transformation of biological form, namely in a process of development of the organism into the environment. Eventually even the conceptual barrier between organism and environment may drop.

Giusseppe Sermonti

Biological structuralism was the red herring of the 1980s in biology, surviving tolerated, neglected, or ridiculed on the margins of mainstream biology. The movement was established in 1986 as the Osaka group for the study of dynamic systems (Sibatani, 1987a,b) and has its platform in the journal *Rivista di Biologia/Biology Forum*. The members comprised a heterogeneous group of biologists, philosophers, and mathematicians.

Webster and Goodwin (1982), leading figures of biological structuralism, described the contemporary conceptual system of biology as resting on three pillars: (1) Darwinian evolutionary theory, stressing history and function; (2) the Weismannian holistic theory of inheritance and development; and (3) Mendelian atomistic genetics. Biological structuralism suggests an alternative that is derived from rational morphology: its primary interest is form and order in living beings. It revived the work of the rational morphologists of the nineteenth century. To illustrate the differences from the mainstream of contemporary biology, Webster (1984, 1987) suggests three pairs of antinomies—the first member of each pair being "structuralist," the second one "Darwinist":

(1) Internal constraints versus external requirements: Internal constraints suggest that not any shape is allowed, even were it preferred by external factors (natural selection). The alternative is given by the neo-Darwinist slogan "It may be that the only reason pigs have no wings is that selection has never favored their evolution" (Dawkins, 1982, p. 42).

(2) Lawful transformations versus heritability with random variations: According to structuralism, morphogenesis is self-regulated, with morphological realms being endowed with inherent stability. It therefore follows that the plasticity of organism is not arbitrary; hence, selection is not the only force deciding morphology: "It is from this perspective that Cuvier and his followers can regard the concept of a structural plan, which every creature is supposed to exhibit and to adhere to, as an explanatory concept—strictly speaking one that allows prediction" (Webster, 1987, p. 195). Darwin, say the structuralists, rejected such assumptions as metaphysical. But how, then, should we treat homology, and how do we give names to body parts in different organisms? the structuralist will ask. In the comparative anatomy of vertebrate bones, the problem is trivial, but what of the case of fish teeth or tree leaves? What is the status of serial homology (the mutual relations of, e.g., segments in the body of insects)? How can sameness and difference be defined? The principle of homology, Webster concludes, was apparently alien to Darwin.

(3) A rational system of transformations (i.e., "structure" in the sense proper) versus purely empirical time-and-space relations: At least some morphological changes and differences can be understood as lawful, that is, as transformations. Here structuralists endorse rational morphology and the heritage of d'Arcy W. Thompson (1917). For rational morphology, the principal question was the origin of the form of living beings. They were looking for a system of transformations (jaw, limb, serial homology), and adaptations to *external* conditions were only ancillary (Webster and Goodwin, 1982, 1996; Kauffman, 1993). The material composition of organisms was of no interest: first, the diversity of forms is much greater than their material composition; second, matter flows through the body, but the form remains. Structuralists praise the attention paid by comparative anatomy and embryology of the rational school to "essential" properties of the typus, to invariants and constants in the internal fabric of organisms.

Toward a Theory of Biological Form

Biological structuralism, then, ends in the critique of the materialistic version of the identity principle as used by Darwinism, of the view that morphological diversity is nothing but variations of unchanging substance put together by chains of random events (tinkering; Jacob, 1977). The point is not, of course, in the replacement of dogmatic Darwinism by equally dogmatic structuralism. The structuralists' aim is to change the science of morphology. This requires

1. elaborating a new theory of morphogenesis;
2. showing that all empirically known morphologies can be inserted into an ideal relation—by finding simple rules for the transformation of morphogenetic fields, and thus proving the equivalence of empirically found forms; and
3. reconstructing the hierarchical system of classification as an ideal system of all possibilities for building biological forms.

Webster takes structuralism as comparative, logical–mathematical formalism that is not interested in "substrate." In other words, the material substance of the investigated object, or the formatting forces in action are beyond its field of interest. Its only aim is to prove an isomorphism between different "contents" (*eidos* in the sense used by Neubauer; see introduction to part II, this volume), an invariance of the relationships between them. It is thus a classifying, systematic science that looks for formal parameters limiting the changes or variations of a given phenomenon.

I suspect that structuralists went too far in neglecting the material continuity and denying the genealogical continuity of organisms. Their need to dissociate themselves from Darwinism played perhaps a much greater role in their disdain of genealogies than did their urgent needs. It is, however, true that structuralism (biological or otherwise) does indeed leave no room for genealogies—thus, strict adherence to a synchronism might have been, at least in the beginning, simply an effort to retain the purity of style.

Goodwin (1982; Webster and Goodwin, 1982, 1996) anchors his thinking in the rationalist (in contrast to the empirical) tradition of Western thinking (he even uses rhetoric not dissimilar to that of E. O. Wilson). He claims that biological processes can be better understood in terms of organizing principles than in the historical and function-oriented concepts of Darwinism:

> Structuralism is . . . simply a twentieth century version of the methodology and conceptual framework of rationalism, founded on the belief that natural processes are intelligible—that is, reducible to certain logical princi-

ples of order. Empiricism, which dominates contemporary biology, takes the opposite view: that the world is as complex as its multifarious phenomena, so that for example, all species are accidents frozen by success, and all accidents are possible. The potential set is thus unlimited, unconstrained except by accident, and success is the arbiter of persistence. Such process is unintelligible in terms simpler than itself. (Webster and Goodwin, 1996, p. 197)

Here we come to the very essence of the teaching. Webster and Goodwin are looking for a research program that would be—by structure and methodology—similar to that of physics! The aim is thus similar to that of objective science (see chapter 1), but the means differ diametrically: structuralism has no ambition to reduce biology to physics. Biological phenomena will stay in their own "causal domain" (Havel, 1996), without reference to other domains of description. The attraction of physics for them lies in the dominance of rational taxonomy and its lack of any need for history. It is irrelevant whether nitrogen came to existence before carbon or vice versa: their position in the periodic table is indifferent to historical contingencies. To disclose such an order for the realm of living beings is the principal goal of all biologists. Biology should also break away from the flaws of historicity and finally transform itself into a true science:

> Physics is thus based upon the things it can be reasonably sure about, and so seeks the universal laws or constraints that define what is possible. That which actually occurs is then understood as a specific realization from the set of the possible by the action of specific conditions. . . . In contrast, contemporary biology does not have a theory of organismic form analogous to the theory of atomic structure; that is to say, it does not have a rational taxonomy. It has only informed guesses at an historical description, a genealogy of species. And it does not have a theory of temporal asymmetry of organismic transformation: there is no principle of directed or preferred evolutionary change. As might be expected of an historical description, there is only a posteriori principle of stability of historically given forms (survival of the fitter organism). Thus biology does not have a theory of how organisms are generated, nor of the principles of their organization, nor of their transformations; that is, it does not have a theory of the origin of species, either ontogenetic or phylogenetic, in the sense that it would have in the physical science. (Goodwin, 1982, p. 45)

Such a state, according to Goodwin, is typical only for post-Darwinian biology, which is obsessed by "origins" and diachronicity. Rational morphologists searching for the plan of Creation since the time of Linnaeus, believed in an order in life; it was they who created concepts such as "typus" or "homology." Darwin, however, replaced organizational principles by genealogies, and biology became interested in content (historical explanations, contingencies) instead of form (universalia, laws). Biology, says Goodwin, will remain irrational and concentrated on historical contingencies packed in the rhetoric of genetic programs, as long as it does not elaborate a scientific theory of organization.

Ontogeny and Phylogeny

A special place in structuralist theory is held by the relationship between ontogeny and phylogeny. In contrast to the neo-Darwinian view, structuralists do not see any diametrical difference between the two processes. Goodwin (1982) claims that this is mainly because the principal question in neo-Darwinism is the nature of the elementary processes of development and how their changes can give rise to the morphological variability that is material for natural selection. For neo-Darwinists, genes are direct causes of development; that is, developmental processes are simply descriptions of causal chains from genes to phenotype. Developmental processes may place some constraints on variation, but if everything must ultimately be explained by genes, such constraints have no informative value anyway. Goodwin does not cast doubt on the model—he even admits that it may be true—but offers an alternative view based on the organization of matter and oriented transformation. It is for that reason that he calls for a taxonomy analogous to the periodic table (see above), that is, independent of the history of a particular line, species, or higher taxon, and compatible with various historical scenarios. He suggests returning to the original conception of homology as a relation of equivalence within a set of structures; such a relation sorts the set into classes whose members share invariant internal liaisons and may change one into another while conserving the invariance. This conception of homology was replaced in neo-Darwinism by an invariant of a different kind—common descent. Goodwin points out again and again that homological equivalence is independent of history: the rules of the game lie in the recurrence of the same generative principles, principles superior to historical contingencies. In contrast to "panglossian" Darwinian biology, he sets up a program of biology less dependent on environment, and independent of time. The essence of Goodwin's (1982) conception is apparently the following:

> What organisms inherit is not simply genes, but a complex organization called the living state that is capable of generation (reproduction) and regeneration because of intrinsic properties ascribed . . . to field behavior. . . . What is reproduced in each generation is an entity with a potential set of forms out of which emerges a specific morphology as a result of external and internal particulars, among which are included the genes. (p. 54)

If, however, all development is a robust natural process with a high probability of generating other states, what is the role of genes? Goodwin (1993) answers that genes, besides enabling metabolism and producing the building blocks of the body, play a key role in influencing the values of parameters— by maintaining them at certain intervals. Changes in parameters lead to modification of morphogenesis: not to the *appearance* of new forms, but only to *modifications* of existing ones within the frames present in advance. No genetic program exists that would enable morphogenetic transformations. Transformations issue only from a cycle in which the dynamics create geometrical forms that feed back to the dynamics. Genes define the extent of these processes, but the organizational principle does not lie in them: rather, it lies in a morphogenetic field that is a function of cells and extracellular matrix. If, then, we want to know the dynamics of development, it is not enough to know the composition of such structures: we also need a system of differential equations describing the dynamics. And we cannot succeed in creating such equations before we know what organizational principles lie behind them. A genetic program is unable to show *how* morphology will manifest itself.

Resurrecting Rational Morphology

Webster and Goodwin (1982) ask why the rational morphology of the nineteenth century was abandoned, and see the reason as the unhappy marriage of empirical atomism and idealistic holism, which became a curse of Western thought. A materialist and functionalist concept of the organism is connected with a holistic idea of the controlling center, that is, the genetic program defining, classifying, and unifying all phenomena and processes at the molecular level: "The organism as a real entity, existing in its own right, has virtually no place in contemporary biological theory" (p. 16).

The structuralists praise the efforts of systematic biology of the last two centuries: classification was a preliminary reduction in face of the wealth of forms. This rational ideal was, however, replaced by the idea of historical, developmental science; older results were reinterpreted, and the prime reason for classification was forgotten. Formal causes were replaced by material or historical ones; the organism ceased to be viewed as a self-organized totality and became a product of contingencies organized from outside by natural selection. Darwin, they say, worked in a tradition of protestant natural theology where "content" is more important than "form." As natural theology supposed the existence of the external creator (God), living beings were automatically taken as mechanical constructs, that is, functional units where the single structural relation was the spatial interconnection of parts. Such an approach tended to emphasize not what connects the organisms, but rather the differences between them. The philosophical basis of the new science lay in Hume's empirical positivism: only what is observable is allowed. Causal relations, society, theories, or "plans of Creation" are not observable; therefore, they must be nothing but subjective constructs. In such a climate, Darwin and his followers reified the abstract *typus* of Cuvier into a "common ancestor" and typological thinking yielded to population biology. Having accomplished this step, Darwin's followers from the fin de siècle sanctioned randomness as a cause of forms and claimed that no constraints exist in the realm of forms. Form became defined as a mere aggregate of "parts," which are functionally coupled to the environment.

Rational morphology received its coup de grâce when Weismann introduced the concept of germinal plasm as the single cause of form. The idea became materialized in germ cells, nuclei, and finally genes. Organisms became artifacts produced by the germ line in order to be transferred into subsequent generations. Dawkins's metaphor of the selfish gene is a modern version of this thinking (see chapter 4). Only within this framework did questions such as "What is the chemical base of organisms?" become relevant: in the thought climate of rational morphology they would be impossible. Webster and Goodwin (1982, p. 36) reproach Wolpert for having resurrected the concept of the morphogenetic field in such a manner that its final form would again be decided by genes (see chapter 9):

> The genome, we suggest, is no more the "directing center" of organismic structure than a lexicon or a dictionary is the directing center of a sentence or a text. The concept of a "central directing agency" or "genetic program" and the organism as an "expressive totality" is the last vestige of a mystifying holism that should have died as a consequence of molecular biology but, paradoxically, appears to live on most vigorously in the molecular biologist's conception of how organismic form is generated. (p. 38)

After the Darwinian turning point, the goals of rational morphology became obscure and the whole area ceased to be considered part of science. Thus, contemporary biology is the result of a merging of German romantic idealism and protestant theology: it is strong in detailed empirical observations and descriptions, but conceptually powerless. Webster and Goodwin think that the concept has been outlived and suggest a return to earlier ways of thinking.

Order for Free

Biological structuralists constantly emphasize that they are offering an alternative to the reigning paradigm. However, they remain on the defensive, particularly because their principal method is modeling, which raises a serious difficulty. On the one hand, they hardly can do otherwise—efforts at reification are incompatible with the very essence of structuralism. On the other hand, this very fact makes them vulnerable — they can even be challenged by the well-known phrase "if true": "Yes, original, exciting, and important — if true.... But how do they know that nature's algorithms are the same as their own, or even close?" (Wilson, 1998, p. 87). The tension between modelers and those who investigate reality itself varies from polite distance to open antagonism.

One of the main protagonists of structuralist modeling is undoubtedly Kauffman (e.g., Kauffman, 1993, 2000). His models show how the elements of a Boolean network (devoid of any meaning, as required in structuralism) build ordered systems with very complex dynamics, based solely on internal relations. Kauffman even shows that such systems are able to resist external interference. If projected onto evolution, then order (structure) will establish itself "for free," *despite* natural selection. The behavior of models even supports the basic postulate of biological structuralism — there is no principal difference between ontogeny and phylogeny.

It should be admitted, however, that a broad selection of equifinal models can be built to solve nearly any problem (see, e.g., Held, 1992; Prusinkiewicz, 1999). An experimental biologist will rightly demand that the ways of a "real" biological object be tested. Leaving aside the question of whether such a demand for reification is justified, it might be impossible to achieve even in the simplest Helmholtzian case when everything could be reduced to causal and local effects of particles.

6

CHANCE AND LYSENKOIST BIOLOGY

Recently we have again seen in the press various papers that openly or indirectly propose the renaissance of Lamarckism, and its principal idea of so-called inheritance of acquired characters. It looks like it is time for it again, after the "defeat" it suffered under the name of Lysenkoism in the mid-1960s, to try its luck under the slightly renewed disguise of so-called epigenetic inheritance.

Letter to the editor of the
Czech magazine *Vesmír*, 1997

Why should we mention at all one of the most regrettable chapters in the history of biology, one that destroyed many scientific careers and discredited, for many decades, a certain way of thinking? The answer is because of this "certain type of thinking." It happened to be seized by a half-learned, vulgar and power-seeking trafficker who discredited it to such an extent that for a long time it was not reasonable even to speak about it.

But even then, there would be no reason to deal in greater depth with the "Michurinist teaching" or "Soviet creative Darwinism," as Lysenkoists called themselves. My reason for doing so is the fact that there are many phrases in Lysenkoist jargon that look very similar to those used by fully respectable structuralists and epigeneticists. Because Lysenkoism is still remembered in many parts of the world, the ideas of this and similar branches are accepted with great suspicion, even if it is clear that neither structuralism nor epigenetics has its roots in Russian biology.

Lysenko may look to us like a self-styled prophet, but he was also heir to a respectable tradition of Russian biology of the late nineteenth to early twentieth centuries. There were three sources that played a role (along with relative isolation from the rest of the world) in forming Russian biology after the 1917 revolution.

First, by the end of the nineteenth century, the Darwinian teaching that flourished in Russia was of a slightly different brand from that in the West. It did not stick so much to Malthusian connotations, which led to a stress on the idea of intraspecies competition. Instead, it took the physical environment as the principal formative force in evolution. As Gould (1991) reminds us, such an orientation should not be surprising in a huge, scarcely inhabited country with a harsh climate. Malthus was much more acceptable for British biologists who lived during the industrial revolution and performed their field research mostly in tropical areas bubbling over with life. Because of the language barrier and long political isolation, we mostly come into contact with Russian tradition only through the bizarre anarchist manifesto by Kropotkin (1902) or in a form digested by the Lysenkoists.

The second source of Russian biology was neo-Lamarckism. The teaching was popular everywhere in Europe and was only displaced by the advent of the neo-Darwinian synthesis. The observations of practical agriculturists such as Michurin or Burbank seemed to be compatible with the neo-Lamarckian views.

The third and perhaps decisive factor in play was Engels's *Dialectics of Nature* (1972). I have already mentioned his critique of mechanicism (chapter 1); here I return to his book because, in my opinion, it throws light on the roots of the Lysenkoist movement and its fundamental dislike of Mendelian genetics, Weismann's teaching, and neo-Darwinism:

> Mechanism applied to life is a helpless category, at the most we can speak of chemism, if we do not want to renounce all understanding of names. . . . Mechanism (and also the materialism of the eighteenth century) does not get away from abstract necessity, and hence not from chance either. That matter evolves out of itself the thinking human brain is for mechanism a pure accident, although necessarily determined, step by step, where it happens. But the truth is that it is the nature of matter to advance to the evolution of thinking beings, hence this always necessarily occurs whenever the conditions for it are present. (pp. 208–209)

"Life as a form of the movement of matter" was to become a major slogan of Lysenkoist biology. The second slogan was about the *progressive* evolution of matter: once a certain level of organization has been attained, the origin of life and of consciousness is absolutely lawful and necessary. We can see that, as in structuralism, there is a tendency to assign to "living matter" properties that cannot be derived from chemistry or physics. In both cases, however, all these properties are tied down by rigid laws of another sort. They are tied, but at the same time they are not, because everything should be seen dialectically. In Engels's words, "Hegel came forward with the hitherto unheard-of propositions that the accidental has a cause because it is accidental, and just as much also has no cause because it is accidental; that the accidental is necessary, that necessity determines itself as chance, and, on the other hand, this chance is rather absolute necessity" (pp. 218–220).

In a normal situation, Michurinist biology would end up in a version of vitalism or structuralism. At this point, however, state orthodoxy entered the game, which resulted in a forced merger between Darwinism, Lamarckism, dialectic materialism, and suppressed vitalism. Its history has been dealt with in great detail (see, e.g., Roll-Hansen, 1985; Sonneborn, 1950; Medvedev, 1969), and when reading it one cannot avoid feeling that from the beginning the teaching aroused considerable sympathies within the community of Russian biologists. The main theses of Lysenkoist teaching may be summarized as follows:

(1) Genetics is a fraudulent pseudoscience. Lysenko did not believe in genetics with its numeric ratios of inalterable traits transmitted into subsequent generations, with mutations as the only source of creative change in evolution. The source of this hate apparently was his distrust of randomness in science, apparently inspired by Engels. The belief that everything, even the development of the human society, is ruled by objective laws, cannot be compromised by random events:

> For the Morganists, living nature looks like a chaos of random disconnected phenomena devoid of any necessary connections and lawfulness. Randomness rules everywhere. Because they are not able to discover the laws of living nature, they seek refuge in probability theory, thus transforming biological science into plain statistics. . . . Living nature has evolved and is still evolving according to strict rules, which are appropriate for it. Organisms and species evolve according to natural necessities that are characteristic to them. By exorcising Mendelism-Morganism-Weismannism from our science we expel randomness from biology. We would do well to remember that science is the enemy of randomness. (Lysenko, 1952, p. 579)

If we disregard the rhetoric, this quotation is indeed somewhat reminiscent of those we encountered in chapter 5, but the Lysenkoists were not structuralists. What alternative, then, do they suggest? Mechanical description cannot be their starting point, because the dialectics of nature do not allow for it (hence the hate of genetics, for which mechanicism *is* a condition). Nor could they endorse vitalism, because it had been labeled "idealism" by the official Soviet propaganda and was prohibited. A compromise, which was, moreover, compatible with Engels, was the verdict that life is a special form of the organization of matter (such as photons or atoms on another level) and behaves according to its own rules, which cannot be derived from physics and chemistry. It is worth noting that, despite the differences in rhetoric, the project is identical to Driesch's vitalistic conception (see chapter 7). The laws of life consist of three principles of dialectics, plus a property that could be summarized as the "assimilation and dissimilation of conditions of external environment." The result is the precept:

(2) Inheritance is a *habit* modified by assimilation of environmental action. Any presupposition of its conservative character is denied: "The living body builds itself from the elements of the external environment, from food. When it assimilates new factors of the environment, the inheritance will change" (Lysenko, 1958, p. 273). Offspring are similar to their parents not because of prescriptions hidden in genes, but because such is the habit in a given species. If, however, the parents have assimilated anything new during their life, they can transmit the modified habit to their progeny. The concept of germinal plasma is thus condemned. The offspring can also be manipulated during its embryonic development, and once determined, the direction can also be transmitted to their own progeny. The practical output of the theory is that breeding (improvement) becomes education.

(3) The tenet of vegetative hybridization aroused particular attention. This maintained that not only can the grafted scion take up a trait of the stock, but even seeds grown from the scion will transmit the stock's trait to the next generation.

(4) So-called creative Darwinism (in contrast to its "plain" version practiced in the West) was the theoretical output of the teaching. Its specific feature was its stress on the Lamarckian aspects of the original theory as proposed by Darwin: "Thus the finding of the possibility of transmission of acquired aberrations—this greatest achievement in the history of biology, whose outlines were laid down by Lamarck and that later became an organic part of Darwinian teaching—all this has been thrown overboard by Mendelists-Morganists" (Lysenko, 1952, p. 556).

(5) Another theoretical outcome of the teaching is the theory of the species. A species is an objective entity, one of the law-led outcomes of the self-forming potential of living matter. The species is thus an analogy of a chemical compound. It follows that a species can leap suddenly into another species, simply by assimilating external conditions in a different way. Wheat will give rise to rye, lentils to vetch, and so forth. It should be noted that new, unknown species were never reported: all transitions have resulted in species that are already known. Species, thus, exist objectively, but not just any species may exist. (Again, here is an analogy with chemical compounds, and with structuralism.)

(6) Creative Darwinism must also square up with Malthusianism. Here, Lysenko (1958) says, Darwin was wrong: there is no such thing as intraspecies competition. On the contrary, individuals are branches of the species' body, and as such they always altruistically cooperate for the good of the species. As a result of the dispute with Malthusianism, a new law was formulated—the Law of the Life of a Species: "Different organs, traits, and physiological processes, all the endless plethora of forms and functions of the animal or plant organism are aimed at direct or indirect cooperation in order to increase the numbers of individuals of a given species, even if such behavior may mean a reduction of the lifespan or even the death of a particular individual" (p. 284). This is not the only place where a teleological "in order to" can be found in Lysenko's papers. He frequently encouraged biologists not to be afraid of the phrase.

Even this brief account shows that there are many parallels between Lysenkoism and structuralism, something the adversaries of the structuralists never fail to recall. Even if the two ideas start from different points, both call attention to the internal dynamics of organisms, which cannot be appreciated by either mechanicism or reductionism. Both allow for internal, immanent rules of development, clarify the difference between ontogeny and phylogeny, and have no fear of teleology.

At this point, however, the similarity ends. Lysenkoism was discredited by its intolerance and slapdash approach to experiments. Experiments, apparently, were not intended as a means of confirming or falsifying the theses professed; they rather served as a demonstration, or illustration, of indubitable (because revealed) truths, therefore leading to the aggressive behavior of Lysenkoists toward all those who called for statistics and systems of control. One has an impression that Lysenko and his followers were hardly aware of what their opponents wanted from them. And, inevitably, the idea became discredited by its political misuse. Nothing of this holds for the structuralists.

7

THE BIOLOGICAL FIELD

The fields have a reality that is almost independent of the
objects that create them. One can do something like shake
a charge and produce an effect, a field, at a distance; if one
then stops moving the charge, the field keeps track of all the
past, because the interaction between two particles is not
instantaneous. It is desirable to have some way to remember
what happened previously. If the force upon some charge
depends upon where another charge was yesterday, which it
does, then we need machinery to keep track of what went
on yesterday, and that is the character of the field. So when
the forces get more complicated, the field becomes more
and more real.

Richard P. Feynman, Robert B. Leighton,
and Matthew Sands

The concept of the field played an important role in biological theory, especially in the 1920s and 1930s. Despite this, it remains rather elusive not only
in biology but even in those sciences that introduced it. I cannot help but feel
a strange uneasiness on the part of authors when I look for definitions of
"field" in physics textbooks, and the same holds in personal discussions with
physicists.

For the sake of my quest, I am therefore introducing a working definition
of a field that will provide a cue for those aspects to pinpoint in browsing
through the biological literature. A field is any entity whose components
know of each other and therefore behave differently than when removed
from the field. The verb "know" stands for coherence and nonlocality. It fol-

lows that (1) changes in any part of the field are felt in all places within the field (coherence), and (2) such changes are inherent to the field, not a product of any external forcing (nonlocality).

Thus, molecules of an expanding gas in a spark-ignition engine do not constitute a field: their movement is not coherent, and the interactions between them are local. The transfer of energy from the point of its liberation to the piston proceeds through multistep, noncoherent, and local collisions; most of the energy ends up on the walls of the cylinder, and a particular collision is not felt by the system, only by the particular molecules involved. The piston will "get information" about the explosion only through the mediation of multiple chaotic, noncoordinated, local impacts of molecules.

Nor do all coherent systems fulfil our definition of field: the coherence can also be imposed on systems from outside, with interactions within the system itself remaining local. This is the case with a marching company of soldiers or majorettes, a collective gymnastic performance, or flow turbulence and similar dissipative structures. Field properties are displayed by the nucleus of an atom, Earth's magnetosphere, a football match, a performing orchestra, or electrochemical potential on a cell membrane. . . . In part III of this book I intend to persuade the reader that a protein molecule, a cell, and a living being also belong in this category.

Contemporary Biology

The idea of a morphogenetic field is not new—its high point was in the period between World Wars I and II. Almost forgotten after World War II, it made a gradual return in the 1970s, when Wolpert came up with his famous "French flag model" (e.g., Wolpert, 1991; Wolpert et al., 1998; figure 7.1). This is based on a supposition that a compound—a "morphogen"—is produced in a restricted area and diffuses from there to the ambient area filled with cells. Depending on the distance from the morphogen source, its concentration changes (in the simplest case by dilution, but regulation can also be involved), and cells along the diffusion pathway can sense its concentration. This value provides the cell with *positional information*, which is the decisive factor for the trajectory of further differentiation (toward different colors of the flag, different digits, etc.). Later, the originally short-term and continuous space of the morphogen would be digitized, and this subdivision remembered by the cells involved and their progeny. Differently specified parts become modules that then become autonomous: the original field breaks down into a mosaic. Note that it is the presence of the morphogen that is decisive for the development toward different colors (digits). In its absence, the default trajectory would be unique and very probably completely different from that which has been forced from outside (e.g., yellow).[1] Wolpert's theory

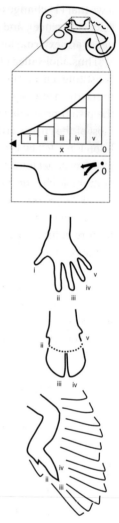

Figure 7.1. Differentiation of the space by morphogen in the limb bud. *Top:* The morphogen is synthesized at point *0* and diffuses along the x-axis, where cells are situated. According to the sensitivity thresholds for the concentration of the morphogen, one of possible developmental trajectories would be decided by the particular cell. *Bottom:* General scheme of the limb bud of jawed vertebrates. The morphogen emanating from the rear differentiates along the postero–anterior axis of the presumptive limb: this is best demonstrated by the differentiation of the hand or foot. The limb bud and the signals involved are universal for the whole group of jawed vertebrates; particular morphology typical for a given class, genus, and so forth, is a secondary establishment. Adapted from Wolpert et al. (1998).

was of a great heuristic value, and today many developmental processes are being explained within its framework. This is especially true of the last decade, when sensitive methods of analysis allowed direct identification and quantitative analysis of putative morphogens, and the construction of causal chains from the morphogen to structure(s).

The model does not, however, satisfy our definition as formulated above.

---

1. For the sake of symmetry, the structuralists' view of the same phenomenon should also be presented. For them, the structure has always been here. The morphogen event is a mere episode, whereas the structure endures, simply changing its configuration over time. For a structuralist, the final gradient is the revelation of the structure, not a cause of the "structuring" of the space.

The Wolpertian morphogen is a chemical entity diffusing through a geometrical space; the gradient of the morphogen endows a positional value on any place within its range. The positional value for a given region is nothing but the concentration of a chemical interpreted by a cell present at a given spot. Interactions in the morphogen "field" are only local. The whole area *is* coherent, but its coherence is achieved by a force from outside, as in the case of a marching company, where coherence is provided by the orchestra.[2] If, then, I speak about the "revival" of the idea of a field, it is first necessary to consider its essence in its heyday.

Neubauer et al. (1989) provide a detailed analysis of the field concept, from Faraday and Maxwell up to the present, and conclude that a field is a property of space, a formal cause that transcends the concrete material implementation. Space, in his conception, is not identical to emptiness, and the properties of space (summarized by the concept of the field) determine the alignment of material "fillings." He takes "field," "entelechy," and "formal cause" as synonyms and calls for a mathematical theory of shape (or *eidos*; see the introduction to part II) that would be complementary to the contemporary "materialistic" biology. At present, however, we are witnessing constant attempts to reify the "transcendental," to make mathematical formulations conform to a material carrier, be it a gene, a membrane, or a gradient of morphogen. In such a situation, the field (in Neubauer's sense) is a very vague conception. In fact, it is superfluous: neither biologists nor phenomenologists modeling morphogenesis on computers are in need of it. I suspect, however, that the situation before was the same and is best illustrated by the development of the views of Alexander Gurwitsch, the inventor of the concept of a "biological field."

The Biological Field of Gurwitsch

The history of the biological field can be seen best in two books written by Gurwitsch. In his book *Die histologischen Grundlagen der Biologie* (The Histological Basis of Biology; 1930) he disagrees with the mechanistic explanation of morphogenesis resulting exclusively from local interactions, and seeks inspiration in Driesch's entelechy (see chapter 9). He considers the Mendelian genetics of his time unsatisfactory because they are preformistic: the gene unambiguously determines the final state (p. 234). Developmental biologists, however, should not be satisfied with a static mirror having the genotype on

2. I admit to a little deceit in a previous paragraph: as far as I know, Wolpert never uses the term "field." In the textbook cited (Wolpert et al., 1998), there is no reference to (morphogenetic) field in the index, nor could I find the word in his other papers. Other authors, however, do not hesitate to use the concept when referring to the Wolpertian model (see, e.g., Gilbert et al., 1996).

one side and the phenotype on the other: instead, they should engage in a study of *processes*. An identical "material essence" may lead to very different developmental pathways and/or final patterns (multifinality), and at the same time very similar forms may be attained from different starting positions (equifinality). Gurwitsch (1930) concluded that mere deciphering of material causes for such phenomena would lead into a blind alley. The matter is not in the material used, or in the "mechanism" of how the form appears: it is the form itself that holds: "Which of the thinkable forms are really utilized in organic patterns? Could some configurations not be biologically 'impossible?' Our conception would triumph should we one day demonstrate that forms not allowed by our field conception were indeed never effectuated. We do not know anything about this at present, and the problem thus remains in the domain of mathematics rather than of biology" (p. 268). Should we, asks Gurwitch, resign the search for a unifying principle and accept biology as pure systematics, a mere endless list of odds? Or should we rely on mere analogies and evaluate the truth of statements hermeneutically? If we are to introduce a unifying theory, then it would not rely on dismembering living beings into elements. Gurwitsch recognizes only two unquestionable variables of biological development—time and field; only the former is measurable, and the field can be described only geometrically, not physically. The whole state of an organism is a function of field intertwined with time; all other factors are mutually dependent.

> The concept of field will be hereafter used purely formally, as the shortest and most synoptic outline of the geometry of embryological processes. We will aim for the simplicity of the whole construction, and the simplest construction will be a priority. We will put aside the basic questions that arise whenever a formulation of a physical field is attempted. Such questions refer to the source and structure of fields. We should, above all, avoid confusion, which might become unpleasantly misguiding under certain circumstances. In a purely geometrical approach, the "source of field," means something diametrically different from its meaning in physics and chemistry. (p. 295)

What can be tested in the laboratory is the flow of material along the field vectors (this aspect is emphasized even more in Gurwitsch's second book, *Teorija Biologicheskovo Polja* [The Theory of Biological Field; 1944]). Gurwitsch, in a way, anticipates the dissipative structures.

At this point I should stress another aspect of *Histologischen Grundlagen* (1930), characterized by following quotation:

> The overall field should not be taken as a synthesis of secondary fields, if we cannot assume as a matter of course that with any displacement of some element in the field, its field will be displaced, too. We should therefore ac-

cept a fact that is quite hard to grasp, that while a particular transplantable part of an embryo can be a "carrier" of its own field, this does not mean that any part would bear a fraction of the overall field. A deeper insight into the ruling relations remains hidden. (p. 305)

I particularly stress this conclusion because in his second book Gurwitch explicitly withdraws it and openly tries to reify the field. He justifies the attempt by the necessity to construct biology from its own premises. I suspect such a stance is his reaction to a development he witnessed in the last years of his life, when *biologists*, in an effort to explain *biological* phenomena, adopted more and more of the concepts of physics and chemistry. Causally oriented biologists even saw their goal as the transformation of biology into biochemistry and biophysics. Gurwitsch, in contrast, prefers a specifically biological definition of the living state. He admits that a certain degree of reductionism is unavoidable, should a complicated and incomprehensible sequence of phenomena be replaced by (faithful) simplification; otherwise we could not speak of science. The reduction, however, must not exceed the boundaries of biology—it should not be a step into the realm of other disciplines. At the same time, however, he comes to the conclusion that the higher order fields he had been proposing for decades cannot represent a universal principle that would become a starting point for a new biology. Such fields exist only for a very short time during embryogeny and therefore do not allow for extrapolations into the future. Gurwitsch therefore adopts a bottom-up approach: he deductively arrives at the concept of *cellular field*, a basic component of the secondary supracellular, macroscopic, field. The cellular field now becomes for him the universal biological principle, the first building block of the future system of general biology. Gurwitsch admits, and even stresses, that the whole system is nothing but a thought experiment, that he has no experimental proof at hand. He speculates that the cellular field plays the role of a regulatory principle: it "orders" the molecules in the cell. As a consequence, the chemical substances in the cell occur—in contrast to ordinary chemical systems—in disequilibrium, and their movement is given by the orientation of vectors (lines of force) of the field. The behavior of molecules within a field cannot be described chemically without introducing new assumptions and parameters to chemistry, because no structures exist at the submolecular level, only structured processes.

But it is not only energy potential that is formed according to "instructions" from the field (the field itself does not perform any work). The anisotropy of the field is species specific, and therefore the properties of the field also determine the morphogenesis typical of the species. The cellular field is in fact the single species-specific invariant! What is important from our hermeneutic point of view is that the cellular field has never ceased to exist.

Paradoxically, however, this new view of the cellular field is as strictly defined as several years later the gene would also be: in some authors' formulations it is enough to replace "field" with "gene" to obtain statements fully acceptable in contemporary molecular biology. The "cellular field" would today be expressed as cell-specific regulation of gene expression.

By discarding the idea of overall field as wholly geometrical, primary, and invariant, Gurwitsch slips into the reductionist jargon of his time. His cellular field is nothing but one of several ways to explain morphogenesis (before the discovery of DNA and the genetic code) by short-distance causal actions.

A Structuralist Comeback

With the arrival of molecular biology and the neo-Darwinian synthesis, the concept of field has quickly evaporated. One of its comebacks in biology occurred in the 1980s, with authors who were later among the founders of biological structuralism. The field was taken as a primary state, and "the occurrence of mosaic properties is then due to the presence of forces resisting the field property, analogous to friction in the case of macroscopic motion" (Goodwin, 1982, p. 47).

Goodwin, like Gurwitsch, tries to define the necessary and sufficient conditions for generating species-specific form. Each developmental model should contain initial and final conditions, plus a description of how the field operators determining the sequence of controlled transformations work. Such a description issues from rules (or constraints) that will choose the particular solution (i.e., form) out of the set of all solutions that can be implemented by a given field. We can follow, states Goodwin, a parallel line and describe living beings as entities *composed* of molecules, cells, or organs, but such statements are of a similar value as those stating that chemical elements "are composed" of protons, neutrons, or electrons. We will get the properties of chemical elements not from a list of parts, but only from the solution of a Schrödinger equation, which takes atoms as fields. Similarly, an all-embracing biological theory cannot do without the concept of complementarity, with cellular and molecular theory on one side and the conception of the biological field on the other. Goodwin (1982) argues that the conception of a "genetic program," as defined by contemporary theories of morphogenesis, cannot lead to a solution, because specific gene products as such cannot represent the species-specific principles of form. The genetic setup of an organism represents a potential with a much broader set of morphologies than that ultimately implemented into a particular body. The field works as an organizer, a selector of realizations.

This potential can also be described by probability distributions over a range of morphologies, so that each species of organism may be seen as a set of possible forms, one of which is most probable and tends to be used as an identifying characteristic of that species. Evolutionary transformation may then be defined as stabilizations of different initial and boundary conditions so that the mean of the probability distribution is shifted, a process involving a change in certain internal constraints some of which may be determined by specific genes. (p. 50)

Goodwin thus takes developing organisms as entities endowed with a broad morphological potential—*morphogenetic field*—which can be understood as an analogy of quantum superposition in physics. The newly developing organism has the character of a field, which subsequently decays (collapses) into a mosaic represented by the adult. It should be realized that the collapse can take place on one level (e.g., early embryo) while the field remains at another (e.g., organ primordia or limb buds).

Goodwin's morphogenetic field is identical to "structure" (in the sense of structuralism), that is, endowed with wholeness, self-organization, and transformations. The structure is given in advance, and an organism emerges as a deterministic, passive solution of the "field equation." When I maintain (in part III of this book) that the form of an organism is enacted as a hermeneutic achievement, for Goodwin it is simply a selection from forms that are given in advance.

Experimental Biology

Let me now show how much room is left for the idea of the field in "mainstream" biology. I have already described Wolpert's "field," which had an enormous impact on the thinking of developmental biologists in the latter half of the twentieth century. Wolpert's approach is purely pragmatic, and his *gradient* can be taken as a special limited case of the morphogenetic field.

Cells within the gradient will obtain three types of information: (1) if the maximal concentration of the morphogen is known, then the actual concentration informs the cell about its distance from the maximum; (2) the vector of the concentration gradient provides directional information and can enable the polarization of the area; (3) the declination (steepness) of the gradient provides information about the size of the whole area. Each cell thus obtains *local* information concerning its absolute and relative position in the area, as well as its polarity—the idea of a field has indeed no space in the scheme.

Some authors, however, have started to use the term "field" in a broader sense, in the context of contemporary terminology. W. A. Müller, in *Developmental Biology* (1996) provides the following description:

> A morphogenetic field is an area whose cells can cooperatively bring about a structure or a set of structures. Another way to define a morphogenetic field is an area in which signal substances—"inducer," "morphogen," or "factor"—become effective and contribute to the subdivision of the field into subregions. . . . Morphogenetic fields define developmental potencies; these are not necessarily exactly coincidental with developmental factors. Usually fields are initially larger than the area fated to construct the particular organ. Fields exhibit the faculty of regulation. When cut into two, each half will give rise to a complete structure, albeit of half the size. (p. 183)

This definition, and its development on subsequent pages of his book, is a very interesting unification of two views. Müller's model considerably enlarges the potential of Wolpert's concept by adding dissipative structures. He can reconcile Wolpert's French flag model (which, as I have shown, does not conform to our conception of field) with another concept, Turing's reaction–diffusion model. This model does not require an organizing center, and the space becomes differentiated from intrinsic forces. The reaction–diffusion models also operate with "inductors," "factors," and so forth, but the order imposed on the space is of different nature—it has the character of a dissipative structure (figure 7.2).

Of other well-known textbooks, I will quote from that by Gilbert (1994). Here the field is defined as "a group of cells whose position and fate are specified with respect to the same set of boundaries. A particular field of cells will give rise to a particular organ when transplanted to a different part of the embryo, and the cells of the field can regulate their fates to make up for the missing cells in the field" (pp. 691–692). The definition is somewhat restricted compared to Gilbert's activities oriented toward rehabilitating the concept of the morphogenetic field. I would highlight particularly the manifesto *Resynthesizing Evolutionary and Developmental Biology* (1996) that he published together with two developmental biologists, J. M. Opitz and R. A. Raff. The article begins with a declaration reminiscent of Gurwitsch:

> Homologous developmental pathways . . . are seen in numerous embryonic processes, and they are seen occurring in discrete regions, the morphogenetic fields. These fields (which exemplify the modular nature of developing embryos) are proposed to mediate between genotype and phenotype. Just as the cell (and not its genome) functions as the unit of organic structure and function, so the morphogenetic field (and not the genes or the cells) is seen as a major unit of ontogeny whose changes bring about changes in evolution (p. 357)

Gilber and colleagues first analyze how the concept of the morphogenetic field—the central explanatory principle of developmental biology—could have completely disappeared from the vocabulary of biologists after World

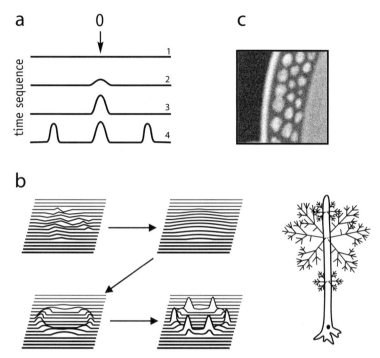

Figure 7.2. The reaction–diffusion model. (*a*) In a homogeneous solution, we have compounds x and y with the following properties: (1) x catalyzes the production of both x and y; (2) y inhibits the production of x; and (3) y diffuses quicker than x. If the concentration of x at point O increases by a random fluctuation, the production of both compounds will increase in that place. The concentration of x will rise further at point O, whereas y will diffuse to the surrounding area and will avert possible fluctuations in x near the peak of O. Further fluctuation can therefore rise further only where the influence of a higher concentration of y is not apparent. The result of the whole process is a uniform division of space, concerning maxima and minima of x (time-point 4). Adapted from Kauffman (1993) and Müller (1996). (*b*) Differentiation of whorls in a unicellular alga *Acetabularia*: the model of the developing field and a sketch of the plant. Adapted from Harold (1990). (*c*) Turing structures produced in a chemical reactor. Adapted from De Keeper et al. (1991).

War II. The manifesto is not, however, meant as a historical survey, but as an ambitious attempt to found a theory that would unite three separate areas: homology, macroevolution, and developmental genetics. The field thus receives the exceptional status of an explanatory principle not only for ontogeny but also for the evolution of morphologies. If the project succeeds, it will, after many decades, lead to a common platform of developmental and evolutionary biology.

The properties of field are summarized in ten points (paraphrased from Gilbert et al., 1996, pp. 366–368):

1. Fields are discrete units of embryonic development. They are produced by the interactions of genes and gene products within specific bounded domains. They are therefore defined in terms of information that becomes translated into spatial entities. Changes in field properties will result in changes of the phenotype and may lead to evolutionary transformations.
2. Morphogenetic fields are modular, that is, independent of other fields present in the embryo (except on the single primary field of the early embryo, of course). The interactions between the modules can change without affecting the characteristics of the modules themselves. (For modules, see chapter 13.)
3. Unlike the classical concepts (e.g., Gurwitsch), the conception of field is based on genetically defined interactions among cells. Products of genes high in the hierarchy of regulations (e.g., homeotic genes; see chapter 13) play probably decisive roles in establishing the field.
4. Morphogenetic fields can be serially homologous (paralogous) or orthologous.[3] Evolution depends on the replication and modification of morphogenetic fields.
5. Homologous genes/proteins can play different roles in different fields. This point is a reminder that speaking of homology makes sense only within a single frame of description.
6. Developmental anomalies such as pleiotropic and polymorphic syndromes should be explained within the frames of the theory.
7. The field acts as an "ecosystem." This means that the genetic background influencing the formation of the field is largely redundant. Mutations or deletions—even of key genes—may have no phenotypic consequences, because the void place (niche) will be immediately occupied by its functional equivalent. How the "ecosystem," that is, the reservoir of redundant regulatory genes, survives for a long time is explained by population genetics models (e.g., Cooke et al., 1997; Nowak et al., 1997).
8. The gene exerts its effect by operating within the field. This means that in many cases its effect depends on the genetic background into which it was introduced.
9. The character of the field is to a great extent influenced by symbolic signals (inductors) and the extent and quality of their processing. The development of the field will depend on the setup of this interaction network; its changes, or even "transfers of competence" (when the inductor adopts another signaling pathway), will result in changes of size and/or morphology of the phenotype. The field can thus be tuned to certain inputs. Here, I think, there is space for the application of both individual and species experience—for epigenetics and, in a broader sense, hermeneutics.
10. Cells, not genes, are units of body structures and function. The mor-

---

3. Serial homology concerns the repetition of homologous modules in a single body (e.g., segments in an earthworm or vertebrae). Orthology is the relation of homology between organisms (e.g., the forelimbs of dogs and whales are orthologous, whereas the wings of hens and butterflies are not).

phogenetic field can be seen as a major unit of ontogenetic and phylogenetic change.

Gilbert and colleagues thus suggest an alternative to the purely genetic
model of development and evolution. This, however, is not antagonistic to the
genetic model (as is the case, e.g., with the model of Goodwin) and offers connections of benefit to both. The whole treatise deserves greater publicity and
discussion, though, to my knowledge, only one (highly negative) response exists.[4] From the point of view of this book, an eleventh point (perhaps first in
importance?) should be added, stating that the field has never ceased to exist.

Resonance

I cannot end this chapter without mentioning another prominent personal-
ity who stands quite outside the mainstream trends—Mae-Wan Ho (see, e.g.,
Ho, 1993, 1994). Ho makes a very serious attempt to describe living beings
as self-structuring fields. Her conception is close to that of Neubauer (see introduction to part II), but she makes an important move from phenomenological description to reification. Ho was inspired by the Fröhlich theory of
resonance (see, e.g., Pokorný, 1995; Pokorný and Wu, 1998). The theory enables modeling of coherent systems synchronized through many levels of organization. Her experiments, together with extensive study of references, led
her to several important conclusions:

(1) Living beings can be characterized by high-efficiency energy transfers,
with minimum losses. Ho interprets this fact as evidence that energy transformations in living beings are of a different order from those described by
chemical kinetics. The latter are defined for reactions in homogeneous space
involving very high numbers of molecules, and characterized by quantities
based on the averaging of states of large numbers of particles (temperature,
concentration, free energy, entropy, etc.). Such quantities, however, cannot be
defined for the interior of living beings—they have no meaning there, because the space within the cell is highly structured. Ho refers to McClare's
(1971, 1972) model of resonant and lossless energy transfers and transformations. The model explains the contraction of skeletal muscle, which is coherent across nine orders of size scales. This means that 10^{20} molecules of
ATP are split in a coherent (i.e., coordinated, nonlocal) manner, which ensures almost 100% efficiency of the process. Ho (1988) supposes similar

---

4. In a letter to the editor entitled "Resynthesis or revisionism?" Lipshitz (1996) protests
against similar activities and states: "Major 'rediscoveries' or advances in our scientific understanding do not come from compendia of poorly understood phenomena or from erudite-sound-
ing speculations; they come from mechanistic hypotheses and their empirical tests" (p. 616).

arrangements in other heavy energy converters, such as metabolic pathways, oxidative phosphorylation, photophosphorylation, and so on.

> Intercommunication can proceed so rapidly through the liquid crystalline continuum of the organism that in the limit of the coherence time and coherence volume of energy storage—the time and volume respectively over which the energy remains coherent—intercommunication is instantaneous and nonlocal. There is no time-separation within the coherence volume, just as there is no space-separation within the coherence time. Because the organism stores coherent energy over all space-times, it has a full range of coherent space-times, which are furthermore, all coupled together. (p. 93)

Although Ho herself admits that this conception of nonlocality is not generally accepted, I consider it very appealing.

(2) Living cells exhibit optical polarization, which dead cells do not (Ho, 1993). This phenomenon is interpreted as proof that living things are highly ordered, to the same extent as crystals where polarization of light can be observed. This means that cells do not contain anything like homogeneous solutions (see also Hess and Mikhailov [1995] for support of this notion). For a very similar concept of evolution based on nonergodicity, see Kauffman (2000).

(3) Living organisms emit coherent "biophotons," which dead or poisoned ones do not. Moreover, these living "lasers" work over a broad range of wavelengths (Ho, 1993; Chang et al., 1998). Ho asserts that these results support the postulate that the coherence in living systems is quantum in nature[5] and interprets living organisms as highly coherent systems interconnected through many orders of space (10^{-10} to 10^1 m) and time (10^{-14} to 10^7 s).

Ho's theory, perhaps alone among all "holistic" theories, allows for the formulation of testable hypotheses. The results of measurements to date are ambiguous, owing to shortcomings in the new methods. For Ho, however, the main message is still clear: "One comes to the startling conclusion that the coherent organism is a macroscopic quantum object, it has a macroscopic wavefunction that is always evolving, always changing as it entangles its environment. This wavefunction is the unique, significant form of the organism" (Chang et al., 1998, p. 94). I do not feel competent to judge how these words align with the paradigms of quantum physics, but I admit that I find the ideas very attractive. One postscript: the morphogenetic field, be it quantum in nature or not, is also a concern of hermeneutics, because it was never "empty." The question as to how it came into existence I leave aside.

---

5. In this respect, Ho is not alone; I refer here to the works of quantum physicists who suppose that quantum processes bear on the living state and conscience (see, e.g., Hameroff, 1994; Penrose, 1997). It is beyond my powers to judge such ambitions, but I must say that those quantum physicists I consulted remain very skeptical.

8

EPIGENETICS

And, after all, I am a biologist; it is plants and animals that I'm interested in, not clever exercises in algebra or even chemistry.

Lamarck's theory could quite well be interpreted to mean not that the individual organism that acquires a character during its lifetime will tend to transmit this to its immediate offspring, but that, if members of a population of animals undergoing evolution acquire a character during their lifetime, this character will tend to appear more frequently in members of a derived population many generations later.

Conrad H. Waddington

Ontogeny and phylogeny today represent two complementary areas of biology. The difference can be best characterized by the slogan "Whereas ontogeny is controlled and purposeful, evolution is effectuated by random events." Mixing the two looks like a heresy, which threatens to contaminate the paradigm with opinions surpassed long ago.

Yet the differences between these two approaches is not that clearcut. First, the actual *process* relating genes to morphology remains unexplained: though the realm of experimental (molecular) embryology is one of the most dynamic in biology, we have learned more about what organisms have in common than about the essence of species-specific appearance. Second, the new synthesis, the leading paradigm of evolutionary biology, arose out of population genetics characterized by free permutations of genes and traits (mostly of adult organisms) and gradual shifts in statistical weights. It has almost no room for ontogeny.

The concept of *epigenetics* was introduced in the 1940s by Conrad H. Waddington, to give a name to causal *interactions* between genes and their products that lead to the realization of the phenotype (Waddington, 1975, p. 218), in both ontogeny and phylogeny. Epigenetics, for him, was an antipode of a one-way (genotype-to-phenotype) comprehension of morphogenesis, and against barriers erected between developmental and evolutionary biology. But the concept had its own life and often caused serious misunderstandings. To map the semantic field, I first present four contemporary definitions of epigenetics.

1. Lodish et al. (1995) in their textbook of cell biology state: "An epigenetic condition or process is one that is passed from a specific cell to its progeny without any alteration in the germ line coding sequence of the DNA. The differentiated state of cells, which is passed on to progeny cells, is generally determined epigenetically" (p. 1286). From this definition, it follows that, in humans, for example, the whole process of ontogeny (except genetic changes in lymphocytes and production of germ cells) can be understood as epigenetic — a long-known process has simply been given a new name.

2. Russo et al., editors of the compendium *Epigenetic Mechanisms of Gene Regulation* (1996), give a broader definition of epigenetics: the "study of mitotically and/or meiotically heritable changes in gene function that cannot be explained by changes in DNA sequence" (p. 1). Note that this definition does not exclude the heritability of gene states via gametes.

3. Wilson (1998) broadens the definition to take in even the inherited operations of the sensory systems and the brain, that is, rules that provide them with rapid orientation and problem solving in anticipated situations: "Epigenetic rules . . . are innate operations of the sensory system and brain. They are rules of thumb that allow organisms to find rapid solutions to problems encountered in environment. They predispose individuals to view the world in a particular innate way and automatically to make certain choices as opposed to others" (p. 193).

4. Maynard Smith (1990) and Jablonka and Lamb (1995) introduce the concept of "epigenetic inheritance system," defined as a system that enables the transmission of functional states or structures from one cell generation to another, even when the stimulus that induced the particular state or structure is no longer present.

Thus, one single heading covers organelles and other cell structures, cells, canalization of phenotypes in ontogeny, speciation, possible Lamarckian inheritance, and instincts. Culture and language are, of course, epigenetic phenomena *sui generis*. This can lead to a conceptual gibberish that is not easy to understand. It may therefore be useful to have a closer look at how the concept was understood by its founding fathers, Ivan Ivanovich Schmalhausen and Waddington. They were contemporaries, but Waddington is much better known: he spent his whole career at the peak of the world biological community, whereas Schmalhausen lived in isolation in the U.S.S.R., due to war and Lysenkoist oppression. Both acknowledged the mutual isomorphism of their ideas. Waddington, however, was more acceptable to the scientific community because he published in English (for many decades, Schmalhausen was known only through a poor English translation of his book *Factors of Evolution. The Theory of Stabilizing Selection* [1946]), because his formulations were more cautious, and, last but not least, because he tested his hypotheses experimentally. Both authors tried to unify developmental and evolutionary biology.

Reaction Norm and Canalization

Two key concepts will be useful in the discussion that follows: the "reaction norm" and "canalization." The term reaction norm refers to the set of all possible phenotypes that could be produced, in various environments, over a single genotype (Schlichtling and Pigliucci, 1998, p. 51). It follows that the boundaries of phenotypic expression can never be set.[1] The reaction norm is usually represented by one or more typical phenotypes that occur in "common" environments and a set of many different ones occurring under specific or extreme conditions. The term was introduced in 1909 by Woltereck (*Reaktionsnorm*) and further developed in the 1930s and 1940s by Schmalhausen. A concept that is closely related is "plasticity," that is, the degree of phenotypic change evoked by a change of environment. Plasticity is bound to the reaction norm, but the latter may not be plastic. The plastic responses characterizing the reaction norm can be described as amount, pattern (i.e., monotonous, intermittent), rate, reversibility, and competence—an ability to respond to environmental clues at a given time or stage (Schichtling and Pigliucci, 1998). Symmetrical to the reaction norm is canalization, that is, projection from a set of genotypes onto a single phenotype (see futher discussion later in this chapter). For those who opt for the explanation of ontogeny at the gene level, the reaction norm concept presents a way to understand the enormous plasticity of gene expression. This holds especially if the concept is broadened to the level of a population (i.e., a set of genomes) and used to explain variability in the penetrance of various alleles.

The term "reaction norm" is often compared with the quasi-Lamarckian Baldwin effect (Baldwin, 1896), which was formulated to explain the fixing of

---

1. The reaction norm should not be confused with the "reaction range," which denotes the limitation of the genotype in some respect; for example, if there are no genes for glycolytic enzymes available, none of the possible phenotypes will be able to split sugars.

acquired characteristics in psychology and behaviour. The Baldwin effect can be expressed as follows: The greater the ability of an individual to adapt to external conditions, the greater its fitness, that is, production of progeny; the progeny will also inherit the tendency of being able to adapt (learn). In the terminology of the reaction norm, it holds that organisms capable of high phenotypic plasticity, if confronted with environmental changes, have a high probability of producing a minority phenotype that will be compatible with survival and with the production of progeny. If an environmental change lasts for many generations, the bearers of such phenotypes will have the opportunity to accumulate mutations that will shift the reaction norm toward a new maximum in place of the original minority phenotype (figure 8.1). An apparent Lamarckian inheritance will find an explanation in the Darwinian scheme. Baldwin, as a devoted Darwinist, formulated the principle for just these reasons.

The reconciliation of evolution with ontogeny, however, could also proceed from another direction—by presuming the evolutionary emancipation of development from random mutations and its role in setting the *direction* of evolution. Such was the approach of Schmalhausen (1986): "Liberating the organism from the *determining* influence of the environment involves the establishment of a system of internal factors of development which determine the specific course of morphogenetic processes" (p. 2). In contrast to the biological structuralists, in Schmalhausen's concept the structure of developmental relationships has an evolutionary dynamic and can assimilate changes by adaptive modifications, that is, by the selection of fitter phenotypes (within the limits of its plasticity).

Adaptive modifications will be evoked by standard situations again and again: their stability is acquired in the evolutionary history of the species. However, even nonstandard factors may occur (e.g., cathode radiation), in which case organisms will react by producing "morphoses," that is, phenotypes outside the reaction norm. Morphoses are individual and labile improvisations to nonstandard external cues, whereas adaptive modifications react to factors that are assimilated, familiar. Morphoses perhaps may be characterized as new hermeneutic achievements in a Gadamerian sense.

The role of the environment in producing modifications or morphoses is, however, limited—it is only a trigger, an inductor. Subsequent development proceeds autonomously as a result of *internal interpretation* of the signal received:

> The dependence of individual development upon certain environmental factors is a truism. However, what matters in this interaction between organism and environment is that the morphogenetic reaction is typical of the organism under given conditions. After a very brief period of induction, the reaction proceeds autonomously without the influence of determining

factors. This type of development is termed "autoregulating." This autoregulation is typical in various degrees of all normal morphogenetic reactions and of all adaptive modifications. (Schmalhausen, 1986, p. 6)

Schmalhausen then tried to specify the role of the hereditary material and of the (cyto)plasm.[2] (Cyto)plasm is the specific *substrate of ontogeny* (p. 26)— the site of all species-specific morphogenetic processes. It is the (cyto)plasm that will decide the modifications (i.e., concrete realization of possibilities). (Cyto)plasm has peculiar properties—it is variable in ontogeny, but maintains high evolutionary stability (p. 28). Evolution proceeds marked by a constant increase in the internal autonomy of ontogenetic processes. It is the organism that decides its future behavior, based on historical experience.

In the course of evolution, ontogeny thus becomes less and less dependent on the environment. The effect of the environment will gradually become limited to triggering a cascade of species-specific and internally controlled responses. The internal environment is thus buffered and pays no attention (over a broad range of values) to external conditions. This fact opens up a space for a *new* type of evolution driven almost exclusively by *internal resources*. The appearance of new variants is anticipated by the acceptance of a new genetic scheme (by the population in a given biotope), and the cooperation of different factors leads gradually toward better cohesion of the ontogeny. Selectively neutral factors may also exist—they are simply carried along at the beginning, but they slowly invade the network and eventually become part of it, and thus become indispensable for ontogeny. Sometimes the process can be circumvented by a long leap, but the complexes of small mutations and "gene modifiers" play a much more important role. Stable morphophysiological systems arise as a result of the evolutionary process:

> As the systems of correlations become more complex, they lose their genetic character; in other words, the effects on individual genes can no longer be distinguished (more precisely their disruption by mutations has lethal consequences). Morphophysiologic interrelationships and their systems may be regarded as entities that are not capable of analysis in genetic systems. (p. 219)

Particular changes in function thus decide the directionality of evolution: swimming comes first, followed by the appearance of fins; burrowing will precede the mole's limbs, and so forth. Gradually the functional adaptations become a genetic default: the mole will develop its limbs even if it has never

---

2. In Russian, the word used is *plazma*, whereas the English translation uses "cytoplasm." I follow the usage of the translator in my text, although I feel that *plazma* may designate a more general concept, perhaps synonymous with "body." I stress the fact typographically as "(cyto)plasm."

had a chance to burrow, and ducks reared in the backyard will retain their webbed feet.

I now turn my attention to Waddington (1975). Throughout his career, he remained a strong opponent of the neo-Darwinian synthesis and its playing with numbers, which left no room for ontogeny and its evolution: "Evolution of organisms must really be regarded as the evolution of developmental systems. . . . I still think that when modern population geneticists express the variation in a population by means of a timeless frequency curve, which deals only with the adults, this is a simplification that needs justification. (p. 7; see also epigraph at the beginning of this chapter).

In 1941 Waddington published an apology of Goldschmidt's theory of evolution and stated that rather than deciphering the physical–chemical mechanisms of development, evolutionary theory needs a vision of possible interactions between evolutionary processes. It needs a system of concepts that will allow a weight to be assigned to observed differences, for example, between variants or between species. In another paper the same year he introduced his concept of the *canalization of development* as a tool to explain the fixing of adaptive traits:

> Adaptive characters are inherited and some explanation of this must be provided. If we are deprived of the hypothesis of the inheritance of the effects of use and disuse, we seem thrown back on an exclusive reliance on the natural selection of merely chance mutations. It is doubtful, however, whether even the most statistically minded geneticists are entirely satisfied that nothing more is involved than the sorting out of random mutations by the natural selective filter. . . . Developmental reactions, *as they occur in organisms submitted to natural selection,* are in general canalized. That is to say, they are adjusted so as to bring about one definite end result regardless of minor variations in conditions during the course of the reaction. (Waddington, 1975, p. 16)[3]

On a small scale, canalization will manifest itself in the discreteness of cells and tissues—there are no intermediary morphologies (see below for similar models by Kauffman). On a large scale, it is manifested as a "wildtype" constancy, despite many different regimes pressuring the system away from equilibrium: "Canalization is a feature of the system which is built up by natural selection . . . it ensures the production of the normal, that is, optimal, type in the face of the unavoidable hazards of existence" (p. 19). Canalization, as Waddington admits, is identical to Schmalhausen's autoregulation. Both authors also agree on the details of the process, which can be divided into three phases:

---

3. All quotations are taken from the selection of Waddington's papers reprinted in Waddington (1975); for the original references, see therein.

1. Gradual conversions following an internal logic: there is no threshold for reaction to external stimuli, and the intensity of the response is proportional to the intensity of the stimulus.
2. The environment becomes a canalizing switch (trigger): a threshold of stimulus can be distinguished that, when exceeded, will evoke a different mode of response.
3. Genetically fixed canalization is either strictly encoded or switched on only by "symbolic" (e.g., hormonal), not environmental triggers.

Genetic Assimilation

Waddington constructed his experimental research on the assumption that "natural selection will act, not solely on fortuitous variants resembling the form produced by the environment, but on the sensitivity of normal individuals to the environmental stimulus; and the genotypes sensitive to the external influence will also reinforce the action of any genes that tend to produce similar phenotypes and will canalize their activity toward the exact effect that is being selected for" (p. 23). Waddington worked with the fruitfly *Drosophila* as an experimental model. He submitted the early developmental stages (eggs, pupae) to unusual environmental stresses (high temperature, chemicals) and obtained a variety of malformations that resembled well-known genetic mutations. These phenotypes, however, were not caused by mutations: their offspring—when no longer submitted to abnormal stimuli—yielded normal morphologies again. Waddington called such mutationlike phenotypes "phenocopies."

If, however, sensitive developmental stages were submitted to the noxious agent repeatedly in subsequent generations, particular phenotypes started to appear that became independent of the external factor—that is, they became genetically fixed. Thus, "genetic assimilation" of phenotypes occurred under direct pressure from the environment: " 'Genetic assimilation' is a name that has been proposed for a process by which characters which were originally 'acquired characters,' in the conventional sense, may become converted, by a process of selection acting for several or many generations on the population concerned, into 'inherited characters' (p. 59). This result led Waddington to a critique of the neo-Darwinian conception of evolution based on selection from random and nondirected mutations. He argues that such an assumption is extreme, because it ignores the results of developmental biology. Waddington maintains that natural selection not only acts as a filter for organisms whose properties are close to the optimum required, but also favors individuals that have a tendency to produce such phenotypes independently of external conditions.

Waddington is also the author of a classic icon of ontogeny: the epigenetic landscape (figure 8.1) with discrete valleys—"chreods"—that determine the ontogenetic pathways. The environment may act either by shifting development toward another existing chreod (plasticity within the boundaries of the reaction norm) or even by ploughing the landscape to give it a new pattern (genetic assimilation, appearance of new reaction norm). The whole process of genetic assimilation depends on how broad the reaction norm is. It can be evoked in a normal population with a large supply of appropriate mutations, but not in inbred strains: "The explanation in terms of genetic assimilation is not alternative to an account in terms of random gene mutations, but is supplementary to it; and what it adds to the theory is the more important, the more one is dealing with evolutionary change in complex organs or organ systems which must be affected by numerous genes that have to be integrated with one another" (p. 92). If the effect of both the environment and the processes determining the reaction norm are taken into account, the image of natural selection becomes much more plastic than in models where only genes and traits are considered.

Contemporary Trends

Here I summarize approaches toward epigenetics in the late twentieth century:

(1) Neo-Darwinism has been very resilient also because it is able to absorb new trends and bring them under its own jurisdiction. Richard Dawkins, for example, recognizes epigenetic processes as a matter of fact but rejects as redundant the claims that feedbacks might exist, on any possible time scale, from phenotype to genotype. He maintains that evolution can be fully explained by variational replication of replicators (regardless of whether these are pieces of DNA, centrioles, or memes). He often ridicules naive critics who appear to believe that neo-Darwinists waste their time looking for "genes for" this or that trait (e.g., Dawkins, 1987, p. 296). It goes without saying that the phenotype is a collective piece of all genes that is plastic and that therefore can react flexibly to external pressures, and so no unequivocal projection to phenotype is possible.[4] The genotype is obviously not a blueprint but a prescription, a recipe for how to assemble the body. In his famous "cake analogy" (p. 297), Dawkins discusses the consequences of replacing the word "yeast" in the recipe with "baking powder." Preparing a cake is an epigenetic process:

---

4. How such epistatic interactions could stabilize the phenotypes of large sexual populations is shown by Flegr (1998), who shows that a panmictic species is not capable of a further speciation event and simply survives unchanged before it becomes extinct. The only feasible way to establish a new species is to remove the maximum of the reaction norm distribution—for example, by genetic drift in a small, isolated population.

a

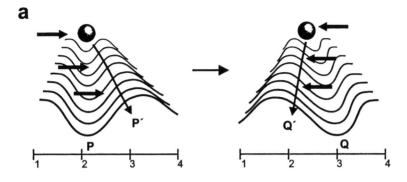

b

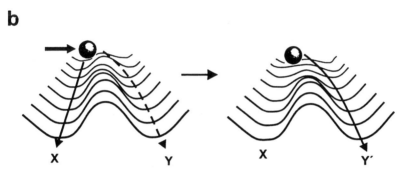

Figure 8.1. The epigenetic landscape. Ontogeny is compared to the trajectory of a ball that is headed (canalized) toward the lowest point of the valley (chreod). Such a point is characterized by a particular phenotype. (*a*) Quantitative traits. Under normal conditions the development will end in the phenotype *P*, characterized by a value of 2. Environmental pressure (*horizontal arrows*) will shift the development toward *P'*, with a value of 3. If the pressure persists over several generations, the new development becomes fixed by shifting the chreod, and a typical trajectory will aim toward point *Q* with a value of 3. The former conditions that led originally toward point *P* are now sensed as a stress—they will shift development toward point *Q'*, with a value between 2 and 3. (*b*) Qualitative shift. A normal trajectory aims toward the phenotype *X*. Stimulus (environmental factor or a mutation, *horizontal arrow*) enables the ball to cross the internal barrier and take the chreod leading toward the phenotype *Y*. Genetic assimilation consists of lowering the barrier, that is, reshaping the myriad coordinations in the developing organism. The process may result in a complete removal of the barrier when no further initiation is required for the new trajectory, and the phenotype *Y* becomes a default. Adapted from Waddington (1975).

mutation of the recipe will change the whole cake, and it is impossible to say that "part" of it was coded by yeast. Such a change in a recipe is hereditary—all subsequent cakes baked according to it would bear the new trait. On the other hand, the fact of cutting away a piece of cake will hardly influence the phenotypes of cakes that will follow. Natural selection will sort out from this variability what appears to be the fittest. Dawkins is right in that, if the recipe is a design for constructing a machine, that is, if ontogeny is a mere mechanical processing of a program written in advance, there can be no alternative to his views.

Maynard Smith and Szathmáry extended the concept of an "epigenetic system of inheritance" (see above) to evolutionary processes (Maynard Smith, 1990; Maynard Smith and Szathmáry, 1995). Events such as bounding the replicators into compartments, their confinement into chromosomes, the appearance of symbiogenetic (eukaryotic) cells, multicellularity, colonies of animals with castes, communities of primates, and language all belong to this concept. The attainment of any level is an epigenetic event; hence, heredity is more and more a matter of factors other than molecular replicators (i.e., nucleic acids). What is transmitted is also the setup, the organization of structures and relations. These structures and relations thus become units of selection, because they are submitted to natural selection as wholes, not just as a bunch of genetic replicators. The whole model is, in principle, an extension of Eigen's theory of hypercycles (Eigen and Winkler-Oswatitsch, 1992; see figure 4.1), and of modular views of evolution (see chapter 13).

By attaining a "higher" level, the former selection units will irreversibly lose their autonomy. Evolution becomes an accumulation of complexity. A view of evolutionary epigenetic transition thus absorbs the classic mutation—selection theory, genetic assimilation, and even memetics. The only constraint—which authors on this topic do not forget to stress—is the sharp definition of an individual (at a given level of organization). Only when it is possible to recognize parents and their (variable) offspring is the functioning of natural selection ensured. (From this point, the development of an ecosystem cannot be considered an epigenetic process, because we cannot define selection units; see chapter 10). Maynard Smith and Szathmáry thus developed the Darwinist theory to absorb epigenetic phenomena and made it resilient enough to accept possible further discoveries.

(2) Stuart A. Kauffman began from Waddingtonian and structuralist positions. In his book *The Origins of Order* (1993) he specifies his position as "not against Darwin, but against Darwinism" (p. 472). He developed mathematical models of evolution and/or ontogeny with a high degree of internal correlation, which can evolve independently of selection pressure: they can even resist it. From the behavior of models, he concluded that development on time scales of both evolution and ontology is highly canalized by internal correlations.

Kauffmanian models serve as a mathematical corroboration for Waddington's epigenetic landscape, with its chreods and jumps into different regimes. Moreover, they answer the question of why self-sustaining order exists in organisms even though either chaos or a "frozen" timeless state seems much more probable. Kauffman shows that "living" models are able to maintain themselves at the narrow interface between both extremes and to evolve within this space. The features of models are then elaborated to explain ontogenetic as well as phylogenetic events. Kauffman warns that the difficulties people have with his models come from considering both evolution and ontogeny as processes dependent on a program, which they understand as being analogous to the programs of common serial computers. Here, of course, even a tiny change in the text of a program will lead to its breakdown. Ontogeny, however, is not the result of a serially processed algorithm: a better analogy of organisms is a parallel network where a gene influences a limited number of other genes and is regulated by a small number of regulators. On the one hand, the interconnection between gene functions is very loose, and on the other, repeatedly stable regimes of behavior will appear. Such regimes will appear as a consequence of canalization. Kauffmanian models thus assign a much higher autonomy to epigenetic processes than do previous models. Furthermore, he seeks to reconcile his views with both classical Darwinism and rational morphology.

(3) Concerning epigenetics, Jablonka and Lamb are probably the most radical of contemporary theoretical biologists. The preamble to their book *Epigenetic Inheritance and Evolution: The Lamarckian Dimension* (1995) states:

> We accept the Darwinian theory of evolution by natural selection of heritable variations that affect fitness, but we contend that the nature of these variations is a poorly developed part of this story. In the present, neo-Darwinian version, the theory is based on two assumptions: first, that all variation in the hereditary material are random, and second, that all hereditary variations are variations in DNA base sequences. We question both of these assumptions. (p. vi)

The statement is undoubtedly overly harsh: Richard Dawkins belongs among the hard-core neo-Darwinists, and despite this he is the founder of memetics, which does not operate with variations in DNA bases. Perhaps "variations in replicators" would be a more appropriate expression. Concerning the randomness of variation, Jablonka and Lamb are of course right. They take Maynard Smith's epigenetic systems of inheritance and show that, together with culture, they are systems of inheritance with Lamarckian features. They first present the Lamarckian teaching in a more favorable light than the caricature of "inheritance of acquired characters," usually illustrated by Weissman's experiment of cutting off mouse tails. They argue that a more realistic presentation will show that Lamarck's ideas should be summarized as follows: living beings are poised toward change, and when they change they do so as a single coherent whole. The change may be caused by either internal or external factors. The change *may* be adaptive and *may* be transmitted to the progeny. With Lamarck, as with Waddington, Schmalhausen, and

Kauffman, the problem is always dealt with by an organism actively, in a creative way. That is why it is nonsense to cut off tails and declare the Lamarckian inheritance experimentally falsified when no taillessness appears in subsequent generations. On this point Jablonka and Lamb disagree with neo-Lamarckism. They argue that Lamarck always disclaimed any direct influence of environment on the structure (of animals): the response is always a result of internal processing and an active approach on the part of the organism. Whereas Maynard Smith and Szathmáry have problems with the viability of an evolutionary novelty at the very time of its appearance (because it presents a minority in the population), there is no problem in the Lamarckian conception: the whole population—or at least its greater part—can change synchronously.

Jablonka and Lamb (1995) list the following properties of inheritance of *acquired* (i.e., not *required*) traits: (1) the change of trait is stimulated by the environment, (2) the change is specific and repeatable but not necessarily adaptive, (3) the change involves a specific change in the hereditary material, and (4) it is transmitted to the progeny (p. 14).

Jablonka and Lamb trump Dawkins's cake analogy described above with the analogy of a musical score and interpretations. If, besides copies of the script of a score (which include copy mistakes), records of the score also exist, these records will influence all future interpretations (copies) and their evolution. For Dawkins, the best analogy of an interpreter is a music box, which cannot, of course, listen to different interpretations: it has only the code at its disposal. Jablonka and Lamb support their theses by a plethora of facts: from lingering modifications (*Dauermodifikationen*) up to Cairnsian mutations and epigenetic restructuring of chromatin, and they discuss their data from many viewpoints.

As an epilogue to this chapter, I add a quotation from McClintock's (1984) Nobel Prize lecture of December 8, 1983:

> The ability of a cell to sense these broken [chromosome] ends, to direct them toward each other, and then to unite them so that the union of the two DNA strands is correctly oriented, is a peculiarly revealing example of the sensitivity of cells to all that is going on within them. They make wise decisions and act upon them. . . . The sensing devices and the signals that initiate these adjustments are beyond our present ability to fathom. A goal for the future would be to determine the extent of knowledge the cell has of itself. And how to utilize this knowledge in a "thoughtful" manner when challenged. (p. 798)

9

THE SPECTER OF VITALISM

The biologist observes the motion of an ameba towards
food, and attributes a purpose to its swimming. The ameba
has nothing to do with this attribution, the ameba just
swims driven by forces in a concentration gradient, and
does not know it. The "purpose" is a mere mental
construction of the scientist observer, it depends on
his/her intelligence, on his race, religion, scientific
beliefs. This implies that the notion of purpose is not
objective, but it is contextual, changing in time, and is
probably different in different societies and traditions
and points of time.

Pier Luigi Luisi

Consider a bacterium swimming upstream in a glucose
gradient, its flagellar motor rotating. If we naively ask,
"What it is doing?" we unhesitatingly answer something
like "It's going to get dinner." That is, without attributing
consciousness, or conscious purpose, we view bacterium
as acting on its own behalf in an environment. The
bacterium is swimming upstream in order to obtain the
glucose it needs.

Stuart A. Kauffman

Biology came into existence as an attempt to produce a catalog that would
bring order to the increasingly exuberant plethora of living patterns, in
order to understand and praise the Creator's intentions. In such a context it
was, of course, unnecessary to pose the question of the purpose of living be-

ings. With the arrival of modern science, and especially after Darwin defin-itively expelled the Creator from the initial set of axioms, the question of pur-pose — in Nature in general, and in living beings in particular — has repeat-edly reentered the field through the back door. Embarrassments of this kind arise whenever it is convenient to suppose a kind of teleology, and awkward constructions are often built just to explain that such a teleology is only apparent.

Why do we feel such embarrassment, and why is it connected with the modern age? Modern science set all natural processes into a three-dimen-sional Cartesian space and linear time: in such a scheme, the whole world be-came a mechanism and was explained as such. Everything would have been in order, were it stated unequivocally that we are dealing with a concept, a model, a map. As Bateson (1988) states, "[T]he map is not the territory, and the name is not the thing named" (p. 30). A map is a projection from a mul-tidimensional world, and as such it undoubtedly presents an excellent tool for constructing an idea of the world; the success of science-based technologies shows how fruitful this approach may be.

Since Descartes, however, this powerful tool has been accompanied by a curse — a conviction that what is being studied is not a projection but the world itself, endowed by nothing but the four dimensions mentioned. Even should additional dimensions be allowed, nothing would project onto them because there is simply *nothing* to project. The territory was confused with the map, and what cannot be found on the map cannot be found in the territory either! But we ourselves happen to live in this territory and so cannot escape some paradoxes that follow from such a "reading" of the map. This is why the idea of evolution, of the role of contingency, of the spontaneous emergence of entities that cannot be derived from initial conditions, became such a nui-sance for the nineteenth-century worldview.

Teleology supposes an existence of goals, attractors, toward which all or some processes in Nature are inescapably heading. Mechanical science does not accept teleology, though paradoxically it is *the* mechanisms whose future is (at least in principle) easy to calculate without any need for guesswork. It follows that for science the problem lies not in the existence of goals them-selves but solely in intentionality, in immanent, internal goal-oriented drive; this because the prime mover of the mechanism lies outside the world itself and its nature is not an object of scientific inquiry. Thus, the "evolution" of the mechanical world is blind, following unequivocal and simple laws of physics. Such a worldview was fully satisfactory for a long time, and in biol-ogy we have been witnessing repeated attempts to stay with it.

The Kantian Solution

One attempt to solve the paradox of intentionality existing in a mechanical world was the Kantian statement that the world of nature and the world of freedom exist independently; the latter, however, overlaps with the former. Our ontological model of the world must, then, be constructed in such a way that it should allow such an overlap; thus finality (*Zweckmäßigkeit*) should be accepted:

> The finality of nature is, therefore, a particular a priori concept, which has its origin solely in the reflective judgment. For we cannot ascribe to the products of nature anything like a reference of nature in them to ends, but we can only make use of this concept to reflect upon them in respect of the nexus of phenomena in nature—a nexus given according to empirical laws. Furthermore, this concept is entirely different from practical finality (in human art and even morals), though it is doubtless thought after this analogy (Kant, 1988, p. 467)

To conceive Nature according to the principle of *finality*, which is inherent to our cognitive abilities, means to weave random and isolated empirical findings into a continual experience. If we are to succeed and orient ourselves, our judgment must necessarily suppose an order in the outer world, and we also behave as if such a world really exists: "For, were it not for this presupposition, we should have no order in nature in accordance with empirical laws, and consequently, no guiding-thread for an experience that has to be brought to bear upon these in all their variety, or for an investigation of them" (p. 469). The teleological judgment is thus "the faculty of estimating the real finality (objective) of nature by understanding and reason" (p. 473). Thus, Kant says, we introduce the analogy of purposiveness not for want of an explanation, but purely for heuristic reasons—it enables us to assume a position that is suited to observation and inquiry. To go back to our analogy of a map, we create a mental map that may not correspond to any "territory": "But the universal idea of nature, as the complex of objects of sense, gives us no reason whatever for assuming that things of nature serve one another as means to ends, or that their very possibility is only made fully intelligible by a causality of this sort. (§61, p. 550).

The whole thread of thought becomes complicated by the existence of *organic* beings, which can undoubtedly take care of themselves. The constitutive parts of these entities undoubtedly "serve one another as means to ends." As if there were, after all, something corresponding to our mental map that also existed in the real world, the difference between a mechanism (a watch) and an organic being comes to the fore:

> I would say that a thing exists as a physical end if it is both a cause and effect of itself. For this involves a kind of causality that we cannot associate with the mere conception of a nature unless we make that nature rest on an underlying end. (§64, p. 555)

> An organized natural product is one in which every part is reciprocally both end and means. (§66, p. 558)

> An organized being is, therefore, not a mere machine. For a machine has solely motive power, whereas an organized being possesses inherent formative power, and such, moreover, as it can impart to material devoid of it—material which it organizes. This, therefore, is a self-propagating formative power, which cannot be explained by the capacity of movement alone, that is to say, by mechanism. (§65, p. 557)

Kant comes to the conclusion that the organization of nature is not analogous to any known kind of causality:

> Organisms [*organisierte Wesen*] are, therefore, the only beings in nature that, considered in their separate existence and apart from any relation to other things, cannot be thought possible except as ends of nature. It is they, then, that first afford objective reality to the conception of an end that is an end of nature and not a practical end. Thus they supply natural science with the basis for a teleology, or, in other words, a mode of estimating its objects on a special principle that it would otherwise be absolutely unjustifiable to introduce into that science—seeing that we are quite unable to perceive a priori the possibility of such a kind of causality. (§65, p. 558)

Kant then introduces the antinomy of judgment (thesis: "all production of material things is possible on mere mechanical laws"; antithesis: "some production of such things is not possible on mere mechanical laws"; §70, p. 563), and on its basis develops a detailed critique of teleological judgment. This leads Kant to a resigned conclusion:

> It is, I mean, quite certain that we can never get a sufficient knowledge of organized beings and their inner possibility, much less get an explanation of them, by looking merely to mechanical principles of nature. Indeed, so certain is it, that we may confidently assert that it is absurd for men even to entertain any thought of so doing or to hope that maybe another Newton may some day arise, to make intelligible to us even the genesis of but a blade of grass from natural laws that no design has ordered. (§75, pp. 569–570)

This brief and undoubtedly incomplete illustration of Kantian thought shows some of the paradoxes encountered in a strict projection of the world into the Cartesian coordinates. The frustration became even greater in biology, which has, from its very beginning, been confronted with the specter of vitalism.

Vitalism

According to *The Shorter Oxford English Dictionary of Historic Principles* (1973), vitalism is "the doctrine that the origin and phenomena of life are due to or produced by a vital principle, as distinct from a purely physical or chemical force." More detailed sources inform us that the founder of vitalism was Aristotle; we can learn that the teaching has flourished throughout most of Western history and was definitively uprooted by modern science. I believe that we can leave Aristotle aside: his scheme of the world was fundamentally different from that of modern science, and the presence of living beings in his world was a matter of course. To assign him the modern label of "vitalist" is therefore quite anachronistic.

Encyclopedia entries, however, paradoxically grasp the very essence of Aristotelian rather than modern vitalist thought. The modern vitalists were not philosophers but *natural scientists* who tried to incorporate life *into* the frames of the (already established) Cartesian world. To better understand their viewpoint, take the following parable about thermodynamics: imagine that the steam engine has been known since antiquity, but whole generations have failed to explain its functioning. Endless tracts exist written in a language that to a contemporary scientist would sound like gibberish or pure mysticism. Suddenly, one day, someone explains how steam engines work, and instantly mythical terms such as entropy, free energy, and so forth, become a normal, organic part of physics. Not only the functioning of steam engines, but the whole area of the forms and transformations of energy then become ordered and transparent.

The vitalists' endeavor was similar: to encompass the phenomenon of life into the body of science. One stream of thought—call it "mechanist"—has always considered the "laws of physics and chemistry" known at the time to be satisfactory for explaining life. Others—the vitalists—felt a need to find and define some additional principle controlling vital processes (hopefully measurable and in simple mathematical relations to magnitudes already known). Thus, both groups' priority was to discover simple laws that govern life. This quest can best be demonstrated by the initial rejection of Darwin's theory by both groups—they held that introducing historical contingencies into pure science was unacceptable![1]

The best illustration of neovitalist endeavor may be provided by paradigmatic works by Driesch (1905, 1914, 1929). The introduction to his *History and Theory of Vitalism* (1914; an English, elaborated version of the 1905 Ger-

---

1. It should be admitted, however, that vitalists were not always happy with the projection of the "territory" into the Cartesian "map"; hence, they unintentionally excluded themselves from science defined on such a basic premise. It is also true that they continued using Aristotelian terms and contributed to further confusions (see, e.g., Müller, 1996).

man edition) states: "The main question of vitalism is not whether the processes of life can properly be called purposive: it is rather a question if the purposiveness of those processes is the result of a special *constellation* of *factors known already* to the sciences of the inorganic, or if it is the result of an *autonomy* peculiar to the processes themselves" (p. 1). "Purpose" is a purely descriptive term for situations where the explanation of living beings' actions is made easier by the idea of an "aim." The whole problem becomes exposed only if we ask whether such purposiveness is explicable by known laws of inorganic nature. Can the processes in organisms be explained as an outcome of "machinery" working in the background? Are organisms analogous to man-made machines, or can purposiveness be attained by different means? Depending on the answer, Driesch distinguished three kinds of teleology:

1. *Descriptive teleology* is a mere statement that there exists a form of behavior classified by an observer as purposeful. This leaves open the crucial question of whether or not it is a mechanism. Depending on the answer, scientists would choose one of following alternatives:

2. *Static teleology* takes vital processes to be special incidences of general rules determining world affairs. Nonliving parts of organisms simply attain a pattern whose outward manifestations appear to be "living": "Life is only distinctive as a combination and not because of its own laws" (Driesch, 1914, p. 5). Static teleology therefore leads necessarily to the mechanistic theory of organisms. All forms of preformism—the doctrine that living processes are nothing but causal developments (*e-volutio*) of what has been around since the very beginning—belong to this category (this is why the preformists of the eighteenth and nineteenth centuries called themselves evolutionists). The neo-Darwinian conception of life can be characterized as a typical static teleology.[2]

3. *Dynamical teleology* or, in other words, *vitalism*, is a conviction that life processes are autonomous. It supposes a *knowable* and *describable* inner principle that arranges and controls processes characteristic for life. All biologists defending epigenesis (as an opposite to preformism) were, according to Driesch, vitalists, whether they considered themselves as such or not.

Driesch devotes much room, of course, to Kant. According to Driesch, Kant's teleology seems purely descriptive; however, as Kant assigns man as

---

2. Of course, neo-Darwinism was able to assimilate the contingency and historicity so greatly scorned by Driesch and his followers. Evolution (in its contemporary meaning) could be imported into biology through reduction of the whole process to the level of the passive existence of molecular replicators. These, apart from the ability to produce replicas, need just one single ability—to *survive* (or better—*to become a predecessor*). It is a trifle of history that the term "evolutionism," originally designating mechanistic preformism, was taken over to characterize the exact opposite of preformism—the emergence of novelty. It is another trifle that the most successful explanation of a mechanism(!) of evolution is the preformist theory of the selfish gene.

a part of nature, he becomes a vitalist—at least with regard to some living beings. Kant, states Driesch, made his analysis complicated for himself because under physics Kant considers only mechanical movements, that is, those that can be disassembled to elementary movements. There is no room for biology in such a physics: even chemistry would not fit into such a world, had Kant taken it into account. Driesch would interpret Kant's famous passage above on Newton and a blade of grass as Kant's hope that, ultimately, everything can be fitted into the mechanical world. Despite all criticism, then, Kant did not take any decisive step away from Cartesianism. Driesch comes to the conclusion that the methodology of Kant's *Critique of Judgement* (1790) may be an asset for both protagonists and adversaries of vitalism. Driesch's evaluation of natural history (*Naturphilosophie*) is very similar: both static and dynamic teleology can find support in it, and so from the viewpoint of vitalism the whole doctrine remains worthless.

For a biologist at the end of the twentieth century, it is surprising to learn that, at least according to Driesch, most of nineteenth-century biology adhered naturally to vitalism; moreover, it was never uprooted in the struggle of ideas! It simply became worn out by the indolence of its protagonists and the lack of opponents. The mechanistic biology that prevailed in Driesch's time simply moved into a vacant niche.

History Is Not Science!

It is important to realize that Driesch's critique of Darwinism is rooted *mainly* in a belief that history is a transgression that does *not* belong to science. The methodology of older, "typological," rational morphology was much more deserving of the label "scientific," but, alas, it was completely abandoned. Among biologists, says Driesch, only von Baer held the torch of true science high and resisted the "fortuitous science" (*Zufallslehre*) of the Darwinists, the view that living processes are nothing but the results of physical processes, and maintained henceforth that "the whole life process is in no way the result of physico-chemical events, but rather a ruler of those" (*ein Beherrscher derselben*, 1905, p. 136). Driesch regretted that from the beginning of the nineteenth century, biologists lost their interest in morphogenesis (*Physiologie der Formbildung*). In his opinion, it is that very science that remains a source of inspiration for vitalist thinking.

After this introduction, Driesch (1905) presents the outlines of his own vitalist teaching, which he afterward corroborated for a quarter of century. His aim was both modest and insurmountable: "To investigate if there are processes in living beings which cannot be converted into natural phenomena (or combinations thereof) known from non-living domain; that is, processes with their own autonomous rules. If we succeed, we also would like to establish the extent and depth of such autonomy, what such an autonomy denotes and what will follow on from its existence" (p. 171).

Driesch, as one of the pioneers of experimental embryology and discoverer of regulatory processes in early embryos, centers his efforts on the explanation of regeneration, that is, the processes following amputations of different body parts in embryos or adult organisms (polyps, ascidia, newts, plants). He became particularly involved in the study of lens regeneration in newts. In this case, says Driesch, one can hardly claim an evolutionary adaptation: it is difficult to imagine that newts would ever be in a danger of losing a lens; that is, the regenerative capacity by no means is an adaptation (as opposed to, say, losing an eye or a whole limb). To understand such phenomena, one has to presume the existence of harmony (causal, structural, or functional) and purposiveness in organisms. Driesch's aim was to prove this suggestion. First, he assumes for each part of a developing embryo a value—prospective value (*prospektive Bedeutung*)—which assigns a fate trajectory to the particular developing region. Even more important is another value, prospective potency (*prospektive Potenz*), which expresses the totality of all possibilities that *may* become open for the given region (see figure 9.1).

We can estimate this potential only if the embryo experiences extraordinary conditions (e.g., after the destruction of some of its parts). The potential is very high in regulatory embryos and zero in mosaic ones.[3] The very existence of regulatory embryos allows Driesch to state that a living being cannot be considered as machine: as every regenerating part is the bearer of a "field," it has a "holographic" image of the whole body. He terms such body parts with comparable regenerative potential "equipotential systems," whose properties can be estimated from the value for prospective potency, $S = f(a, g, E)$, where a and g are geometrical variables—distance (*Abstand*) and size (*Größe*); the quantity E is a nonvariable factor he called *entelechy*. For Driesch (1905), entelechy had a different meaning from the analogous concept in Aristotle: "It is a short expression for the physical-chemical structure found in every system, for a tectonics, for a mechanism (understood in the broadest sense), for a manifoldness, a structure, which puts in a typical pattern and controls a plethora of physical and chemical substances and forces" (pp. 206–207).

Today's equivalents of entelechy would perhaps be species-specific morphogenesis; close to it would be conceptions such as field, structure (in sense of biological structuralism), reaction norm, information, complexity, organization, and so forth. If ontogeny were strictly determined, then the potential S would be distributed step by step to all parts of the organism. In such a case,

---

3. A regulatory embryo can compensate for losses and gains; in mammals, for example, cutting the embryo in two will lead to two individuals. In a mosaic embryo, destroying a cell will lead to the deletion of all structures destined to appear in the progeny of that cell. Cutting such an embryo would result in two half-individuals.

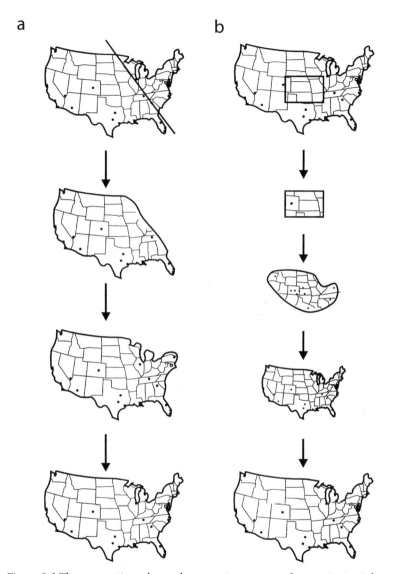

Figure 9.1 The prospective value and prospective potency of an equipotential system. (*a*) The prospective value is the measure of generative and regenerative capacity by the area characterized by given coordinates. (*b*) The prospective potency characterizes the ability to regenerate the whole from *any* fragment of the embryo or body. Adapted from Driesch (1905).

the quantity E would itself represent a mechanism. The complexity of such a mechanism would, however, be comparable with that of the organism itself; that is, no reduction, no clearing of concept would be gained. Even such a simple case of ontogeny would thus escape scientific inquiry. But harmonic systems, like regenerating embryos, are even more complex! Here each particle of the regenerating organism bears a latent image of the whole, and for *E* it would not suffice to be a simple mechanism: it should contain an endless regression of mechanisms. Driesch (1905) states: "The quantity *E* cannot thus be a typical physical-chemical variable, the less one belonging to the set of the 'extensive' mutually dependent manifoldness. It is rather a case of a natural factor sui generis, which, as a new basic factor, complements what is known from physics and chemistry" (pp. 207–208).

Entelechy is an expression of the regularities proper to the living body (*Eigengesetzlichkeit lebender Körper*; Driesch, 1905, p. 242), a divisible principle that upon division remains "whole." It seems that Driesch would be content if entelechy were—in some distant future—to be defined as a quantity that is in well-defined (constant) relation to other quantities (e.g., energy, mass, etc.). Everything should remain strictly "scientific" in the sense of the natural sciences of the end of the nineteenth century. It cannot, in fact, be otherwise, if we assume that it holds, that "[f]or the highest, scientific degree of reality, things exist in endless, three-dimensional space, and in endless time" (p. 229).

Spontaneity Forbidden

What seems to be forbidden in Driesch's worldview is spontaneity. The following quotation from Driesch (1914) is very reminiscent of those by Helmholtz (see chapter 1): "The degree of manifoldness of a natural system can never increase of itself, i.e. without a cause as its quasi-sufficient reason. To allow this would be to abandon the rational theory of becoming. . . . Whenever there is an increase of the degree of manifoldness in the one spatial becoming that is to be rationalized, there *must* be a quasi-reason, i.e., a cause, for this increase that is outside the system itself" (pp. 197–198). Compare this statement with the solution by Kauffman presented below! Driesch also explained the relation of entelechy to the system of contemporary physics, especially thermodynamics. Entelechy is not a violation of the second principle of thermodynamics: it is simply a principle, which can *suspend possible change* of a thermodynamic system in a disequilibrium, and "afterwards relax the suspension in one of endless possible directions" (1914, p. 261). To use contemporary language, we are in a realm of potentials, activation energies, self-organizing systems, dissipative structures, and the like: "Entelechy only allows that to become real which it has itself held in a state of mere possibility—not that has been in this state simply as a result of physico-chemical influences" (p. 205). After this, Driesch states that nonmechanical causality does indeed exist in nature, whereby vitalism has been proved.

Driesch was a pioneer in investigating the realm of systems far from equilibrium, and his single fault, I think, was that naming his principle "entelechy" led to considerable misunderstanding. Of course, he did not forget to warn again and again that it is not to be understood in the Aristotelian sense, but those who quoted him left out the warnings and thus caused many misunderstandings, with sad consequences for the whole development of biology.

Driesch was not a mystic, despite being accused as such throughout the entire twentieth century; his ethos of investigation is shared with that of contemporary biologists (e.g., E. O. Wilson). He opened a new realm of science—the realm of "transitory" properties of things—and from there he tried to infer eternal properties, further generalizable to terms and their relations. He aimed at objective reality; paradoxes are not allowed in his science. He saw as very important the constants that define the general outlines of the world being investigated. Entelechy is one such basic constant: "To ascribe an entelechy to the body means to endow it with a set of possibilities, a set which, as a natural factor, cannot be further divisible and is consciously conveyed only by a long sentence" (Driesch, 1905, p. 230).

Entelechy can perhaps be best understood as a "chemical" version of spontaneous generation. In Driesch's time, of course, no one any longer believed in the spontaneous generation of organisms. Chemical compounds, however, can originate *de novo* again and again, and this repeated creation according to existing and known (or knowable) rules may serve as an analogy for the repetitive appearance of the organismic shape. Driesch, as an opponent of the role of history and contingencies, apparently did not consider a competitive explanation based on an uninterrupted sequence of cell generations, hence his distinction from both descendence (evolutionary) theory and genetics. It is not surprising that biological structuralism considers Driesch one of its founders: "The primary properties of entelechy can perhaps be characterized as 'primary knowledge' and 'primary drive.' These expressions are, however, used in a purely analogical, descriptive sense. We use the term 'primary' to distinguish what we mean, from 'secondary' knowledge and drive, which are based on 'historical realities' and 'experience'" (1905, p. 243).

It is strange for me that Driesch's name became a synonym for "unscientific" biology: at least his books mentioned here give very little reason for such negative fame. Drieschian vitalism is a respectable attempt to "save" the autonomy (i.e., nonreducibility to physics) of living beings in contemporary natural science. Similar attempts in this direction were those of the materialists—vitalists of the Enlightenment (e.g., Diderot) or, in the twentieth century, biologists such as Gurwitsch, Waddington, Schmalhausen, and the biological structuralists. All these various directions of thought have much in common but usually refer to each other only marginally or not at all. None of them founded a long-lasting tradition or an established and generally accepted methodology. In this sense, the objectivist program (represented, e.g., by neo-Darwinism) is much more goal oriented and coordinated. It is, however, questionable whether it is more successful: the anxiety *not* to leave the

Cartesian world where "the laws of chemistry and (Newtonian) physics rule" may be—as in the case of Driesch—also condemned to failure. Should biology, psychology, and similar areas of human knowledge become sciences with a status similar to physics, they would have to abandon their vain attempt to confine biology to the Cartesian space and do what physics did several decades ago: transcend it. There is no need to return to Driesch, Gurwitsch, or even to rational morphology in order to "save" modern science —which, by the way, neither needs nor asks for such salvation.

The impossibility of escaping a holistic standpoint was felt especially in the realm of developmental biology. When in the 1920s it became obvious that vitalism had become depleted of explanatory potential and dogmatic, that is, of no practical use in experimental *science*, the term "organicism" was coined instead (von Bertalanffy, 1932, 1960). The aim of the movement, again, was to explain the obvious fact of emergent properties of complex systems, where one moves from a "lower" level of description to a "higher" one. This tamed form of vitalism survived in developmental biology for the rest of the century and, according to Gilbert and Sarkar (2000), will also have much to say in the coming century. For myself, I do not see much difference between the organistic statement that "different laws are appropriate for each level" and the vitalistic "there are life-specific laws." Moreover, organicist statements can be easily applied to any complex dissipative system, which means that they do not provide the answer to the basic question: "What is the difference between the living and the nonliving?" We no longer speak of *entelechy*, but is our understanding sharper when we speak of "information," "complexity," "structure"? Below, I refer to the attempt of Stuart A. Kauffman to push the problem toward a solution.

Purpose Today

Mahner and Bunge, in *Foundations of Biophilosophy* (1997), state, with a grain of irony, the schizophrenic situation of most biological sciences, which are unable to live either with teleology or without it. On the one hand the very existence of biologists is proof that the statement "at least some living beings are teleological" is undoubtedly true, but on the other hand, we see an understandable unwillingness to allow cosmic, vitalistic, or whatever teleology to enter the realm of objective science. That is why, according to Mahner and Bunge, biologists (e.g., Monod, Mayr) try to escape the paradox by introducing "teleonomy," a seeming finality. "Seeming" it is, because in fact wherever we feel—from the outside—the existence of a final cause (e.g., in ontogeny), it is nothing but a realization of a program, an algorithm selected during evolution by mechanisms already deciphered by neo-Darwinism. Obviously, neo-Darwinism has nothing in common with teleology. Ontogeny, the story goes on, is not teleological but teleonomical, that is, determined not by a final cause but by natural selection. All this, say Mahner and Bunge, is nothing but a word game—they see no distinction between the two terms, and therefore suggest abandoning them completely, because it is no problem to explain a seeming finality in a truly scientific way: "Purposive behavior can be explained, at least in principle, in terms of processes occurring in highly evolved central nervous systems. One way of explaining purpose is in terms of learning and expectation, where each of these is conceived of as a particular activity of certain neuronal systems" (p. 370).

All this would confine purposive behavior only to animals whose nervous systems have reached a certain level of complexity. If we wish to encompass all living beings in the scheme, we should turn to cybernetics. Here, Mahner and Bunge show that self-regulating systems with feedback loops should not be understood as teleological/teleonomical: "Developmental processes are lawful and thus reach a certain end state given certain circumstances. Yet 'lawful' is not cointensive with 'teleonomic'" (p. 375). Hence, the metaphor of a program, an instruction, is not a way of smuggling teleology into biology: those who inundate biology, either literally or metaphorically, with "what for?" questions merely reveal their early childhood indoctrination. Biology can easily do without teleology/teleonomy. Contemporary neo-Darwinists follow this advice: I have shown already in chapter 4 that a perspective based on the occurrence of passive replicators is fully satisfactory for the theory.

The neo-Darwinist purpose without teleology, together with the consistent application of the machine metaphor of life, is the prevailing paradigm in biologists' communities. However, it is not without alternatives, and in the pages that follow I illustrate views that do not conform with it.

Teleological Trends

Undoubtedly, the greatest twentieth-century protagonist of the idea of a goal-oriented universe was the paleontologist and Catholic theologian Pierre Teilhard de Chardin. In his posthumous work *The Place of Man in Nature* (1956), he presents a vision of the progressive integration (drive) of the universal spirit, from atoms on, through the origins of life to humans, and further to planetary consciousness (the noosphere), up to a mystical attractor of all evolution—the Omega point. It is, however, apparent that for Teilhard such an "evolutionary stream" is nothing but a kind of potential, an outline of possible trajectories to be developed, not at all a belief in a blind, strictly driven trajectory that the world would follow by itself (such is the caricature of his teaching in many books). The whole process is directional, but neither necessary nor predestined. Galleni (1994) sees in Teilhard's work the accomplishment of finding a meaning of the scientific quest: "He was . . . convinced, that one evolutionary phenomenon involved the whole universe and that it had a precise goal. It represents the convergent path of matter toward a more precise goal. . . . In this way Teilhard was able to find a narrow but useful path to confront together the Darwinian mechanisms of evolution with the theological necessity of the emergence in our Universe of the thinking creature" (p. 123).

I return to Teilhard's view of a teleological planetary superorganism when discussing the Gaia theory in chapter 10. At this point, it is worth mentioning other personalities with related views. The existence of evolutionary trends was, in the twentieth century, alive in paleontology: early in the century the Russian paleontologist Leo Semionovich Berg published his *Nomogenesis* (1922) . After the World War II, the French zoologist and paleontologist Pierre-Paul Grassé in particular propagated the idea of evolutionary trends in the lines of different animal taxons. The first chapter of his book *Evolution du Vivant* (1973) states: "Evolution means the existence of genealogical lines (filiation), among other conditions. It is no mass of random, incoherent variations succeeding each other without any rule. In fact, evolution is a canalized and ordered unwinding of successions characterized by trends which will become more and more apparent over generations" (p. 27).

Grassé interpreted paleontological findings as a sequence of events aimed toward attaining a given final state. This aim—the "idiomorphon"—is defined as a (macroevolutionary) tendency toward the realization of a plan, a tendency lasting for tens of millions of years. The pathways leading to idiomorphon are by no means straight, but no random variation, not even great cosmic cataclysms, can shift the line from its general direction. Thus, evolution is creative (in contrast to variation inside the species, which can be random), and its goal is often being attained along several parallel lines. Natural selection plays only a role of "genetic hygiene," deleting aberrant variations, but without any creative potential. At the end of his book Grassé exclaims: "In embryogenesis we can observe ordered tendencies and regulations and nobody would seek to deny such phenomena. Yet in the case of phylogeny, where tendencies are equally apparent as in the developing egg, disputes arise and some biologists feel offended by the idea of directed evolution. Is it really so difficult to stick to facts?" (p. 378). I do not need to stress that such views are incompatible with the Darwinian paradigm. Grassé acknowledges its role only in the realm of intraspecific variations; beyond that he considers it as a truth revealed, but not a scientific truth because it is not supported by fact.

I show in chapter 14 that even differences between ontogeny and phylogeny may be a question of point of view. If so, the disputes around teleology/teleonomy may appear more benign than they seem today. Waddingtonian epigenetic landscape may become a fruitful metaphor not only for ontogeny but also for evolutionary processes. Organisms may easily exhibit some control over their evolutionary trajectories, some "feeling" of what is the "norm" in the given lineage. Such an idea will then help to designate a path, a strategy, a chreod (see chapter 8) leading into the future. The future is present as a potential that will act on the one hand as a buffer against disturbances (in Schmalhausen's sense), and on the other as an outline defining future trends, an opening to the exploitations of new dimensions.

A "Vitalistic" Cruise of Kauffman

A new impulse to the seemingly endless debate was given by the recent book *Investigations* (2000) by the American biologist and mathematician Stuart Kauffman. He first introduces the term "autonomous agent" for systems that are able to act on their own behalf. Living beings undoubtedly fulfill this definition. What, however, should the properties of a physical system be for it to be able to act on its own behalf, that is, to become an autonomous agent? Such a system must be able to increase its own organization, and the same holds for "biospheres" built by agents.

The configuration space of a biosphere cannot be defined in advance. It follows that no thermodynamic law can be applied to *all* nonequilibrium thermodynamic systems. Kauffman (2000) asks:

> If there cannot be general laws for all open thermodynamic systems, might there be general laws for thermodynamically open but self constructing systems such as biospheres? I believe that the answer is yes. . . . To roughly state the candidate law, I suspect that biospheres maximize their average secular construction of the diversity of autonomous agents, and ways those agents can make a living to propagate further. In other terms, on average biospheres persistently increase the diversity of what can happen next. In effect, . . . biospheres may maximize the average sustained growth of their own "dimensionality." (pp. 3–4)

However, there is a lack of concepts in physics to grasp the ever-increasing number of dimensions for increasing organization. Concepts such as matter, energy, entropy, and information are useless. Kauffman therefore approached the problem through the concepts of work and working cycles. For a system to work, constraints must exist that canalize liberated energy (e.g., piston and cylinder) and ensure a closed work cycle, that is, a return to the initial state. Work performed can be used to build ever more canalizing devices. Thus, constraints enable the system to perform work, and work is necessary to build constraints. Kauffman's analysis ends with a definition of an autonomous agent as a self-reproducing system able to perform at least one thermodynamic work cycle:

Work is more than force acting through distance; it is, in fact, the constrained release of energy into a small number of degrees of freedom. It is
the constraints themselves, with . . . a kind of rigidity, that largely constitute the organization of the process. But . . . in many cases it takes work to
construct the constraints themselves. So we will come to a terribly important circle, work is the constrained release of energy, but it often takes work
to construct the constraints. (p. 83)

Investigations is a continuation of a program Kauffman started in *Origins of
Order* (1993). In *Investigations*, however, he takes a decisive step by leaving the
world of computer models and entering the physical world. Kauffman takes
a combinatorial space of 100 million catalyzed chemical reactions; each reaction leads to more and more new products, and the increasing molecular
diversity leads spontaneously to a state when a collectively autocatalytic and
reproducible network of chemical reactions becomes established. The networks are flexible enough to absorb ever-appearing changes, but these cannot modify the configuration of networks too profoundly. (Kauffman suggests
an analogy with the Anglo-Saxon law system, where each cause is significant
and creates a precedent, but no new precedent can change previous interpretations.) Organisms, niches, and searching procedures constituting the
network are in an endless process of mutual construction — the network becomes alive. One of its most important properties is its ability to search for
new sources of usable energy. Coupling to such a new source will allow the
system to create new working cycles, which in turn allow a further search
into the space of possibilities. Kauffman comes to the conclusion that the ability to organize work is crucial, and yet there is no concept available to characterize it further. Work, as stated above, means reducing the degree of freedom of the system: such a constraint on the one hand becomes the memory
of the system, whereas on the other hand it presents a barrier that directs
evolution in preferred directions.

Kauffman (2000) tries to apply his vision also to the econosphere and even
to the whole universe, though we do not need to follow these directions here.
What is more important, and what connects him with all vitalists who preceded him, is that he makes a honest attempt to disclose laws valid in living
beings. As a working hypothesis, he suggests the "fourth law of thermodynamics": "As an average trend, biospheres and the universe create novelty
and diversity as fast as they can manage to do so without destroying the accumulated propagating organization which is the basis and nexus from
which further novelty is discovered and incorporated into propagating organization" (p. 85).

Some of Kauffman's formulations are very similar to those of Teilhard and
Driesch. But is this vitalism? If we take Driesch as a reference of vitalism, the
answer is no. There is, in Kauffman's work, no sign of the stiff scientism so

typical of Driesch. Quite the opposite is true: Kauffman is focused on creativity, spontaneity of the living. But how to name the quality "scientifically," to formulate a concise theory, to develop testable hypotheses and appropriate methods for testing?

Biosemiotics

Compare the views of Kauffman with the following quotation written some hundred years before him by the founder of American semiotics, Charles Peirce:

> Hence, it would be a mistake to conceive of the psychical and the physical aspects of matter as two aspects absolutely distinct. Viewing a thing from the outside, considering its relation of action and reaction with other things, it appears as matter. Viewing it from the inside, looking at its immediate character as feeling, it appears as consciousness. These two views are combined when we remember that mechanical laws are nothing but acquired habits, like all the regularities of mind, including the tendency to take habits, itself; and that this action of habit is nothing but generalization, and generalization is nothing but spreading of feelings. (quoted in Emmeche, 1997, p. 89)

It is beyond my power to summarize all the areas touched by the influence of Peirce, especially in linguistics. Here I mention only the last three decades of effort of a group of scholars calling themselves biosemioticians (see, for example, Sebeok and Umiker-Sebeok, 1992, and Hoffmeyer, 1996). If organicism (holism) tries to escape vitalism via materialistic realism, biosemioticians set forth another path: they maintain that, in contrast to inanimate matter that can be characterized by causal processes (action and reaction), the essence of the living is in *semiosis*, manipulation with symbols. Whereas "natural laws" represent generalizations about natural processes, that is, help to arrange original heterogeneity into a small number of simple and homogeneous rules, the process of semiosis leads toward greater heterogeneity, elaboration—evolution (compare with the evolution of Kauffman's "biospheres" above). Emmeche (1997) hopes that effort in this direction will lead to the integration of semiotics, biology, and physics and thus to the comprehension of emergence of new orders of complexity. We can follow the description of a universe perfused with signs, with organic wholes participating in never-ending interpretative process. The whole scenario is isomorphic, or complementary to that of hermeneutic circle described in chapter 2. The principal terms in biosemiotics are meaning and understanding and the processes that create them. Actually, for the uninitiated, it is often difficult to perceive the difference between semiotics and hermeneutics: one has a feeling of dealing with two parallel traditions. I consider crucial the following thesis, which is not far removed from vitalism or organicism:

> The world is material, but all matter is organized into forms and these again can be further organized. There are qualitative differences between these organized forms. What exist are not just fundamental particles, energetic fields, and their organization: Reality has during its evolution become organized into characteristic primary levels (the physical, biological, psychical and social). Entities at higher levels possess emergent properties, some of which are ontologically irreducible to lower level properties (also called material pluralism or irreductive physicalism). Semiotic phenomena may be characteristic of some, but not necessarily all levels. (Emmeche 1997, p. 89)

We get the view of unfolding "semiosphere" (Hoffmeyer 1996, 1997, 1998) not incompatible with the visions of Kauffman or even Teilhard de Chardin. All living beings participate, as *experienced* entities, in this process:

> We can say that when life, and thus natural selection, emerged inside the Earth system we had already passed beyond the secure sphere of physics into the sphere of communication and interpretation. In this sphere the dynamics of history (evolution) changed and began to become individualised, so that each little section of history became unique and henceforward no big formulas could be erected covering the whole process. Organic evolution is narrative rather than lawlike, and if quantification is wanted, it should be searched not at the level of genetics, but at the level of the constrained thermodynamic system framing organic evolution. (Hoffmeyer 1998)

Semetic, instead of genetic, processes and interaction are considered the driving force of evolution.

The common denominator of the efforts and theories described in this chapter is the effort to find a plausible holistic theory of life. All help us to focus on phenomena that are not easy to grasp, let alone develop methods of studying them. The principal drawback of all these theories is that they have so far failed to develop methods that would allow their incorporation into the framework of standard biology. The current state of affairs allows one to hold three positions: (1) all efforts described are nothing but vain and speculative: reductionist biology will finally reveal the problems shown here as pseudoproblems; (2) we shall witness the establishment of holistic biology; (3) some problems concerned with life will always remain outside biology established as a natural science and will overlap into cultural and historical domains of knowledge. As I hope I have shown, I take the third stance.

I have shown how biology has been struggling with the task for the past century. Biological field theory, structuralism, epigenetics, general systems theory, organicism, and many other theories attempting the holistic or top-down approach in science all remain somehow suspicious from the point of view of "true," prosperous, reductionist science. The objective for the twenty-first century is clear: either to create a concise holistic theory of life (whatever name it will receive) or to conclude that *some* aspects of life appearance simply cannot be subdued to the scrutiny of objectivist biology as we know it today.

10
SUPERORGANISM

We live in a world where order everywhere prevails; and
where final causes are as well known, at least, as those
which are efficient. Thus, the circulation of the blood is
the efficient cause of life; but life is the final cause, not
only for the circulation of the blood but for the revolution
of the globe. . . . Therefore the explanation, which is given
of the different phenomena of the Earth, must be consistent
with the actual constitution of this Earth as a living world,
that is, a world maintaining a system of living animals
and plants.

James Hutton

It must be borne in mind that nature itself does not seem
to care about the self-identity of anything beyond the
organism. Our concern about self-identity reflects our
demands on nature. We might feel uncomfortable with the
position that ecological units mainly exist in our minds,
but at the present stage of ecology we should accept this
position as a null hypothesis that helps sharpen our
thinking.

Volker Grimm

The idea of the planet as a single living organism can be traced back to
antiquity, and during the Middle Ages and Renaissance it was a familiar component of the hermetic tradition. But it was apparently the founder of geol-
ogy, James Hutton, who introduced it into modern science. The idea experi-

enced its most recent rebirth in the 1970s as the Gaia theory, coined by James E. Lovelock (see, e.g, Lovelock, 1975, 1990). The thought climate in ecology at that time was receptive to such an idea: ecosystems were then seen as perfectly tuned teams of organisms mutually cooperating for the welfare of the whole community. As physiology is a typical goal-oriented teleological science, it is not surprising that a more "scientific" name for the Gaia concept is geophysiology. Contemporary ecological thought seeks its roots (its basic level of description) in the neo-Darwinian paradigm, and when seen from this perspective, ecosystems emerge as results of the "invisible hand" of the "market," where selfish individuals aspire to the survival of their own line. They interact with other individuals—of their own and other species—and as a result we observe the emerging behavior of a community. "Objectively," the superorganism does not exist. From such a position, there is no need for a holistic notion; hence the Gaia theory is largely criticized and even ridiculed. Below, I examine the theory and its adversaries more closely and try to analyze its perspectives.

Organism

The first point to consider in comprehending Gaia theory is the concept of an organism itself, because it is by no means unequivocal. In chapter 9 I showed that Kant considered an entity whose parts can "serve one another as means to ends" as an "organic product of nature." It is not a mere machine, because in addition to "motive power" it is also endowed with inherent "formative power." An organism is a product of nature that is able to take care of itself. It is frustrating that no real progress has been made beyond these ideas during the nineteenth and twentieth centuries. For illustration, compare some encyclopedic entries for "organism":

- Henderson's Dictionary of Biological Terms (1989) offers a laconic "any living thing," without further specifying what a "living thing" is.
- *The Cambridge Dictionary of Science and Technology* (1992) gives a list: "animal, plants, fungi, and microorganisms."
- *The Shorter Oxford English Dictionary on Historical Principles* (1990) defines an organism as "an organized body, consisting of mutually connected and dependent parts constituted to share a common life; the material structure of an individual animal or plant." Such a definition can easily encompass even biosphere or planetary superorganism.
- *Merriam Webster's Collegiate Dictionary* (1993) gives a similar definition: an organism is "1: a complex structure of interdependent and subordinate elements whose relations and properties are largely determined by their function in the whole; 2: an individual constituted to carry on the

activities of life by means of organs separate in function but mutually dependent: a living being"—again, a circular definition: organism is a living being, but we do not know what a living being is.
- *Random House Webster's College Dictionary* (1990) defines the organism as a "form of life composed of mutually dependent parts that maintain various vital processes." What, however, is meant by "vital processes"? Are there other forms of life that could not be defined as organisms?

None of these definitions can conceal Kant's influence. Kant knew that "organism" is a term created for the sake of our classification, that it would be hard to delimit it as an objective entity. He therefore based his definition of an organism simply on a list of its parts and properties, and today we have nothing more than this. In that case, however, it is not clear what is meant by statements (see the epigraph by Grimm at the beginning of this chapter) that nothing *above* the level of organism (community, superorganism) has an objective identity (even if "everybody knows," intuitively, where the problem lies).

Life

A quest for a definition of the term "life" is very similar to that in the case of "organism." This is not a light-hearted statement: the problem *is* serious, and it is evident that we may not have paid enough attention to certain fundamental biological questions. Again, I can offer a choice of definitions; it is symptomatic that in special dictionaries of *biological* terms the entry for "life" is absent or is present only in composites (life cycle, etc.):

- *Encyclopaedia Britannica* (1995) devotes 17 pages to the entry for "life" but admits at the outset that no general definition exists, and continues with simple descriptions of properties supposed to constitute life.
- *Merriam Webster's Collegiate Dictionary* (1993) gives two sufficiently general meanings: "1. a: the quality that distinguishes a vital and functional being from a dead body," and the more vitalistic "b: a principle or force that is considered to underlie the distinctive quality of animate beings."
- *The Shorter Oxford English Dictionary on Historical Principles* (1990) says essentially the same: "life is a property that distinguishes an animal, plant or living tissue from dead tissue or non-living matter"; again, a list of functional activities is added.
- The Short Czechoslovak Encyclopaedia (*Malá Československá Encyklopedie*, 1987) gives defines life as "1. A form of existence of matter that will lawfully appear at certain conditions of its evolution; and 2. A common property of all organisms by which living matter differs qualitatively from non-living." To make sense of such a definition, one already needs to know a lot about what life is.

- From the perspective of Cairns-Smith's *Seven Clues to the Origin of Life* (1985), "life" can also be understood as an epiphenomenon of the evolution of "nonliving" organisms: "Life is an informal term for the seemingly purposeful quality of evolved organisms. If organisms are prerequisites for evolution, 'life' is rather a product of that process" (p. 125).
- A similar definition comes from Kauffman (2000): "Life is an expected, emergent property of complex chemical reaction networks. Under rather general conditions, as the diversity of molecular species in a reaction system increases, a phase transition is crossed beyond which the formation of collectively autocatalytic sets of molecules suddenly becomes almost inevitable" (p. 35).

It is apparent from this short survey that it is extremely difficult to find overall definitions for fundamental terms that would allow for clear distinctions between life and nonlife, between life and "intelligent" machines, between Gaia–thermodynamic machine, and Gaia–living being. Rather, these definitions must be constantly renegotiated. Encyclopedia entries can serve only as a starting point for more serious analyses of the phenomenon called life. It has been mentioned in chapter 1 that the difficulties with defining life may be due to the fact that it extends through many hierarchical levels (Havel, 1996).

I have addressed various mechanical metaphors of life and their critics in chapters 1 and 6; here I mention only the theory of life offered by Mae-Wan Ho (see, e.g., Ho, 1993, 1995). The key word in Ho's thinking, as discussed in chapter 9, is *coherence*: "[L]ife is a process of being an organizing whole" (Ho, 1993, p. 5). All processes in living beings are interconnected through many hierarchical orders by vibrational transfers of energy. This enables, first, the free energy to be transformed and then carried through great distances and across many hierarchical levels without substantial loss; second, the whole body can behave as a single coherent whole. Hence, for Ho, extrapolation from a multicellular organism to a superorganism is quite easy.

Individual

The third and possibly even the key concept of our analysis is that of the "individual." If we start from our common experience of multicellular animals, we encounter no difficulty. An individual is identical to an organism; it is a member of the population of the species, the bearer of one unique variant from an endless possible genotypes that can be projected onto the particular, species-specific genome. An individual is also an item in the line of the organism, and usually it is also able to propagate the line by bearing progeny. However, anomalies are found in, for example, castes of eusocial species, asexually reproducing lines of genetically identical individuals, individuals arising by polyembryony, and, of course, animals living in colonies. What should be taken as an individual—a single polyp or the whole coral reef? Similar difficulties can be encountered in plants and fungi—organisms with unfinished growth and, moreover, with a broad palette of asexual forms of reproduction. Can we consider a mycelium that extends to the area of a whole forest to be an individual? In organisms such as slime molds, we should first decide which of the levels of organization can be taken as an individual. Finally, in symbiogenetic organisms (e.g., lichens, corals, ciliates, mycorrhiza, or even organismal ecosystems such as the human body, with its intestinal, vaginal, gingival, and surface symbionts), the problem takes on yet another dimension.

In contemporary biology, evolution is often viewed as a linear time sequence of individuals, with organisms interconnected only through their common descent, their genidentity. It becomes obvious, however, that bacteria do not always multiply in a clonal way: the horizontal transfer of genetic information plays a much more important function here, and instead of the "tree," their genealogy assumes a network topology (Maynard Smith, 1991, 1992; Maynard Smith et al., 1991, 1993). Eukaryotic organisms may also become members of such a web, although at the present level of knowledge, treelike genealogies seem more plausible.

At the beginning of the twenty-first century, three theories of superorganism deserve attention: Lovelock's Gaia theory, Wilson and Sober's (1989) superorganism, and a teleological planetary organism connected with Teilhard.

The Gaia Theory

Of all the definitions to be found in Lovelock writings, I consider the following to be most comprehensive:

> The Gaia hypothesis, when we introduced it in the 1970s, supposed that the atmosphere, the oceans, the climate and the crust of the Earth are regulated at a state comfortable for life because of the behavior of living organisms. . . . [This] homeostasis is maintained by active feedback process operated automatically and unconsciously by the biota. . . . Life and its environment are so closely coupled that evolution concerns Gaia, not the organisms or the environment taken separately. (Lovelock, 1990, p. 19)

Planetary homeostasis has been maintained not only on short time scales, but also during the *entire* time span of life's existence on the planet. The planet has faced many changes—both self-generated and cosmic, both gradual and catastrophic—but has never become uninhabitable. This motif is further developed by a notion of self-preservation: "[L]iving organisms have to regulate their planet, otherwise the irresistible forces of physical and chemical evolution will soon render it uninhabitable" (Lovelock, 1996, p. 22). Very soon after its beginning, life had to either take on the burden of maintaining these favorable conditions or perish. Gaia actively (but unconsciously) enters feedback loops, thereby constituting geophysiology. A classic example is the average temperature of the planet, which for four billion years has remained within the narrow interval of $10-22°C$. It is a notable achievement when one realizes that solar luminosity has increased by one third during this period and considers the temperature extremes present on the neighbor planets. Events such as glacial periods did not change the average temperature by more than $5°C$.

The idea of a superorganism inevitably aroused a wave of misunderstanding and criticism. From the very start, the theory had been leading a constant rearguard defense against cohorts of planetologists, climatologists, and biologists. The arguments very often slip into the fuzzy language of metaphors, analogies, and even poetry, which inevitably weakens the scientific discussion and facilitates the task of its opponents. If we set aside various mythopoetic fantasies, inspired mainly by the very name "Gaia," the most frequent objections can be summarized as follows:

(1) The planetologists maintain that the evolution of the planetary environment can easily be modeled even without assuming the presence of biota (the evolution of oxygen being the single exception). Goody's *Principles of Atmospheric Physics and Chemistry* (1995) states: "[L]ife, in its turn, has subtle but important effects on the atmosphere, for example, it is probably responsible for the existence of free oxygen" (p. 1). Its chapter devoted to geochemical cycles does not deny the contribution of biota but places no particular importance on them; abiotic explanations lead. A single page (in the introduction) is devoted to the Gaia theory, where Goody states: "This proposal falls foul of the accepted tenets of neo-Darwinism, but has focused attention on what is undoubtedly correct, that the atmosphere is strongly conditioned by events taking place in the biosphere" (p. 5).

(2) Similarly, Williams's *Molecular Biology of Gaia* (1997) rightly states that Gaian regulation would require the existence of regulatory pathways and mutual cooperation of organisms. Both notions would violate the neo-Darwinist paradigm of evolution as he understands it. Another superb monograph, Ehrlich's *Geomicrobiology* (1996), completely ignores geophysiology, Gaia, and the superorganism: there is not a single mention of them in 700 pages!

(3) The climatological argument is based on the fact that, even on short time scales (thousands of years), it is impossible to assess the trends in the development of such decisive elements as clouds, albedo, oceanic gyres, atmo-

spheric gases, and so forth. Thus, it is impossible to presume any system that would be able to support the planetary homeostasis for billions of years. Despite the fact that the vital parameters of the planet have remained within very narrow boundaries of values, Lovelock's opponents prefer the null hypothesis "it just happened."

(4) Ecologists point to the fact that the biological feedback loops assumed by Lovelock are too long (in space and/or time) to be able to maintain their integrity. Individuals are essentially selfish, and such vast cycles would be quickly parasitized and broken down. Lovelock strikes back by showing that such complicated cycles started as simple one-step feedback circuits. He maintains that the whole system evolved automatically, without any anticipation on the part of its members and even without communication among them. He presents a couple of "Gaian" interpretations of homeostatic circulation on the planet (see, e.g., the description of feedback regulation of precipitation, sulfur circulation, and temperature by dimethylsulfide; e.g., Lovelock, 1990).

It is no doubt that a steady homeostatic state may become established in ecological communities. The stable regime of such systems will differ from simple machines only in its greater complexity. Why, then, all the tension between Lovelock and the ecologists? I believe that it is only because Lovelock, instead of using neutral concepts such as "global ecosystem," introduced new ones such as Gaia, organism, and geophysiology. Earth was first proclaimed to be a living being and then reduced to a thermodynamic dissipative system with fluxes of matter and energy, with kinetic constants but without any memory or self-reference. Such a model is hard to distinguish from the classical models of climatologists and ecologists, and it is no wonder that it is considered superfluous. In chapter 14 I attempt to abandon such models, return to the original statement "Earth is alive," and try to find a path that will go beyond Lovelockian models.

(5) Gaia is also rebuffed by the neo-Darwinists, because the evolution of an organism, which is unique and eternal, is considered counterintuitive from the viewpoint of neo-Darwinian theory. As all organisms should be products of (neo)-Darwinian evolution (i.e., having predecessors and being products of natural selection), Gaia cannot be an organism. The theory received a particularly scathing reception from Richard Dawkins in *The Extended Phenotype* (1982). He considers it to be a culmination of the so-called "pop ecology" (pp. 234–235) at one time disseminated by educational broadcasts of the BBC.

(6) Another serious aspect involved in the discussions is the extreme sensitivity of the scientific community to teleology. Lovelock is often accused of this heresy, and he strongly feels the need for a defense. Why such tension? No biological school will doubt the fact that contemporary organisms bear the memory of the past experience of the given line. Replicators themselves were molded by such an experience. After all, physiology and ontogeny are teleo-

logical (or teleonomical, if you wish), owing to the fact that organisms possess a layout, a phase space of the permissible states they grow toward. An extrapolation of this understanding to the evolutionary line, to a sequence of generations, however, is not possible within the current biological paradigm. But Lovelock does not follow this line of defense; teleology remains his weak point.

Self-organization is an inherent property of all complex systems (from hydrodynamic turbulence, to weather, to the behavior of the stock exchange). They have a true evolution over time, they increase in complexity, they even may be goal oriented, and their robustness can vary from unstable to highly resilient, homeostatic (Prigogine, 1980; Jantsch, 1979; Eigen and Winkler-Oswatitsch, 1992; Kauffman, 1993, 2000). The global ecosystem, then, even if it is not alive, need not be considered a "chaotic time bomb" in the same sense as it does not fit the idea of a mechanical clockwork. If stability were the only issue, the whole system could be described without a postulate of a superorganism; we could stay with the terms "global ecology" or "global climatic system," and the whole theory of Gaia would indeed be superfluous. I do not, however, consider such an attitude to be very instrumental for our understanding. The issue is, after all, to create a coherent view of the evolution of life on Earth.

The World of Daisies

To silence his opponents, Lovelock developed a popular model of planetary regulation of temperature known as Daisyworld (e.g., Lovelock, 1990). This is a model of a planet inhabited by daisies of different shades (in the limiting case only two—white and black). The model is able to react—by changing the albedo of the planet—to the changing luminosity of its sun and hence maintain the surface temperature within narrow limits. A dead planet does not have such a buffering capacity—its surface temperature will blindly follow the amount of energy input. The model is undoubtedly adaptive, but in the same sense as are all the feedback machines of our common experience. In what sense is Daisyworld more alive than a household refrigerator? Why should it be declared to be "alive"? It has no memory or experience, there is no information on how daisies came into existence, and its existence in time is not true evolution, Darwinian or not. The world itself and the daisies do not change: the only variable is the fraction of individual daisy species and the number of their niches. Lovelock is, of course, right that Daisyworld works without any planning, but it is also without memory, without context. It is nothing but an adaptation to a change forced on it from outside, according to given set points in the system. This behavior does not qualify Daisyworld as an organism.

With time, the idea of a Gaian superorganism has become more and more a question of chemical and thermodynamic equilibria (such as weather or climate), with organisms playing the role of catalyzers and feedback regulators (see, e.g., Lovelock, 1997; Lovelock and Kump, 1994). Of course, any organism can be described as a thermodynamic machine, but such a description will not encompass the principal difference between organisms and machines. What remains from the original view is the insight that the evolution of the planet is a closely coupled coevolution of biota and Earth's surface.

And yet the second half of the 1990s witnessed a remarkable shift in ideas. The name Gaia is no longer taboo in scientific articles dealing with evolution (see, e.g., Hamilton and Lenton, 1998; Lenton, 1998), and Gaian research has become a regular part of science. Despite this, I think that the metaphor of the living planet can be developed further. Gaia suggests an organism that is almost as old as the planet itself and has evolved without a mutation–selection mechanism. Could not such a view be transferred to lower levels of "ordinary" organisms and enrich our view of *their* evolution?

I also want to stress another aspect of the Gaian metaphor that is only very faintly emphasized in the original conception: the basic attributes of every living being—memory and experience. Lovelock's Gaia has no memory: when solving problems she cannot make use of experiences, say, from the Holocene or Permian period, and this distinguishes her from more familiar kinds of living beings, even if we consider them as nothing more than "survival machines." Their experience is inscribed in genetic memory and is manifested in the behavior of an individual or a species. Could something similar be found at the planetary level? My answer is yes; I return to this problem in chapter 14.

Neo-Darwinian Superorganism

Selection on the individual level lies at the center of neo-Darwinian evolution; the only questions are whether the basic unit of selection is molecular replicators or whether phenotypes—"gene vehicles"—also play a part. The previous tradition of group selection has been resolutely rejected. Within such frameworks the very idea of superorganism is inconceivable, and so it is interesting to learn that Wilson and Sober (1989) nonetheless found the concept of the superorganism inspiring. They corroborate the definition of organism as a form of life composed of mutually dependent parts that maintain various vital processes (see *Random House Dictionary* definition above). It follows that the concepts of organism and individual are synonymous. Organs or genes, therefore, do not suit the definition, but nor do some autonomous beings if they are not units of selection. In some cases, such a unit is presented only by a higher order "body" of which they are part. In short, an organism is any entity that can be subjected to selection. Classic examples of a superorganism are clonal aphids, myxoamoebae unified into a mold, and, of course, eusocial insects. Such kinds of superorganism present no problem to the neo-Darwinian theory; however, they should be strictly distinguished from aggregates consisting of "true" organisms, such as a flock of birds or a forest.

For Maynard Smith and Szathmáry (1995), too, selection units higher than the gene cause no problems, as long as they can be clearly defined as replicators. The authors stress that the main drawbacks of all holistic models of evolution ignore the selection units and thus lack any factor that would enable evolutionary change.

Teleological Superorganism

As stated above, the founder of geophysiology, James Hutton, and his philosophical predecessors never doubted the purposefulness of the planetary organism. In contemporary objective science, however, there is no room for teleology (the apparent teleology of the ontogeny or physiology of *individuals* can be explained and causes no problems). Those who study superorganismic entities are therefore endlessly balancing between the Scylla of being accused of teleology and the Charybdis of disseminating a mere banality that the "superorganism" is not an organism at all. But it is also possible to argue that teleology—like causality—is nothing but a tool to arrange data into a comprehensive scheme. If so, the causal and teleological explanations may become largely symmetrical. For the sake of symmetry, I consider it useful to introduce a teleological view of the problem, even though, as I have shown, it is not at present a subject of the experimental sciences.

The main protagonist of a goal-oriented planetary evolution in the twentieth century was Pierre Teilhard de Chardin (see, e.g., Teilhard de Chardin, 1956), who in the 1940s laid the foundations for a new science—geobiology. His phraseology is almost identical to that of Lovelock; the difference is not in the topic but in the theoretical background:

> First, the world of life, taken as a whole, forms a single system bound to the surface of the Earth; a system whose elements . . . are not simply thrown together and molded upon one another . . . but are organically interdependent. . . . Second, this organic sheet is not physically separable from the general mass of the Earth it covers. The Earth is not merely a spatial support for, but the very "matrix" of this living envelope. . . . We already have Geophysics and Geochemistry. Now, completing the triad, appears Geobiology. (quoted in Galleni, 1995, p. 32)

Galleni considers Teilhard's views to be a struggle for fulfillment, to find a meaning for the scientific quest. Ironically, when comparing the visions of Teilhard and Lovelock, his conclusions are in strong contradiction to what Lovelock himself declares in his apologies: "Teilhard . . . perceives that the evolving biosphere has a preferential direction leading to more complex and cerebralized forms and finally to the formation of Noosphere. Similarly, Lovelock maintains that the biosphere, acting as a whole, has a well-defined task: to maintain dynamic homeostasis. These assertions reintroduce teleological concepts; their relationships are worthy of discussion" (p. 32). A very strange synthesis of both theories emerges here: Gaia *needs* to maintain homeostasis, and her adaptive answer to this call is the increasing complexity of the evolving biosphere.

Galleni makes another inspiring move: he adapts Waddington's epigenetic landscape (see chapter 8) into a Teilhardian "evolutionary landscape," which would canalize evolutionary events according to *existing* chreods. Canalization is not identical to selection: it also involves self-approval on a given trajectory. The role of selection becomes secondary, and evolution would primarily follow the "shape" of the landscape: " '[O]rthogenesis' . . . simply means that, historically, life developed and continues to develop (in ourselves, for instance) by addition, or (what comes to the same thing) by continually reaffirming itself along certain definite lines" (Teilhard's letter quoted in Galleni, 1995, p. 36). From all the problems and confusions caused by the theory of the superorganism, one is of the utmost importance for me: Is Gaia alive? If so, what are the parameters confirming the fact? I return to these questions in chapter 14.

11

THE LANGUAGE METAPHOR OF LIFE?

The difference between meaning in a formal system and in a language is a very important one. . . . It is in this: in a language, when we have learned a meaning for a word, we then make new statements based on the meaning of the word. In a sense the meaning becomes *active*, since it brings into being a new rule for creating sentences. This means that our command of language is not like a finished product: the rules for making sentences increase when we learn new meanings. . . . [I]n a formal system, the theorems are predefined, by the rules of production. We can choose "meanings" based on an isomorphism between theorems and true statements. But this does not give us the license to go out and add new theorems to the established theorems.

Douglas R. Hofstadter

The language metaphor of living beings has a long tradition, which was reinforced at during the last decades of the twentieth century by the discovery of linear genetic texts and the genetic code on the one hand, and the emergence of programming languages on the other. This reinforcement has, however, its reverse side in that what the metaphor is pointing at is not always clear.

Starting with the weaker metaphor based on "machine" language, the molecule of DNA is above all a "program" for copying itself base after base. If the copying device were purely mechanical and independent of the actual sequence of bases, then the chain of DNA need not contain even the elementary command COPY ME: it could be catalyzed, for example, on the surfaces of some minerals. In this case, however, we should ask whether such a molecule would deserve the name "information medium." No penalty for mutation would exist, and the "survival" of DNA in its progeny would be assured by simply polymerizing gibberish from the monomers at hand. In such a case, the entire language metaphor would be void.

The sequence of bases becomes a message only when successful copying is a function of the sequence copied, when different versions of the inscription compete for their transfer into the next generation. The situation is complicated by the fact that DNA should also contain program(s) of a different kind—instructions for building the copying device, which would be able to understand and perform the COPY ME command. Moreover, bases are not virtual bits—they are "bodily" in nature; that is, they must be synthesized in advance, which requires instructions as to how to build a generator of bases and so forth. In sum, the molecule of DNA is supposed to contain the following:

1. Programs ("genes") for protein synthesis: proteins, in their turn, will mediate the construction of the copying device.
2. Labels (binding sites) for elements of the reading machinery: this enables it to orientate itself in the text and to select preferences for transcription.
3. A database of all genes, even those that are not currently in use.
4. Memory reaching back into the deep past, to the very beginning of life: the memory is embodied in the structure of genes and in the structure of the genome, that is, the set of genes, their regulatory elements, their quality, and their arrangement on the DNA chain. This structure largely determines the rules for handling the genetic text.

The computer metaphor of life was very inspiring in the 1960s, when computers started to be part of our lives and when an extensive study of bacterial genomes began. These genomes are fairly small and relatively "dense" with genes and their regulatory sequences. Moreover, in bacteria morphogenetic processes seldom complicate the situation. It was supposed—and many still believe it even today—that the knowledge gained from bacterial models could simply be extrapolated to eukaryotic organisms with their complicated morphogenesis. Later findings showing that in some multicellular organisms genes constitute only small islands (of the order of a few percent) in an ocean of so-called noncoding DNA caused some embarrassment. It could easily be an inscription in an unknown code, even though parasitic sequences or spacers also exist among this material.

Texts and Explanations

The answer to the question of whether DNA does or does not have the character of text written in a natural language had been sought through the analysis of very long regions that do not contain any instructions for how to make proteins. Methods used to analyze texts written in human languages were applied. Texts written in a natural language comply with the so-called power law (or Zipf law), which can be stated as follows: We take a long natural text (10^5 words or more) and determine the frequency f of any word used. We order the frequencies from highest to lowest and appoint them an ordinal number: rank r. If the text is written in a natural language, the frequency of a word will be directly proportional to its rank: $f \propto r^{-k}$. In a double-logarithmic plot of f against r we get a straight line with a slope k. For all natural languages, k is close to 1.0 (>0.7).

In a text written in a known natural language, it is of course no problem to distinguish individual words: problems arise from strings without punctuation or spacing, or written in an unknown language, as is the case of DNA. In the latter case, "words" will be defined arbitrarily as short sequences of constant length (usually three to seven "letters"). All possible permutations of letters (or nucleotides) will be allowed as words, and the frequency and rank of such artificially created strings can then be determined. In a random string, all "words" will occur with the same frequency (i.e., it would be impossible to state the rank), whereas nonrandom strings will exhibit a nonrandom distribution of frequencies. If, the argument goes, such a distribution satisfies Zipf's law, the string can be considered as a text written in a natural language. Mantegna et al. (1994) have performed such an analysis and concluded that DNA *is* a text written in natural language, albeit with a proportionality constant (k) much lower than in human languages. Their paper, however, was received with considerable reservations, either because of the approach chosen or because of the interpretation of results (Voss, 1996; Bonhoeffer et al., 1996; Israeloff et al., 1996). Tsonis et al. (1997), moreover, argue that the results are even more consistent with the exponential law, not Zipf's law.

Popov et al. (1996), on the other hand, believe that DNA is a text of even higher sophistication than are human languages. Whereas strings in the latter contain only a single message, DNA strings present a superposition of several different linguistic schemes: DNA is a meta-text.

Bodnar et al. (1997) approached the linguistic analysis of DNA from a different angle. They took it for granted that DNA is a language and submitted it to standard linguistic, cryptographic analysis. They started with text structures whose meaning was known (e.g., regulatory sequences); this made it possible to decipher motifs that would represent thus far unknown labels (signaling sequences) for the structures manipulating (reading) the text. Such a cryptographic approach helps in analyzing very long nucleotide sequences, which are produced by genome-sequencing projects. Frequently there no information as to what their function might be, and knowledge of the distribution of control points in the text should help immensely in deciphering the meaning of the whole message. The analysis would further stimulate attempts to identify a generative grammar of DNA (e.g., Searls, 1992).

This whole description suggests that some obfuscation might have occurred. Bodnar et al. obviously did not analyze the *language*, but only the formal structure of *strings of symbols*. They simply state that the genetic text appears to be nonrandom, even in parts where no genes are located (of course, molecular biology came independently to the same conclusion). Even if the genetic text does have some parameters suggesting texts written in a natural language,[1] the question of who is the reader of such texts remains unanswered. The principal question is not how the language is written, but whether anyone can "speak" it. Authors cited earlier in this chapter obviously take the computer metaphor of life for granted. For them, "reading" a genetic text means "machine reading," even in cases when texts are written in natural and not computer language. From the point of view of our hermeneutic task, this whole area might be less important than it would have initially seemed.

Atlan and Koppel (1990) questioned the heuristic value of the metaphor of DNA as a program for how to build a cell. After all, the only known instance of such information processing is decoding (and control thereof) of the triplet code used in protein synthesis. They recall that as early as the 1970s, François Jacob (1974) warned against an overly textual understanding of the metaphor of a "self-programming program" whose algorithms, moreover, are unknown. Despite warnings, the metaphor has taken on its own life, and DNA is usually considered to be a quaternal string analogous to the binary string of a computer program. This preoccupation with the code can be seen behind the drive to identify the complete sequence of the human genome. Atlan and Koppel (1990) comment: "In order to deal with questions of biological function in a practical way one should be able not only to know the primary structure of DNA, but . . . understand how a given genome is expressed into a given phenotype. For this matter mere knowledge of DNA strings is insufficient, except for some specific cases where the determination of a given phenotypic character is expressed into a given phenotype" (p. 337).

There is no doubt that an unequivocal relation between some genes (alleles) and the phenotypical traits can be found, especially in cases where a

---

1. It should be noted that the validity of Zipf's law is not limited to languages. It was originally formulated as a rule according to which communes of different numbers of inhabitants are distributed in a country, and it also holds for the distribution of species in ecosystems. A theoretical justification of why such disparate systems behave according to the same rule is still lacking.

certain modification of a gene was preferred in the evolution of basal metabolism. It is, however, questionable whether we can proceed further in this direction and identify more than trivial functional adaptations to external factors. Atlan and Koppel deprecate the whole idea of DNA as a computer program, with cellular and supracellular structures degraded into the role of hardware. They consider the phenotype a result of multilevel information processing, with the genome simply the source of species-specific data. In this case, a program would also process the data, but it would consist of, and at the same time be executed by, the entire multilevel structure. How should we decide between the two views? Atlan and Koppel try to answer the problem by introducing the mapping function (M), which describes the process of the production of the phenotype (or phenome, in their terminology). Two extremes can exist: M is either a simple interpreting device or something that supposes the existence of a structure. If the genome is projected onto the phenome, and the output is determined by the input only, then the input (i.e., DNA) represents the program, and M is a mere *interpreter*, capable of decoding and executing the program. The process of mRNA translation into protein is very close to such a state (if we do not pose the question of where the ribosome comes from). The opposite extreme is a situation in which M will determine the output; that is, the phenotype is not encoded in the inputs. Inputs (e.g., DNA) would represent data only. An example of this might be a centriole or the cortical structures of ciliates. Most real cases lie between the two extremes, but closer to the second one: the differentiated cell is more like a program that in principle computes the same metabolic function (e.g., respiration, digestion) throughout *all* species. In addition, the mapping structure is characterized by the parameter of *sophistication*[2] and is endowed by *memory* of a different kind from that in databases.

Organisms and the Art of Being Acquainted with the World

I now return to the metaphor of living beings as a natural language and attempt a hermeneutic view. We should be able to work with phenomena such as understanding, memory, forgetting and remembering, invention, and intentionality. My approach will stress the historical, that is, the diachronic na-

---

2. Sophistication relies on the need to define the complexity of a system. Complexity is often defined as the length of the algorithm that is necessary to describe the system. Simple or trivially iterated systems have a low complexity. The complexity is highest for random systems (e.g., gas in thermodynamic equilibrium), because such systems cannot be reduced to an algorithm shorter than the list of the states of the system. Complexity thus defined is useless for living systems where the description is long but nonrandom. Atlan and Koppel (1990) therefore differentiate between random and sophisticated complex systems.

ture of living beings and their ability of mutual communication (given either by their common origin or by relations that have been constantly enacted). This view does not reject the levels described by neo-Darwinists or structuralists. There is no doubt that natural languages possess means that make it possible both to be highly precise and to save time: various automatisms, phrases, idioms, quotations, styles, and so forth. The point is that these levels are not the *only* means of expression.

In the hermeneutic metaphor, individuals, species, the whole hierarchy of the tree of life can be taken as analogues for expression, enunciation. They are the results of *culture*, which operates freely within constraints set by natural selection on the one side and structures on the other (both abstract structures of structuralism and real structures of our bodies). Again, this view is "vitalistic" to the extent that the body is a subject interpreting its genetic text through a filter of its individual experience, but also the experience of the line extending back to the prehistory of life. It has a very clear image of the "norm," of the "typus" that is relevant for a given species and in a given environment. Endowed with this background, it embeds meaning in whatever it encounters in its environment, internal or external. Hence, the language metaphor is not a question only of the gene–body dualism, however important that may be. The central focus is self-knowledge, the self-presentation of organism.

Kull (1998, 2000) is the author of a semiotic metaphor of organism as a self-reading text, moving in circles of endless self-representation and re-representation. I am, however, quite uneasy with the very meaning of the concept of "text." Instead of strings of digital symbols that produce meaning through the reader, Kull obviously perceives practically any appearance of life as text; texts are not strings but *processes*, and whole organisms become *self-reading texts*. The whole concept thus becomes rather incomprehensible to me: it is not easy to grasp what, then, is *not* a text in an organism.

The Interface

I return here to the interface between an understanding being and its environment. What is its nature, and what flows across it? Is it information, and if so, how can it be defined? Here I refer to Fiala (1991), inspired by the autopoietic systems of Humberto R. Maturana, who distinguished two kinds of system. Allopoietic systems process inputs and produce outputs; their internal organization is not particularly interesting and can be taken as a black box. Identical inputs will cause identical outputs (i.e., the behavior of the system), and the system is producing something other than itself (thus *allopoietic*). By contrast, autopoietic systems are autonomous of their environment; they are capable of self-reflection, and they define they own borders. "The system inscribes its own cognitive structure, it is not inscribed in it" (p. 37). An autopoietic, highly organized system can maintain its integrity only because its coupling to the environment is loose: external inputs could otherways even destroy it (recall a similar thesis by Schmalhausen discussed in chapter 8). The system therefore must *anticipate* its interactions with its environment. It is this anticipation that embodies its knowledge of the world, its interpretation, its intelligence. The system develops by establishing, disturbing, or shifting its own borders. The interactions of an autopoietic system with the environment are *not* an information flow: its behavior is determined only by its internal structure. "Objective information does not exist without a system, which 'accepts' it," states Fiala, who continues:

> Does the system, then, accept information or not? We are so entangled in object language that we invite such questions. Information does exist—we can point to any library. But in what sense does it exist? The text in a book does not in itself carry any information. If you wish to persuade me of the contrary, you will remove the book from the shelf and ask me to read it. Fine: in this instant information receives its "existence," but this existence does not reside in "that information," but in my own structure as an observer. In this sense, there is no such thing as a text without its reader. (p. 46)

Texts are read in a community of standard observers, and it is *they* who decide what is "objective information." Scientific texts can serve as an illustration: if the status of scientific information is given by consensus, then it ceases to be information; it has no power to *in*-form. Scientific statements are valid only in a community of scientists: they do not require the presupposition of objectivity. They do not explain an independent, objective reality, but only the experience of observers. *Communis opinio doctorum* again.

To sum up some results of my quest so far: the genetic text, structure, and genidentity are necessary but not sufficient preconditions for the hermeneutics of the living. What, then, do we need in addition? The answer is language, with its discourse. Not computer language with its unequivocally defined concepts, but a natural language with all that it can encompass: its ability to express things in very precise terms, but also its metaphors, ambiguous propositions, wit, and so forth.

What, Then, Is the Language, and Who Is the Speaker?

If the original presuppositions concerning living beings become more and more complicated, if we need more and more new assumptions, additions, and exceptions, their heuristic value becomes obscure. In such a situation, there are two possible outcomes: either to believe that intensive research in the chosen direction will lead to a new level of unification, a new paradigm, or to resign and look for different views, images, and parables. The hermeneutic approach may be one of the options to hand. The conformation of a single protein, the state of a protein network, cell differentiation, an individual—all these can be understood as statements in a given semantic field. To take this approach, however, we must rid ourselves of mechanistic conceptions:

> Are the principles which determine and control the life process at the molecular level, indeed mechanical? I doubt it. We know today that the laws of classical physics describing the behavior of mechanic systems are nothing but averaged demonstrations of the situation in the microworld. The rules of the microworld are anything but mechanical. When speaking of a single molecule of an enzyme whose state is determined by single atoms and particles, to speak of "averaging" is nonsense. In what sense, then, can we speak about "machines"? Yes, we speak of a proton turbine, sodium pump, hydrogen bridges, electron cascades, single and double bonds, but we always should remember that these are examples and conceptions applied to a reality of a completely different order. (Neubauer, 1990, p. 144)

Even if the language metaphors seem strange, the "machine" ones are by no means more natural. I therefore suggest forgetting about inveterate icons of, say, a protein molecule as a very long, intricately folded yardstick of amino acids, of the lock-and-key models depicting binding the ligand, and so forth. Why not take it as a field of force, holonomic and nonlocal? In such a view, conformational changes would become results of reshuffling of the field, expressions of Neubauer's *eidos*. Through a similar prism, we can also observe other "hierarchical" levels and come to a conclusion that, at all levels, living beings have the nature of a semantic field that encompasses all of them. The fields can combine into higher order fields, or disappear—collapse into a mosaic. At some levels—for example, ecosystems—the field character can become suppressed (or simply obscured?); at other levels, it may become obvious.

Whatever happens to living beings is interpreted by experience that is present as a field of different orders; episodes of life become parts of the overall field. The fate of such imprints can vary: they may disappear quickly, become diluted, change their meaning because of a different reading; they may be even absolutized by natural selection as the only reading allowed.

Science has not paid attention to intentionality, because research was directed from the perspective of large numbers: the phenomena that were studied were those that could be generalized and averaged, and if this was not immediately possible, *standard conditions* were created. From such standardized conditions, science attempted to explain the world. It is obvious that much of what has been found under standard conditions can be also applied to every-day practice: bridges are solid and do not collapse, planes can fly, the Path-finder will land on Mars, chemical reactions can be reproduced in any labo-ratory with the proper equipment, inbred mice look and behave identically. All this, however, is no justification for an inductive claim that the world *is* as it is described. And here science once again comes up against the second branch of human knowledge—call it humanities—which has never ceased to stress the conditional nature of our knowledge. Physicists lived through this encounter some hundred years ago, and biology is (I hope) on the edge of rediscovering it today. My main effort in this direction is to stress the idea of the semantic field combined with the intentionality of the living, which is the subject of part III of this book. I ask such questions as, What happens if we try to appoint as the standard observer not the scientist, but living organisms belonging to a given species, with a consensus on how to interpret the genetic text? What happens if we replace the observer with all species on a biotope and determine the consensus to be the behavior of the community? What if we take cells in a multicellular organism as observers, and the consensus as the morphogenetic pathway? My quest proceeds in these directions.

Part III

Life as a Hermeneutic Category

Part III

LIFE AS A HERMENEUTIC CATEGORY

The bacterial cell is a precisionally fine-tuned machine.
The day has long passed when the question should be
asked whether there is more than the laws of chemistry
behind the functioning of the bacterial cell. We now see
the bacterium as an extraordinarily sophisticated set of
interrelated molecules that harmoniously work together
in highly predictable ways to ensure the growth and
selective survival of more of its kind. At the heart of
these remarkable, at most clockwork-type, machines are
the DNA molecules that encode, with total precision, sets
of commands that bring into action molecules needed to
cope with ever-changing nutritional potentials. What
is equally important is that DNA has the capacity to
incorporate within its structure new changes that will
permit further evolution of the cell into forms needed
to prosper successfully upon the Earth's continuously
changing face.

James D. Watson et al.

From the very beginning of our experience in this world, we learn that the
world does not behave arbitrarily. Stones fall down, beetles can fly and whales
cannot, and it is not worth wrestling with an angry dog. Later we learn further constraints that cannot be acquired from everyday life: planets travel in
their orbits according to rules that can by described in physical terms; the
speed of light cannot be exceeded; we are mortal. . . . A beginner in experimental biology also very soon recognizes the constraints of the science. High

on the list are thermodynamic principles and the precept that the laws of physics and chemistry hold in living organisms "as anywhere else." Nothing can be done against such inescapable limitations: the universe has been built that way and we must make do with that degree of freedom that is available inside the barriers. It is strange that a complementary situation is seldom discussed: the barrier undoubtedly defines the *limits* at one level of organization; it brings order into chaos. At the same time, it represents a gate into *new spaces*, into realms that would never become available were the barriers absent. Constraints such as those of thermodynamics do exist, but this allows emergent dissipative structures to arise; the structures themselves, however, cannot be derived simply from the knowledge of constraints. Similarly, entities such as replicators, their durability, inheritance with modifications, and natural selection introduce limitations into life that may sometimes be very hard but that at the same time mark out the playing field for the game called life—they do not influence the game itself. Limitations such as the genetically determined metabolism, the reaction norm, instinctive behavior, and so forth, continue this trend and are undoubtedly often very advantageous. As soon as situations exist where a scheme that has once been worked out will always (or usually) apply, it is very worthwhile embedding it in the repertoire of automatisms—it will save time and energy. But this does not mean that the living being itself is an automaton. On the contrary, an automatism allows and opens new explorative spaces (which may differ in different species) for experimentation with oneself and with the environment. The outcome of such activity may not always be advantageous for its bearer, but neither is such simply a result of a blind causal chain, mechanistically manipulated by selfish genes. Without "selfish genes" phenotypes might never have come to existence, but once they appeared something new had arisen that had no counterpart in the nonliving world. This principle of setting barriers, or gates, which drive evolution into new phase spaces that would be otherwise impossible to reach, recurs in many other domains. All automatisms and lawfulness, whose existence is contingent because, historically, other forms of automatism and lawfulness could have appeared in their place, are on this list.

During billions of years of evolution, an enormous body of experience has been incorporated into automatic, mechanical behavior. Indeed, for decades experimental science—biology—could afford to ignore anything else. During that period, *science* also developed barriers, so that nothing but mechanisms was *allowed* within its realm. Such a barrier also became a gate of a kind—a gate toward the immense success of the biological sciences. But, as biology is a construct of the human spirit, it is still possible that something important may remain beyond the barriers.

In parts I and II of this book, I attempted a survey of different research alternatives in biology that have circulated in the twentieth century. Some of them have become safely established inside the barriers; some never found their way in, and some have been thrown out. I also stated that the genetic script, structure, and genidentity are necessary, but not sufficient, conditions for biological hermeneutics. The goal of part III is to identify what is needed "in addition" and to show that life can be considered a hermeneutic category. Life has never ceased to exist and has again and again been confronted by actual conditions, by memory, by forgetting, and by reinterpretations of the remembered. It has the characteristics of a field, a culture, a statement, and of course sometimes also of a machine.

Our investigation faces many difficulties, the largest of which is, paradoxically, the fact that we ourselves are alive, and so the necessary distance between the observer and the observed cannot be ensured. But *this* is the very knowledge that gives rise to hermeneutics: such amalgamation has lain at the core of the experience of the humanities. It is the main reason why I think that, first, the life sciences should and must cross the barrier that has appeared during the last four centuries between the two great domains of human knowledge. The second, much more important message is that everything that lives is hermeneutic in nature.

In addition to this "ontological" task, there are also drawbacks that have arisen out of the course of history and whose roots lie in *our* culture, worldviews, education, and attitudes. Some of these are discussed below.

(1) There is a deeply imprinted thesis about the controlled path of ontogeny and random erring of evolutionary processes, that is, a strong distinction between determinism and teleology at the one hand and contingency on the other. I have already shown that among contemporary biologists—though not those of the mainstream—such statements are being cast into serious doubt.

(2) Whatever is computable or can be expressed by a mathematical relation is automatically considered to be more "scientific," more "real." This is why definitions such as "evolution is a change in the genetic composition of populations" or "the study of the mechanisms of evolution belongs to the realm of the population genetics" (see, for example, Dobzhansky et al., 1977) satisfied many generations of biologists. After all, such an approach yields clear results. On the other hand, efforts to grasp some phenomena through natural language are frequently suspect as being "mere speculation."

(3) If something cannot be computed, we try at least to arrange our empirical data into a system. Whatever can be classified into a logical hierarchy is considered more "scientific" and therefore more real. In biology this started with Linnaeus, continued with rational morphology, and flourishes today as, for example, cladistics or molecular phylogenetics. A flood of publications on the subject "this and that organism has an orthologue of a gene (protein) described already in a dozen of other organisms" is proof of such a drive toward systemization. Satisfaction, however, may be replaced by frustration if systems describing the same entity appear to be incompatible.

(4) If possible, we seek noncontradictory causal chains. This is why the argument that "the genes control this or that" has greater appeal than the "soft" natural language. After all, even the humanities often tried to find a base that can be relied upon, for example, controlling factors of history or even historical laws.

(5) The quarrel between "idealism" and "materialism," apparently discredited long ago, smolders in the background. The dualism between the perfect (gene) and the imperfect (body) has very deep roots in our culture. This is why in the history of life the principal role is played by the immortal gene, whereas the bodily side of the living creature is considered a mere epiphenomenon. As idealism in science is very suspect, we tend to reify ideal concepts (genes) into a material medium (DNA), and after some time we are even unaware of the operation. The gene undoubtedly "is" a piece of DNA!

(6) Anthropo-, zoo-, or eukaryocentrism: it is really astonishing how many theories of, say, evolution, are centered on multicellular, sexually reproducing animals. This group then becomes paradigmatic for explaining the notions of evolution, ontogeny, organism. . . . Light-hearted extrapolations are made to groups with completely different life strategies (bacteria, plants). The relative isolation of evolutionary lines in multicellular animals is perhaps what hinders our appreciation of the evolutionary role of horizontal transfer of genetic information in different groups, or the role of symbiogenesis.

(7) One excuse for our "centrism" may be the fact that we are apparently unable to think on several scales of time and space in parallel. If we are forced to do so, we tend to choose one level as "basic" for our description and to extrapolate from there to other levels. We tend to see paradoxes—incompatibilities of descriptions obtained at different levels—as mistakes, as incompleteness of either our theory or the experimental method, or even the cognitive functions of the experimenter.

The list is far from exhaustive. It gives only some examples of where the hermeneutic approach could bring new understanding and provide new formulations of testable hypotheses—within or beyond the framework of contemporary traditional biology.

The three chapters of part III focus on three areas: chapter 12 is devoted to proteins and their "ecology"; chapter 13, to the ontogeny of multicellular eukaryotes; and chapter 14, to the biology of the prokaryotic superorganism— Gaia.

12

THE SPEECH OF PROTEINS

Cells detect extracellular signals by allostery and then give those signals meaning by "regulated localization." We suggest that this formulation applies to many biological processes and is particularly well illustrated by the mechanisms of gene regulation. Analysis of these mechanisms reveals that regulated localization requires simple molecular interactions that are readily used combinatorially. This system of regulation is highly "evolvable," and its use accounts, at least in part, for the nature of the complexities observed in biological systems.

Mark Ptashne and Alexander Gann

The focus of this chapter is the linear strings of digital molecular symbols, that is, nucleic acids. These molecular sequences are often compared to a code or an algorithm—a program. Here I explore the possibility that they might represent genuine written texts. If so, then how are they read and who is the reader? The metaphor can be formulated in two ways:

(1) The weaker variant will take the set of DNA sequences coding for proteins for a dictionary of "words." The cell is "consulting" the dictionary saved as the sequence of DNA, selecting appropriate words (i.e., synthesizing proteins), putting these words (i.e, proteins) into a proper grammatical form, and embedding them into "sentences" or longer "utterances" that will constitute the phenotype—*parole*. Note the distinction from the more common metaphor of coding sequence: an entry in the dictionary is not the code of a given word.

(2) In the stronger variant, the string of DNA is a genuine text that is read

and interpreted by the cell. The cell will behave according to how it interprets the text; the interpretation is based on previous understanding, momentary contexts, and/or layout for the future. This metaphor is again in opposition to the metaphor of the genetic script as a program or an algorithm. A text written in natural language is not an algorithm: it requires a reader, not hardware.

Both metaphors stimulate the top-down analysis rather than the more common bottom-up procedures of molecular biology. They offer a complementary view that might, I believe, contribute to a better understanding of what living beings *are*. I appeal to the reader not to take the preceding sentence as an empty phrase: complementarity of the discrete (digital) with the continuous (analogue) may lie at the very heart of understanding the living; their superposition may be the only way to glimpse the *being-in-the-world* of living beings. We instinctively turn toward the digital because it is more easily reproducible, measurable, apprehensible. We tend to forget that the digital text needs a reader whose nature is *not* "digital."

At this point, I take a short digression for those who are not acquainted with molecular biology.

Proteins

A molecule of protein is huge compared to "ordinary" small molecules (a protein molecule can be from several thousands up to millions of daltons in size; compare this with 2 daltons for a hydrogen, 18 for water, and 180 for glucose). The function of practically any protein resides basically in two areas: (1) specific binding of ligand(s) (i.e., a small molecule or a small region on a macromolecule) and (2) performing some specific action after the ligand is bound (or released). Any molecule or part thereof can serve as a ligand; the binding takes place in a special region of the protein molecule called the binding site (every ligand requires a specific binding site). The protein molecule can bear several binding sites for different ligands, each usually situated on a different region — the domain — of the protein molecule. The performance of the protein molecule resides in its ability to change its conformation (shape) upon binding of its ligand(s). This new constellation brings about a specific function for which the protein has evolved. It may help a specific chemical transformation of the bound ligand(s) (as in enzymes), transport of the ligand from one compartment to another (as in translocators), binding of antigen (in antibodies), signal transmission (receptors), and so forth. The given function may require not just one but several identical or different protein molecules that are part of a higher order structure. Such spatiotemporal structures (networks) are typical for both inside the cell and the extracellular space. It is true that many proteins will maintain their specific conformations even when isolated and in a homogeneous suspension, but such conditions are highly artificial. Such a homogeneous space (if it exists at all) is very limited inside the cell—perhaps the content of vacuoles and similar cisternae may be close to it. The cytoplasm, however, is by no means homogeneous,[1] and the same holds for the extracellular space (figure 12.1). Space inhabited by bacteria is also highly structured: coatings, sediments, mats, soil particles, and so forth, have a very complicated structure of biogenic origin.

The protein molecule is primarily a polypeptide, that is, a linear, nonrandom polymer of hundreds to thousands of amino acids. Twenty species of amino acids are being regularly inserted into the protein chains synthesized in cells. This means that within a chain of, say, 500 amino acids, the number of theoretically possible strings is 20^{500}—obviously, only a tiny fraction of all possibilities ever came into existence. Only strings that are able to pack into a specific spatial conformation compatible with function were selected during evolution; mutation in the protein sequence (deletion, insertion, or replacement of amino acids) can lead to incompatibility with the function of the protein. A protein molecule is not a replicator; that is, the proper succession of amino acids when producing new strings of the kind must be ensured by a medium different from the protein itself. I return to this point further below.

To attain the specific conformation, however, may not be a matter of course for a given string: virtually endless numbers of possible packings of a given polymer exist. Despite this, in a living cell the protein has only a small number of typical, strictly defined conformations that enable it to perform its specific function. Nonfunctional conformations either do not appear or, if they do, are actively detected and either repaired or destroyed. The question of how to ensure that the protein is confined to functional conformations lies at the core of the so-called Levinthal paradox (Ruddon and Bedows, 1997; Bryngelson et al., 1995; Bohr et al., 1996): if the functional conformation were sought by a random walk through all possible conformational states, then a chain of the size of an average protein domain (i.e., about 100 amino acids long) would require an astronomical time to do this. A newly synthesized protein, however, attains the conformation required with a half-life of several seconds, either spontaneously or with the assistance of other proteins.

The importance of cellular environment becomes obvious when we compare naturally occurring half-lives of packing with those necessary when proteins are synthesized in vitro. Such molecules either cannot attain the "natural" conformation at all, or can do so only after several hours and only in very dilute protein solutions (fewer than 10 µg/mL; Ruddon and Bedows, 1997). In much denser protein suspensions that (to some extent, perhaps)

---

1. See, for example, Goodsell (1991), Porter et al. (1983), Hess and Mikhailov (1995, 1996), Ovádi (1995), Schaff et al. (1997), Clegg (1992), Welch and Easterby (1994), Shapiro and Losick (1997), Matthews and White (1993), and Westerhoff and Welch (1992).

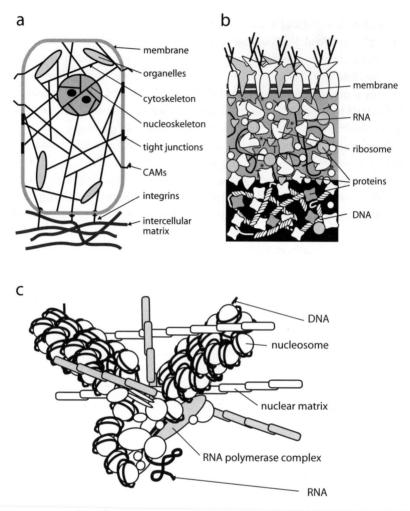

Figure 12.1. Ultrastructure of the "living matter." (*a*) Ultrastructure (highly schematic view) of an animal cell. Note the interconnected network of cytoskeleton, nucleoskeleton, extracellular matrix, and membranous cisternae of various origins and functions. (*b*) Schematic insight into bacterial cytoplasm. (*c*) The structure of chromatin. Regular "spools" represent nucleosomes with rolled-on DNA. In the foreground there is a segment of DNA freed from such a regular matrix—it may contain a gene that is being transcribed. *Round* and *oval symbols* represent the service proteins necessary for such a function (for a more detailed scheme, see figure 12.4); *beamlike formations* symbolize the nucleoskeleton.

simulate the situation within a living cell, the protein is unable to reach the functional conformation at all—in such a chaotic environment, rapid aggregation and denaturation will occur. It should therefore be postulated that the cellular structures into which the new protein has been born play a key role in the process.[2] But even the time necessary for in vitro packing is only a negligible fraction of that calculated from the Levinthal paradox. It follows that the primary sequence of amino acids should be considered one of the major determinants of the final shape: at least some protein molecules "know," even if removed from the cellular context and left to themselves, a shorter path to the goal than random searching through endless conformation space.

The function of a protein, and the evolution of this function, is a compromise between two trends concerning the rigidity of conformation(s) required: higher affinity for the ligand can be attained only by more rigid conformation. Rigidity, however, goes at the expense of the performance that depends on ability to switch rapidly between working conformations (see, e.g., Gillespie, 1991). Upon finding its ligand, the protein molecule can change between "allowed" conformations either spontaneously or by the action of various specific or nonspecific agents present in its cellular environment. Escapes into abnormal conformations are not allowed.

The Buildup of a Protein Molecule

The textbook icon of protein synthesis—transcription and translation—is summarized in figure 12.2a. The shape of the molecule is the function of the sequence of amino acids in the chain; the chain, in turn, was gained by unequivocal decoding (in the process of translation) of another sequence—that of bases in the molecule mRNA. The molecule of mRNA, finally, is nothing but a one-to-one transcription of a special piece in the much longer molecule of DNA. It follows that the sequence of amino acids in a newly synthesized protein molecule is largely, and in some cases (especially in bacteria) even unequivocally, determined by the sequence of bases in the coding sequence in DNA. A decoding machinery providing the task—transcription and translation—must be present in the cell. Side by side with the icon is the "central dogma of molecular biology," that the flow of information is unidirectional, from nucleic acids (DNA or RNA) to proteins. Only DNA is *the* replicator.

The icon is beautiful, economical, and elegant. It enables the construction

---

2. If we transform bacterial cells by, for example, mammalian genes, very often we get precipitates of denatured protein. The bacterial cell will truly perform the synthesis of the polypeptide chain, but it is unable to provide conformation information provided by the mammalian cell.

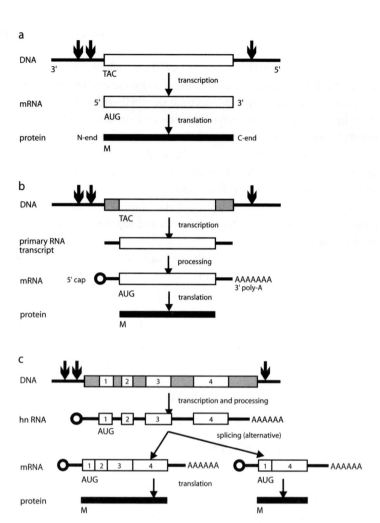

Figure 12.2. The path from DNA to protein. (*a–c*) The first line, 3' to 5', is a short piece of a much longer DNA molecule, with the part transcribed into RNA highlighted as a *rectangle*. In RNA molecules, *rectangles* highlight parts that will be translated into the amino acid chain of protein. *TAC* (*AUG*), initiation codon for the first amino acid methionine (*M*). *Arrows* on the DNA symbolize sites for attachment of the transcription complex (*left*; see figure 12.4) and the site of its release from DNA (*right*). (*a*) An idealized state: the sequence of amino acids in protein directly corresponds, via mRNA, to the sequence of nucleotides in DNA. Both transcription and translation proceed from left to right. (*b*) The coding sequence is only part of the gene, flanked by transcribed but untranslated regions. The primary transcript becomes mRNA after derivatization on both ends. (*c*) Standard situation in eukaryotes: the coding sequences (exons, *numbered*) are interrupted by noncoding sequences (introns). The primary transcript (hnRNA) is processed to mRNA by excising introns and splicing the exons. The splicing can lead to multiple varieties of mRNA, that is, to manifold different proteins that all are products of a single gene (only two shown here).

of causal chains and loops by assuming that a single level—that of DNA texts—is the formative cause of epigenetic structures and processes. These emerge automatically because they are *totally* contained in the genetic text, and the system, led by cues from its environment, is channeled toward one of alternative decoding pathways (i.e., development). The model is compatible with the neo-Darwinian theory of evolution and has indeed become part of its reification.

A more realistic view of the whole process is shown in figure 12.2b, which demonstrates that the definition of the coding sequence on the molecule of DNA and making it available for transcription are not trivial tasks. Before RNA polymerase starts with the transcription, dozens of proteins must bind to the whole area of the string containing the coding sequence in question. The binding sites often extend thousands of bases upstream and downstream of the coding sequence.[3] The process, hence, requires change of the whole higher order structure, of which DNA is but one constituent (in eukaryotes, the structure is called chromatin; figure 12.1c). Thus, the very beginning of the whole process—the identification and selection of a particular DNA string to be read—can be apprehended as a hermeneutic act of the body searching over the genetic text. A related activity is the determination of the quality of the primary transcripts, that is, the selection of those parts of the gene, which will be transcribed into RNA. The genetic text may sometimes start at different positions (promoters) and end at various termini; in such cases we are confronted, in fact, with a set of (partially) overlapping sequences (see also figure 12.3ab). It must therefore be decided *how* the text will be read. Of course, the ratio of different variants, as well as the rate of the whole process, can also be precisely set.

The primary transcript (i.e., the RNA molecule) may enter into a complicated decision process in which exons (i.e., the parts that will finally become components of the resulting molecule of mRNA) are designated. The rest of the chain—multiple and often very long strings (introns)—is cut out of the transcript and discarded (figure 12.2c). It is important to note that the definition of exons and introns in a transcript depends on the cell type and its functional context. Different variants of mRNA—hence different proteins— can be obtained from a single species of primary transcript (see, e.g., Barnier et al., 1995; Kornblihtt et al., 1996).

There is no need at this point to go into all the subtleties of RNA manipulation. Instead, I invite the reader to visit a small corner of the protein zoo, which is depicted in figure 12.3. Schemes of two related genes, CREB and CREM,

---

3. This is why I try to avoid the word "gene." We may define it as that part of the string which is transcribed into RNA—in that case, however, the definition will not include all the flanking labels. Or we include these regions into consideration, at the price that we cannot sharply delineate the boundaries of the gene.

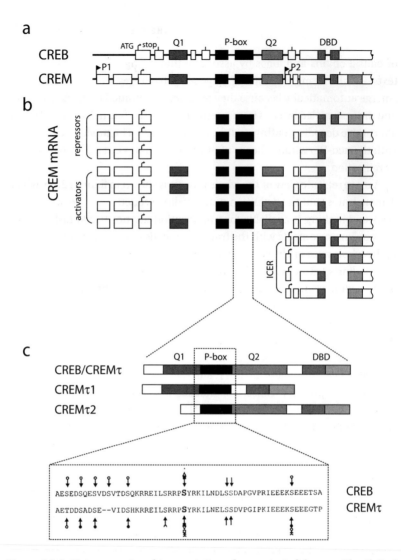

Figure 12.3. Heterogeneity of transcription, demonstrated for one "family" of regulatory proteins, CREB and CREM. (*a*) Schematic outline of the genes. Note two starting positions *P1* and *P2* in CREM. (*b*) The repertoire of CREM products. Primary transcripts are submitted to processing and splicing, which leads to multiple variants of mRNA owing to the selection of exons. Some known variants of CREM and ICER mRNAs are shown here; the set is, of course, fluid both for a given cell type and over time. (*c*) Regulation of protein activity by reversible phosphorylation. *Above,* the protein CREB and three variants of the protein CREM, each containing the domain called *P-box*. *Below,* detail of the sequence of this domain (each *letter* is a symbol for one amino acid, e.g., *S* for serine). *Arrows* point to positions that can be phosphorylated (and dephosphorylated—the modifications are reversible); *symbols with arrows* designate different protein kinases known to be able to phosphorylate the particular site (protein phosphatases not shown). Adapted from Foulkes and Sassone-Corsi (1996).

are shown in figure 12.3a. The genes code for a family of similar proteins that are engaged in performing a plethora of regulatory functions in the cell. Even the layman will recognize the similarity of both genes and will come to the conclusion that resulting proteins will probably display similar qualities.

The protein are able—as homo- or heterodimers (CREB)$_2$, (CREM)$_2$, and CREB-CREM—to bind to specific regions of DNA and thus control the expression of great variety of genes. Each kind of dimer can bind to different parts of DNA, thus regulating expression of a different set of genes. Now consider a situation in which only genes CREB and CREM were transcribed from the whole family, and the product of each gene is only a single species of protein. Simply by manipulating the ratio of CREB to CREM, the occurrence of particular dimers would differ substantially and so would the intensity the transcription regulated by a particular dimer. Now imagine the real potential of creating dimers not with two but with the whole set of proteins produced. Figure 12.3b shows some of possible transcripts of the CREM gene. But the story does not end here. Figure 12.3c shows an example of protein products obtainable by further chemical modifications of a single *domain* of protein (see below).

Nursing the Neonate Protein

As discussed above, native protein produced by translation is seldom ready-made, and the site of its synthesis may not be its final location. Usually it is in a "prepro" form that requires further processing by a variety of other proteins. Even in cases when no chemical modification is required, the molecule may not be able to attain the conformation required: help of specific processing proteins—"chaperones"—is necessary. Other proteins will supply post-translational modifications of the native molecule, for example, creation of disulfide bridges, attachment of prosthetic groups,[4] excision of parts of the polypeptide chain, or derivatization of amino acyl residues by glycosylation, lipidation, hydroxylation, sulfatation, phosphorylation, and so forth.[5] Such processing will bring enormous microheterogeneity to the set of products synthesized according of a single type of mRNA (Fox, 1991; Kobata, 1992). It will result, in turn, in subtle modification of the function of a particular molecule. The derivatization process may continue throughout the whole life-time of the protein molecule.

The protein molecule must be also recognized at the site of its synthesis

---

4. Attachment of prosthetic groups refers to attachment of chemical moieties that are not amino acids and that enable the proper function of the given protein (e.g., RNA in ribonucleopro-tein, hemin in respiratory enzymes, etc.).

5. See, for example, Alix and Hayes (1983), Huttner (1987), Gordon et al. (1991), Lis and Sharon (1993), and Wallis (1995).

(cytoplasm) and subsequently transported and inserted to target compartment (i.e., mitochondria or the extracellular matrix).[6] The process of localization often starts at the level of mRNA, which may be anchored at a specific site in the cell or even transferred from cell to cell (e.g., in oogenesis of *Drosophila*). Similarly, the newly synthesized protein must be quickly and efficiently transferred to the compartments for which it is designed. The rapid delivery is ensured by various types of "addresses," that is, cues on the molecule that are deciphered by the service machinery.

In the development of latent genetic information into the body of the protein, then, we must presume the presence of cellular machinery (or field?) able to perform and control the whole process of proteosynthesis and subsequent embedding of the new protein into the functional context. The very presence of the new protein may change the state of the whole network, and as a result the network may start reading different genetic texts, and so forth. Does the description above differ from that given in any modern textbooks? At the first sight, no. And yet the expression "genetic control" was never used in our story.

Reversible Controls—Chemistry Yields to Semiosis

The system of the epigenetic regulation of a protein molecule has been perfected by the reversible control of protein conformation, which can proceed in parallel in many parts of the molecule. The control can be applied in two ways. The first is *allosteric regulation* by regulatory ligands that bind to specific binding sites on the protein. A second possibility is *chemical modification* of specific groups on the molecule, most frequently phosphorylation and dephosphorylation by a large set of special enzymes—protein kinases and protein phosphatases. These regulatory enzymes are, in turn, also subject to such regulation (figure 12.3c).

In the case of allostery, the regulatory ligand can simply be taken as just another ligand that can finely adjust the processes dependent on other binding sites on the protein molecule. Yet there is an important difference here. Regulatory molecules do not belong to the set of common nutrients as do, for example, glucose or oxygen. Nutrients are "utilized" by all cells in a more or less similar fashion. The most prominent property of regulatory molecules is that they play the role of *signs*. The function of a sign may be carried simply by the amount of the signaling molecule, its concentration gradient in the space, fluctuation of its concentration in time, combination with other signs, and so

---

6. See, for example, Shapiro and Losick (1997), Zimmermann (1998), Gorlich and Mattaj (1996), Pfanner (1998), and Pfanner et al. (1997).

forth. The signaling molecule, therefore, is not a pointer to itself, as in the case of metabolites: it represents something else. This "something else," the *meaning* carried by the molecule, is to be deciphered, interpreted by the cell. And because the signaling molecule refers to something other than itself, it can mediate different meanings to different cells in the body; thus, for example, epinephrine will evoke different responses in the heart, liver or blood vessels. As in the case of reading genetic texts, here also the specific interpretation has been won by the experience of the cell, organism, lineage, species. There, as here, the given interpretations may be strictly unequivocal, but they can be also flexible, exploratory, putting to trial several possibilities . . . sometimes detrimental, sometimes favorable for the interpreter.

The covalent modification (introduced by specific enzymes) is even more impressive. By this process, a genuine *mutation* is introduced into the protein molecule (e.g., the serine residue in the chain of amino acids is replaced by phosphoserine), with all the consequences such a mutation can bring about to the function of the protein. The number of protein building blocks may thus rise from the initial twenty to many tens of different amino acid residues. What is more important, such "mutations" are to a great extent reversible by the action of other proteins. The protein network thus influences the shape and performance of an individual protein at any given moment (figure 12.3c).

The advantage of the above-mentioned regulation is obvious. Instead of harboring many paralogous genes coding very similar, redundant, proteins, only a single crude, half-finished product is coded for. The particular form required is being finely adjusted in the process of protein synthesis (transcription, RNA processing, translation) and ontogeny (noncovalent and covalent modification, addition of functional group, e.g., coenzymes, etc.).

Does not the whole process resemble genuine reading and writing, expressing the right grammatical tense, article, prefixes, and suffixes appropriate for the context, instead of blind decoding the genetic message?

Redundancy—Synonyms in Cellular Functions

Despite the possibility of fine epigenetic adjustment of protein function, many cellular functions are also secured by a high degree of redundancy, that is, by harboring similar paralogue genes. Redundancy, then, is secured either by paralogue proteins expressed concurrently, or by producing a "backup" protein version whenever the primary function aborts. In the first arrangement, the products of different but similar genes will perform different functions, but if one gene of the set is turned down (e.g., by a mutation), the cognate proteins will often take over the missing function and save the normal course of affairs in the cell. In contrast, backup genes remain silent if the master copy is functioning; they become activated only in case of the breakdown of its function (of course, what is backup in one context may be the master function in another). Note that redundancy is typical for regulatory proteins— bypasses in metabolic functions are not that common (figure 12.3a; see, e.g., Nasmyth et al., 1991; Brookfield, 1997a,b; see also discussion of homeotic genes in chapter 13).

In language terms, the same meaning can be expressed by synonyms and circumlocutions when the right expression is not at hand.

It is estimated that an average mammalian cell expresses about 10,000 genes (i.e., about one quarter of its genetic thesaurus). About one tenth of them, the so-called housekeeping genes, are engaged in maintaining basic functions—they are uniformly expressed in every cell. The rest of the set differs from one cell in the body to another, depending on its type, differentiation state, and momentary needs. The number of protein forms attained in the way described above may be, as I have shown above, much higher and, moreover, subject to continual qualitative and quantitative rebuilding.

At the microscopical level, the microheterogeneity of both space and time in the cell is enormously complex. This is why it is hard to apply classical chemistry terms requiring high numbers of identical entities (molecules) to environments in the living body. Even magnitudes such as concentration, pH, and so forth, can be defined only very vaguely for such environments. This leads to uncertainties regarding the functional parameters of proteins in their natural environment. Perhaps what is needed is not a chemical theory of life, but a theory of cellular protein neural networks capable of learning, adaptation, memory trace construction, forgetting, and so forth. Such a model could serve as a starting point toward a deeper understanding of the life of the cell. Bray (1995) considers all short-term behavior of an organism to be a result of the activity of the protein neural network; I would go further and apply this to longer time scales. One example of such a subnetwork of an "ordinary" transcription unit is shown in figure 12.4.

The scheme, however, is misleading in two respects. First, it gives an impression that the whole protein complex can be neatly distinguished, excised from the cell, and studied as such. In reality, such schemes are our abstraction from the cellular field of which the protein complex is normally part. Second, proteins occurring in the nodes of such a network or field should be taken not as points but as fields in themselves. What is more, the field has been around as long as life itself. The whole edifice, then, can be taken as the semantic field of the cell. Such a field does not implicate the existence of a source, a center of emanation as I have shown in Gurwitschian speculations. The reader could object that the "field" is but a metaphor and that strict determination of

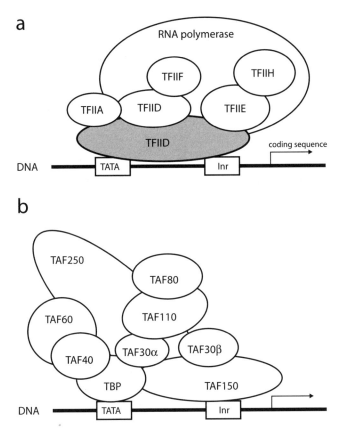

Figure 12.4. Transcription initiation complex. To start transcription of a coding sequence, RNA polymerase must be brought to a very specific context in chromatin, which is ensured by several protein complexes. Regulatory sequences *TATA box* and *Inr* help anchoring the whole complex upstream of the coding sequence to be transcribed. (*a*) Schematic view of the RNA polymerase complex. (*b*) Detail of the factor *TFIID*, which is itself a complex of several proteins. The whole ensemble is embedded into, and constitutes a part of, chromatin (see figure 12.1c).

cellular function has not been ruled out. No one would deny that *some* strictly deterministic processes do occur in the cell, and that *they* should be taken as the starting point of all the reasoning. I only maintain that automatisms should be considered not a *basic* state from which all extrapolations are to be made but, on the contrary, a highly derived and extreme case. I try to justify this view in the next section.

Note that the whole molecular–biological reasoning could easily be turned upside down to provide a synchronous structuralist model with its network of interactions leading toward phenotypic attractors (faithfully and blindly, as in the preceding case). Here the *structure* becomes the formative cause of living processes, and genes become mere parameters of canalizing functions. In such a perspective, new phenotypes in evolution are nothing but the discovery of ever-present possibilities. The evolution of the genetic text (by, e.g., the accumulation of mutations) may contribute to organismic evolution, but it is neither its cause nor its driving force: new structures can establish themselves even despite mutation—selection processes, because they have always existed as a potential. The only drawback of the structuralist approach is its inability to reify the *structures*, whereas genetics believes that it has performed the trick by reifying the formative principle—information—in the gene, as a piece of DNA. It is not important that one of these complementary views has been dominant whereas the second has been neglected. What is important is that, in my opinion, we cannot *decide* between them. Both are, furthermore, tributaries of a mechanical worldview (however much the structuralists may deny the fact) and can do without any self-reference, intentionality, of living beings.

Dictionary

If we stick to the metaphor of DNA as the dictionary, proteins become words that then become "statements" in the form of higher organizational units. Some statements remain unchanged for very long periods of time and could be compared to various clichés in language (cell structures, such as centrioles or some membranous structures, but also metabolic units—metabolons; see, e.g., Srere, 1990; Ovádi, 1995; Mathews, 1993). Others can be compared to the dynamic and ever-changing flow of speech. An example of the second case may be the short-term coalitions of proteins evoked by the presence of growth factors (see, e.g., Pawson and Scott, 1997).

The classic iconography of biochemical textbooks presents a protein molecule as a spatial distribution of beads connected by cords of different strength. In such a representation, a conformational change is coupled with a *local* disruption of some bonds and the creation of new ones. The word "local" is fundamental in this context, suggesting a final number of interactions, with a conformational change being a process of *gradual* manipulation with each of them separately. The transition between two stable "minima" is thus understood as a passage through a continuum of a great number of intermediary states (defined by their energy content). Problems with this model start when it is declared to be reality itself and serves as a background for generalizing theses concerning cell regulations, differentiation, evolution, and so forth. Moving in such a direction can only end with a machine conception of the cell's "functioning."

I suggest an alternative view that I believe will reveal aspects unknown or underestimated by the classic model. Here the protein plays the role of a field with internal, nonlocal rules of conformational transition (it follows that discrete intermediates do not exist). Different shapes (conformations) represent "grammatical forms" obedient to the species-specific "grammar" of the cell. As I have shown, the speaker (i.e, the cell) reigns over an extensive selection of different "words" and "grammatical figures" present as a plethora of protein patterns, of their modifications, and of multiprotein structures. When necessary, new basic forms of "words" can be retrieved from the dictionary (i.e, the genetic thesaurus) and modified in the process of "speech" according to reigning grammatical rules. Elementary protein utterances then assemble into higher order fields (discourses).

Consider, as an illustration, that the word "dog" has many meanings in the English language. First of all, it denotes a familiar domesticated animal. The meaning is then carried over to any carnivore of the family Canidae or, more precisely, the male of such species. The meaning can then be transferred to denote various kinds of unattractive or despicable persons and even to something worthless or of extremely poor quality, or to an utter failure. The word can also be used for mechanical tools. As a verb, it can be used as a synonym of tracking and chasing or for performing perfunctory actions ("dogging"). One can lead a "dog's life" and learn to "let sleeping dogs lie." Add constellations (Canis Minor and Major), hot dogs, dog days, sun-dog, and dogfish. The word "dog" can have various conformations (dogs, doggy, dogging . . . but, e.g., "doggation" is not allowed in English). Redundancy is ensured by using many synonyms (hound, bitch, mongrel, etc.). The word "dog" bears a "dictionary" semantic field that represents an average value of all meanings; different semantic fields from dog breeding, zoology, poetic language, suburb slang, and so forth, are superposed over the dictionary entry. Still other nuances can be found in individual usage. In the act of discourse, individual higher order semantic fields are constructed. Understanding the meaning of the word as used in a given discourse is a hermeneutic task that will cause the field to "collapse" into a single meaning.

Now, it is true that a language is a kind of "agreement" among the speakers. In English, one can imagine replacement of the word dog by, say, *Hund* or *pes* ("dog" in German and Czech, respectively) or even some invented word like *lihue* (of course, not any word would do, the unpronounceable *ksfrachs* would not be accepted). Perhaps such a replacement would even work, but it would leave a terrible scar on the language for a long time before new bonds to "hot dog," "sun-dog," and the like become established. Isomorphism does exist in other languages—the Polish *dog* and the Czech *doga* for mastiff can be easily recognized, and the same holds for the French *doguin(e)* for pug or Czech *buldok* for a bull-dog; in all such cases, however, the transferred word lacks the original semantic field it had in English and enters the semantic field of the language in question, with completely different grammatical confor-mations. Finally, one has to learn that the word "dogma" has nothing in com-mon with dogs.

The whole problem of characterizing living processes may perhaps reside in the emphasis that is placed on "processes" rather than on "living." Such a functionalist approach is typical of our civilization and spreads into life, sci-ence, medicine, worldviews, and so forth.

Many of us became totally disgusted by the lessons in our mother tongue at primary school. In my experience with Czech and Slovak schools, through these lessons the language became transformed into "language processes" and required endless grammar exercises and dictations; there was almost no time left for discussion and essays. The teacher unequivocally prescribed the "hermeneutics": *she* knew how to interpret the text, and the pupils were re-quired only to memorize it. The situation is similar to many in biology, where specific interpretations found in the textbooks are supposed to be the only ones allowed to be taken into account.

The situation can be compared with that of foreigners learning some words and grammar and being able to compose grammatically correct sen-tences. These words and sentences may even be fully comprehensible to na-tive speaker but will still look very strange to them, and native speakers would never utter those phrases themselves. (E.g., native English speakers living in Czech Republic are always surprised by the phrase "We shall slowly go." They hear it from Czech visitors who are about to leave. Of course, it is a translation of the Czech phrase used at such occasions. In this case, Native English speak-ers will even *understand* it, yet they would never *use* it.) Similarly, we move in science into an unknown language with unknown grammar and try, with a dictionary in our hands, to compose grammatically correct sentences.

In the quest to understand living processes, proteins were removed from their cellular context, and their properties have been corroborated in minute de-tail. Experiments under controlled conditions create a context-free "gram-mar," similar to giving all the tenses of a verb in a language textbook. More-over, most knowledge of proteins came from the study of common metabolic enzymes: they occur in high concentrations, can be easily extracted, and re-main stable upon extraction, and their properties can be easily studied. These proteins have the same role that grammatical standards play in linguistics — and all newly studied proteins are studied in the light of such standards. This approach was, and is, invaluable, especially in the study of the common metabolic enzymes. At the same time, we tend to prescribe only a single "reading frame" for natural "speech acts": only those that were *created* in the laboratory are taken as legitimate.

In the language metaphor, the description of the molecular functioning of cells as relying on automatisms is comparable with the world of laws, public notices, directions for use, recipes and manuals, and, of course, scientific definitions. In all such cases, we tend to encounter simple language, precisely defined meanings of words, and simple sentence structures. The languages of such text forms (of course, only when written carefully) are not problematic, but this comes at a high cost: the meaning can be totally changed or even destroyed by a single typographical error, incorrectly situated negation, or improper synonym. Closer examination would reveal how much effort, processing of the meaning of words, and conceptual refinement has come from the past. What is seemingly simple and uncomplicated carries with it much local and historical context and often cannot be translated to other loci, times, or languages. It is fascinating to consider the presuppositions that should be fulfilled for us to be able to understand far more complex texts, for example, Euclidean theorems.

Even more illustrative is a thesis by Umberto Eco devoted to the genre of comic strips, for which he uses as a sample case one of the earliest comics: reading *Steve Canyon* confronts us with an autonomous genre based on the existence of code shared by the readers. The author of *Steve Canyon* has recourse to this code whenever he has to articulate the message addressed to the intelligence, imagination, or taste of the readers (Eco, 1964). Transfer of such structures into a community that does not know them or accepts only some of their facets leads to endless misunderstandings and conflicts and long-winded explanations. Such abbreviations of linguistic, historical, and local contexts, however, represent only a marginal aspect of the natural language. Language is rather characterized by the intentional fuzziness of the means used and, above all, high redundancy of messages. This is why the context will usually smooth over small stumbles; omitted words or spelling mistakes in texts can usually be tolerated without the breakdown of the message.

Metabolic pathways usually proceed automatically—it is a good measure of credibility that they always work in the expected manner. The cell does not have to bother with an accurate study of the situation or go through a laborious decision-making process—things have already been settled and are part of a shared *code*. Automatic reactions save time; they are quick and usually correct. Because of the very existence of the code, the cell can set aside the trivialities of everyday working and pay more attention to things that *are* truly important. Automatic reactions are characteristic of all levels of living (e.g., cleavage of an egg, gait, instincts, conditioned reflexes, or driving a car). Sometimes there is no way back, and the whole behavior is locked in automatisms (e.g., insect instincts). Sometimes controls allow intervention when necessary (as in driving).

Classic biochemistry came into existence as a description of a biochemical automaton driven by energy potentials, with feedback from the concentrations of metabolites. All the nuances that followed (e.g., regulation of protein function) were absorbed into *this* original conception and became the starting point for expansion to other functions (signaling pathways) and for the description of a cell as such. This approach was conditioned by the existence of defects in the elementary protein grammar, for example, by mutations changing the meaning of the "sentence" (e.g., metabolic diseases such as sickle cell anemia), which is fairly comparable to a typing error in codified sentences in language.

The situation is analogous to the above-mentioned language of notices, comics, road signs, and gestures, where no redundancy is allowed. They represent incredibly efficient abbreviations, but they work "for free" only in the community of users that developed them. Other mutations are not visible at the first sight, but they may supply material for evolutionary modifications.

A protein catalyzing a given reaction or transporting a given ion across a membrane does not usually have many degrees of freedom: it must fulfill the needs of a particular reaction. Different forms of the same protein are usually interpreted as adaptations to a different environment. Two or three replacements of amino acids may be interpreted as a *cause* of why the species inhabits a niche different from that of a closely related species.[7] But living beings need not sit back and wait for an adaptational change delivered by a mutation. A good example of this was recently found in yeast. The yeast cell harbors two types of glucose transporter in its membrane. Changing the ratio of the proteins can optimize the glucose intake in standard environments. In the case of special needs, however, the cell can produce multiple copies of both genes and perform recombination among the "slave" copies (leaving the "master" copies untouched), providing a whole spectrum of transport proteins. The cell is able to experiment with such special copies without changing the "master" copy (Brown and Rosenzweig, 1998). Large-scale recombinations taking place in bacteria are described in chapter 14. In multicellular organisms, similar processes allow, for example, the construction of genes for antibodies and T receptors. But above all, it is in the massive recombination in gametogenesis that new versions of the dictionary are produced. The dictionary does allow adjustments! Another way of achieving an optimal setup is redundancy of performance, that is, a higher degree of freedom, of regulatory pathways, allowing them to express "the same" by different constituents of the pathway or by different pathways.

---

7. See, for example, Gillespie (1991), Graves et al. (1983), Graves and Somero (1982), and Watt (1977, 1983).

Gratuity

Monod (1979) termed this higher degree of freedom, through different ways of reaching the same result, "gratuity": "This fundamental concept of *gratuity*—that is, the independence, chemically speaking, between the function itself and the nature of chemical signals controlling it—applies to allosteric enzymes. . . . The result—and this is the essential point—is that so far as regulation through allosteric interaction is concerned, 'everything is possible' " (p. 78). The specific semantic function here looks as if it is free (*gratuit*); it is not a result of forcing, nor is it inescapable for chemical or other reasons. From this point of view, the proteins and their regulators are arbitrary: *what* is regulated is important, not which proteins perform the process. The difference between a regulatory and a metabolic pathway may serve as a good illustration. In metabolism, only enzymes capable of particular catalytic reactions can be at work. Take a sequence of metabolic enzymes A, B, C, and D catalyzing a sequence of reactions *a*, *b*, *c*, and *d*, respectively. Enzyme B cannot be replaced by an enzyme X, which is unable to catalyze reaction *b*. The pathway would simply stop at reaction *a*. The sequence ABCD is compelled by the chemical nature of the metabolites involved and will very probably be found in most organisms that are able to perform the same chemical task. If, however, we find a *regulatory* pathway ABCD in one species and AXCD and WXCZ in two other species, all regulating the same function, it would merely be an illustration of the historical contingency of the means developed by particular species to regulate that particular function. This is the essence of gratuity.

Another form of gratuity is the submission of many different morphoregulatory functions to a universal and conservative set regulatory proteins (e.g., the set of homeotic regulators; see chapter 13). Thanks to gratuity, the same protein can work in different contexts, for example, as a switch for different metabolic or morphoregulatory pathways. The impression that all such services of a protein are free is, of course, erroneous. The protein has come to its given semantic conjunctions by long evolution, a long process of trial and error. As in the case of linguistic clichés, it is only in retrospect that the service appears free.

Classic examples of gratuity are the regulation of the *lac* operon in the bacterium *Escherichia coli* and the bistable regulatory circuit in the phage λ (Mcadams and Shapiro, 1995; Ptashne, 1987). The gratuity lies in the fact that in other bacteria the induction of the same operon or a phage may be achieved by a completely different set of regulators. I think, however, that the idea of gratuity has not yet been fully exploited. This is because it was, from the outset, applied only to explanatory schemes regarding *mechanisms*, to explain how a certain canonical, unequivocal form of behavior might have arisen in evolution, and how can it be further molded by evolution. If questions are posed in this way, research could not but remain confined to "clichés" of automatic regulatory circles and did not venture into aspects of a language metaphor, which seem much more interesting. Again, clichés do appear in organisms as they do in a spoken language, and they make life much easier in well-examined cases. As they occur frequently, they can be easily distinguished and isolated and their rules examined. Historically, research has been focused on such "clichés" and extrapolations made are thus conditioned by the chosen point of view. Other aspects of "life" that would be much more appropriate for the language metaphor are hidden under vague names such as field, coherent whole, plasma, body, and so forth, and remain neglected. Even worse, they are often even taken as special and complicated cases of the well-known clichés.

Proteins Emancipated

The main objective of hermeneutic biology should be to get rid of the geno-centric view that takes the genome as a recipe for building the body. It should pose questions about the *builder*, who takes the genome as a mere dictionary of the language in which the recipe is written. Proteins—"words" uttered in the language—enter into complicated syntactic and semantic relations, which constitute the cellular *parole*. The cell is thus a materialized *parole*.

From this viewpoint, we can pose methodological questions about what understanding can be gained from the contemporary genomic era, which is witnessing the acquisition of complete sequences of genomes. The genome is understood as a complete dictionary and source book of a cell, an individual, a species. Comparative analyses will undoubtedly lead to a deeper understanding of the richness and evolutionary position of a given language. But now another step is needed: to proceed from the dictionary to utterances. The field of grammar is being mapped very extensively—for example, regulatory and metabolic networks. A new move in the field is the interconnection of gene dictionaries with protein utterances, as illustrated by the KEGG database (Kanehisa, 2000). The semantics of new science is no longer a Cinderella, even if it is still hidden under names such as "mechanisms of the regulation of gene expression."

The utterances of the protein continuum themselves may, in turn, appear to be a higher order dictionary for the ontogeny of a multicellular organism. This aspect is treated in chapter 13.

The Text and Its Reader

In the 1950s and 1960s, living beings were seen mainly in terms of bio-chemical pathways and chemical (equilibrium) thermodynamics. Their

THE SPEECH OF PROTEINS

functioning was limited by energy resources and concentrations of inputs, intermediates, and outputs. Cells were described as machines driven by the difference in the free energy of inputs and outputs. Moreover, the whole image was strictly cyclical. From these cyclical events extrapolations were made to acyclical ones, and ontogeny became a process that is highly controlled by a deterministic genetic program. There is no need to give a full summary here: it can be found in current textbooks and monographs on the topic.

As mentioned above, the older concept of cells as bags full of enzymes and driven by a program was later replaced by the idea of an elaborate network of structures and information flows. Cells have active access to their genetic thesaurus: they select from it and interpret it in an unceasing confrontation with their own time and space (i.e., coordinates within the tissue or organism) and with inputs from their environment. This work with the "source code" is dependent on the quality of the text itself and the "tuning" of the cell (the above-mentioned coordinates, physiology, morphology, and history) and is indeed to be viewed as a hermeneutic task. A medium for this interpretative work, the "search for meaning," is to hand in the form of nonlocal morphogenetic fields, concentration gradients, complicated dynamic networks of macromolecules (extracellular matrix, cytoskeleton, nucleoskeleton), and morphological structures of higher orders and longer duration.[8] DNA is thus far from being the algorithm prescribing how the body will look and how it will behave. It is a genuine text to be read by an *informed* (or better initiated) reader. The cell, the body, is an in-formation of experience (chapter 3). Information is in fact "contained" in the whole cell, a multicellular body equipped with temporal, spatial, internal, and external cues and rules as to how to decipher the meaning of a great variety of signals. Changes in the interpretation of any of this multilayered information accumulated over billions of years can also be considered mutations and may even result in misinterpretations ending in aberrant development, or tumors, but from time to time also to a new morphological variant.

In the quest to recognize the ultimate and simple causes of life, biology became fascinated by a single kind of molecule: those able to perpetuate their structure—nucleic acids, molecules that can serve as a medium for digital encoding of strings of signs. But, strangely, the situation is reversed: whereas *all* molecules in the cell can indeed be perpetuated over generations, in the case of the molecule of DNA this is not true—owing to recombination processes in gametogenesis! Neubauer, in the foreword to the Czech edition of this book (Markoš, 2000), commented:

---

8. See, for example, Edelman et al., (1990), Müller (1996), Gilbert (1994), and Wolpert et al. (1998).

What is the difference between the replication of nucleic acids, and repeated chemical production of other molecules? Why only in the first case
we have a need to stress the identity and continuity? Is it in the fact that all
molecules are "produced" by other molecules, whereas DNA is a product of
DNA as its faithful replica? . . . No: nucleic acids must be built enzymatically
as any other biomolecules. And they themselves participate in many organic syntheses having nothing to do with production of their own copies.
From the chemical and molecular–biological perspective the participation
of DNA on its self-replication is of little importance, and all the emphasis
given to prefixes "self-" and "auto-" only play on words. The conception
that the "cell controls its own replication" describes the cell division truly;
in contrast, the phrase that "DNA controls its replication" will hardly do
justice to the essence of replication. (p. 18)

The difference is in the different order of being. Bodies and their parts (cells,
organs) do appear again and again in each generation, as do molecules, but
they can only more or less resemble each other, whereas molecules can be absolutely identical. This is because bodies are from the order of Neubauerian
eidos, whereas simple molecules are from the order of *structures*. Individual
but identical molecules will—under given conditions—behave uniformly;
the rule does not hold for individual living bodies. I maintain that proteins are
of the order of bodies, not structures or molecules in the sense in which the
term was developed for particles of simple chemical species. A lot of effort
should be developed in the laboratory to restrain their hermeneutic properties
and to study them as *molecular* entities.

13

MORPHOGENESIS

The problem to be explained is how structures are produced
regularly in different generations.

David M. Lambert and Anthony J. Hughes

One testable prediction of the hypothesis . . . is that the
similarities in the developmental regulatory mechanisms
governing metazoan appendage formation will be more
extensive than would be expected from their diverse
morphologies and functions.

G. Panganiban et al.

This chapter is devoted to some aspects of ontogeny in multicellular eukaryotes. No area of biology has seen so many bitter encounters. Several incidents
from history were mentioned in part II of this book; here I confine myself to
the current state of the art.

I start with several formulations taken from a recent textbook on developmental biology (Wolpert et al., 1998) that represent "genocentric" phrases
typical of the current biological paradigm. Slightly reformulated, the sentences will take on quite different meanings. Throughout this chapter, I maintain that both formulations can be taken as true; that is, we cannot decide
which of them is more appropriate:

1. "Cell behavior provides the link between gene action and developmental processes. Gene expression within cells is translated into embryonic
   development through the consequent properties and behavior of those

cells" (p. 12). Change the last sentence to read: "Cells determine the embryonic development also through selective gene expression."

2. "One might be tempted to think of development simply in terms of mechanisms for controlling gene expression. But this would be highly misleading. For gene expression is only the first step in a cascade of cellular processes that change cell behavior and so direct the course of embryonic development." (pp. 14–15). Change the last sentence to: "For gene expression is only one of the steps in a cascade of cellular processes that change cell behavior and so direct the course of embryonic development."

3. "We can now ask how genes are controlling cell behavior" (p. 13)—change to "We can now ask how cell behavior is controlling gene expression."

4. "Genes control development mainly by determining which proteins are made in which cells and when" (p. 13)—change to "The cellular phenotype controls development mainly by determining which proteins will be synthesized and when."

5. "The differences between cells must therefore be generated by differences in gene activity" (p. 13)—change to "The differences in gene activity must therefore be generated by differences in cell behavior."

6. "Comparative studies suggest that, despite immense differences in the details, it is likely that the most basic mechanisms of development are similar in all animals and are derived from the earliest animal ancestors" (p. 24). No reformulation is required, only an appendix: "It means that species-specific ontogeny is basically epigenetic."

Universal Tools

The fact that the basic genetic processes (code, transcription, and translation) are shared by all organisms has been a standard textbook truth for since the 1960s. The same assumption holds for basic metabolic pathways. Such conservatism used to be explained by an entrenchment in states that epitomize energy or functional optima, or simply by historical contingency. Later, however, it also emerged that the regulatory pathways—at both the cellular and the morphogenetic level—are largely universal. Whole organs and developmental trajectories share homologous sets of genes and regulatory pathways (see, e.g., Carroll et al., 2001). At the same time, the structures themselves may not be homologous at all and often appear in a given lineage only after it developed as a separate line through evolution. Thus—as discussed in chapter 12 regarding genes and proteins—the richness of forms and life strategies has as its background a universal dictionary (and grammar) of genetic tools. Again, ontogeny can be understood as something that lies not in the language but in what is being expressed. To further develop the language metaphor from chapter 12: genes play the role of dictionary entries, and proteins are words that could appear in various grammatical forms and, together with other proteins, constitute a plethora of predicates. The cell uses all this to weave a texture of temporal and spatial expressions. The multicellular body can be taken as expression, and differentiated cells (including the extracellular matrix) are involved in syntactic and semantic relations. The dictionary would not be genes but whole modules (e.g., signaling cascades). In this metaphor, ontogeny is a species-specific (or genus-specific, phylum-specific, etc.) *explication* of a very old and conservative text shared by the greater part of, or even all, living beings. Like any explication, this, too, is subject to "cultural" shifts in evolution (recall my analogy between the species and culture in chapter 2). Morphology, then, is highly emancipated from proteins (of course, not absolutely: recall clichés and similar historical contingencies discussed in chapter 12).

Modules

The term "module" can refer to a very heterogeneous set of entities. It can be applied to functional units in genomes that can shuffle between the genes, thus increasing functional variability of proteins coded (Patthy, 1995). It can also represent structural, regulatory, or functional units in cells that may never be "present" in their totality at the same time (Hartwell et al., 1999; very similar is the approach of Kanehisa [2000], though it does not use the term "module"); finally, molecules are understood as autonomously developing units in ontogeny (Gilbert et al., 1996).

What is common to all these conceptions is that modules serve as a kind of archetypal "scaffolding" for explication, that is, forming some phenotypical trait. The scaffolding is relatively stable in its internal relations. Its existence is a *necessary* condition for building the trait in question, but the trait itself cannot be *derived* from the existence of the scaffolding. What we observe as differences between modules in different lineages are more like dialects than different languages. Modules can become interconnected with other modules in a variety of ways, thus enabling new combinations of ontogenetic pathways.

There could, of course, be another explanation for the conservative character of modules—it could be due to the necessity for *horizontal communication between the lines.* This supposition is fully relevant at the level of the genetic code—especially in bacteria and archaea. As I show in chapter 14, frequent and extensive genetic exchange across the bacterial world calls for a universal and conservative genetic language. To explain the conservation of modules by the necessity of horizontal transfer, however, would be quite challenging. The lineages represented by the species tend to be well, if not hermetically, isolated. Such an exchange might have some importance immediately after the divergence of lines in so-called hybridization chains: great chunks of genetic material can move from species to species by interspecific hybridization.

Another possible justification for a universal language of modules may be symbiosis: its existence will allow the partners to "understand" (or manipulate?) each other to differing extents. It is not that important whether the partners exchange their genetic material (mitochondria, chloroplasts) or not (lichens, ciliates, parasites). Such higher order phenotypes require intimate interconnections between the regulatory systems of the constituting species. The establishment of multifarious symbiotic associations is typical in the biosphere, and the existence of a universal modular language undoubtedly makes it easier. It may even appear that symbioses (even despite the risk of parasitism) are advantageous in evolutionary terms, to the extent that there is a pressure to maintain the universal language *despite* genetic isolation.

Examples of Universal Modules in Evolution

Perhaps the most popular (and best known) example of a module is the system of *Hox* genes in animals, collinear with the body axis and corresponding to morphological modules that can be recognized on the body (e.g., segments).[1] The genes are expressed in an order that corresponds to their position on the chromosome, along the presumptive anteroposterior axis, and thus establish a map of the anteroposterior specification of embryonic structures (figure 13.1).[2] The products of homeotic genes thus assign an "address" to the body structures (e.g., the third thoracic segment in an insect, or the second lumbar segment in humans). Incorrect addressing caused by incorrect functioning of the homeotic coding leads to so-called homeotic mutations, when structures appropriate to one type of segment appear at incorrect, ectopic sites.

Many other regulatory modules are of such archetypal nature, for example, systems specifying the dorsoventral axis in animals, the proximal–distal axis of appendages, the establishment of boundaries between body compartments, the neurocranium, and left–right asymmetry of the body. Similar archetypal regulations can be found in vascular plants.

What is important to stress is that the role of these morphoregulatory modules apparently ends with the establishment of a projection of the "morphogenetic map" by giving instructions that are very old in evolutionary

---

1. On the system of *Hox* genes, see any textbook of developmental biology, for example, Wolpert et al. (1998), Müller (1996), and Carroll et al. (2001).

2. The colinearity of homeotic genes on the chromosome and their expression along the anteroposterior axis may, according to some authors, be the *single* common property of *animals* (Slack et al., 1990; Richardson et al., 1997).

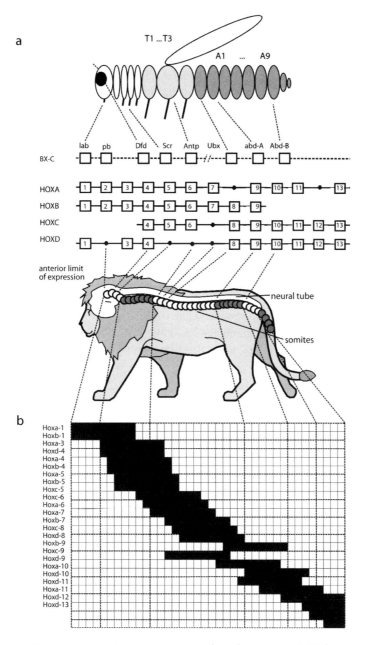

Figure 13.1. Antero–posterior axis in animals and *Hox* genes. (*a*) Scheme of the correlation between development of body segments and *Hox* gene expression. Note that the expression does not start from the fore of the body: in insects the anterior limit of expression is at the level of gnathencephalon; in mammals, of the rhombencephalon. (*b*) The homeotic code of the somite mesoderm in mammals.

terms. These instructions will be remembered by cell lines for the rest of the life of the organism. The systems themselves will not influence the particular morphology typical of the given species—this is left to the interpretative power of the developing embryo (see fig 7.1). This conclusion comes from the fact that transgene animals can be constructed with some of the regulatory genes replaced by their homologs from another phylum. For example, homeotic *null* mutants in *Drosophila*, which are otherwise lethal or lead to a deformed morphology, were successfully saved by transformation with the corresponding gene from a mouse (Lutz et al., 1996).

After the morphogenetic field of the embryo has become fragmented into structures (which, again, can be constituted as second-order morphological modules), the regulatory modules can be reused again and again to establish projections of lower order structures. Homeotic proteins become involved, for example, in specifing limbs and wings in insects, whereas in vertebrates they give instructions on how to articulate the appendages—proximodistally as well as anteroposteriorly (Herault et al., 1999; Carroll et al., 2001; Davidson, 2001). Such recurrent usage may end in specifying tiny differences between orders or species (see, e.g., Abouheif et al., 1997; Rogers and Kaufman, 1997; Warren et al., 1994; Panganiban et al., 1997). In such secondary roles, the modules do not function as homeotic: their mutation will not lead, for example, to a homeotic mutation of an appendage (i.e., a normal structure at an abnormal site), but rather to an abnormal appendage (Duboule, 1995).[3]

> Some transcription factors appear to be specialists: they specify a particular fate or behavior whenever they are expressed in a cell; the myogenic factors might approximate this role, for example. The *Hox* gene products lie at the other extreme: they are versatile generalists. They operate in many different cell and tissue types, where they modulate, sometimes dramatically but more often subtly, a wide range of developmental processes. In each of these cell types, expression of a *Hox* gene means something different—to divide or not to divide, to make or not to make a bristle, to die or not to die. In any given lineage, that meaning probably changes several times during development, in response to hormonal and other developmental cues. (Akam, 1998, p. R678)

It may be that genes and, even more, the morphoregulatory modules possess a kind of reaction norm (semantic field) that, in different organisms, species, and so forth, must be negotiated again and again, put into context, focused. But compare the preceding quotation with the following, which is symmetrical to it:

---

3. The principle is not confined to homeotic genes: other crucial modules of early morphogenesis can ultimately be used in establishing such trifles as eyespots in butterflies (Brakefield et al., 1996; Pigliucci, 1997).

Conventional wisdom has it that genes at the top of linear hierarchies are likely to be "entrenched." This means that any small change in activity will cascade into a major change in morphology that would almost always be deleterious, and hence that such genes are unlikely to contribute to evolution.... By contrast, the more interactions there are in a pathway, the more likely it is to evolve toward a stable state, in which modification of the activity of one gene is buffered by the whole. In this case, the paradox emerges that, despite phenotypic uniformity, the underlying genetic architecture may remain quite labile and in a state of perpetual flux. (Gibson, 1999, p. R88)

Morphogenesis thus seems to be a very specific "statement" that is composed from a relatively limited number of expressive tools—regulatory modules (the repertoire of cell types is similarly limited). In such a case, it is appropriate to try a thought experiment that will take into consideration not the tools but instead a top-down regulatory parameter. From this point of view, the regulatory modules are activated only secondarily and enable the project to be "materialized." Below I opt for this perspective, as it allows a more plastic view of the hermeneutic nature of lineage-specific morphogenesis. The "new head" problem may serve as a good example.

How to Make a Head

The interplay between genetic modules and morphology becomes very plastic when comparing the evolution of the head in insects and vertebrates. If the colinearity of the *Hox* genes with the body axis is curious as such, even more curious is the fact that in neither group does it correspond to the whole length of the embryo: on the anterior end the homeotic code starts at the level of the gnathal (bearing oral appendages) and rhombencephalic (hindbrain) segments, respectively, for insects and vertebrates. In both groups, thus, only part of the head is outlined as serial modules defined by the *Hox* code: gnathencephalon in insects, and the viscerocranium (chordocranium) in vertebrates (see, e.g., Gans and Northcutt, 1983). The foremost part of the head—comprising the neurocranium containing the brain, plus other structures—is also segmented in insects, whereas in vertebrates the segmentation is apparent only in the anlagen of the forebrain (Figdor and Stern, 1993). In embryos, as well as in the later stages of both groups, this anterior part of the head is easily distinguishable from the rest of the trunk (figure 13.2). These facts led to the formulation of the "new head" theory (Couly et al., 1993; Gans and Northcutt, 1983), which states that the neurocranium is an evolutionary novelty flanking the anterior part of an older, segmented wormlike body plan. This older part was originally defined by the *Hox* code from the very first segment. A rough idea (very rough, as I show below) of such a "headless" vertebrate could be represented by amphioxus or an annelid. It follows that the neurocranium in insects and vertebrates developed in parallel after the two lineages became separated, and show no homology (in contrast to those body parts that are defined by a homeotic code). The whole problem became even more interesting when it became apparent that the development of the anteroposterior structures of the "new head" is regulated, in both groups, by homologous modules known as *Otx* (figure 13.2).[4]

If the "common ancestor" of both lineages was indeed headless, the homology found at the level of the regulatory modules would witness the parallel mobilization of genetic systems previously used for other ends. A second possibility is, of course, to reject the whole concept of a new head and to conclude that even in the common ancestor there were structures at the fore end that were projected independently onto the homeotic code. A more detailed investigation of the anatomy of the amphioxus supports this second and rather more digestible alternative. It appeared that it is by no means a "headless vertebrate": even here the homeotic code starts somewhat further back, and its eye spots and hindbrain are homologous with the brain structures of other vertebrates (Garcia Fernandez and Holland, 1994).

It is much more probable that the whole network of developmental regulation existed even before the separation of protostomes and deuterostomes. As I have already shown, both lineages use the same system of anteroposterior coding. The same holds for the projection of the dorsoventral axis. It uses the same elements but with a reversed polarity—what determines the dorsal part in one lineage is ventral in the other, and vice versa. It seems that the evolution of deuterostomes started with the reversal of the dorsoventral body stance, followed by the necessary anatomical adaptations and the perforation of a new mouth (Arendt and Nübler-Jung, 1997). In this scenario, the head was well defined before the split of the two groups, and their neurocrania are thus homologous (Finkelstein and Perrimon, 1991; Finkelstein and Boncinelli, 1994).[5] Similarly, Arendt and Nübler-Jung (1996) discovered analogies in the brain ontogeny of the two groups, both in structures and in the genetic modules engaged. Of course, anatomical convergence and concurrent cooptation of homologous regulatory modules cannot be ruled out, but Arendt and Nübler-Jung see it as very improbable and prefer the existence of a common ancestor, a gastroneuralian. Indirectly, this assumption is supported by the discovery of the role of the homolog of *Otx* in the development of the fore end of the nervous system in flatworms (Umesono et al., 1999).

---

4. See, for example, Finkelstein and Perrimon (1991), Finkelstein and Boncinelli (1994), Matsuo et al. (1995), Sharman and Brand (1998), Bally-Cuif and Wassef (1995), Figdor and Stern (1993), Lumsden and Krumlauf (1996), and Shimamura et al. (1995).

5. Dickinson (1995), however, prefers the "new head" hypothesis, and argues that in the common ancestor the otd/Otx proteins served a different function.

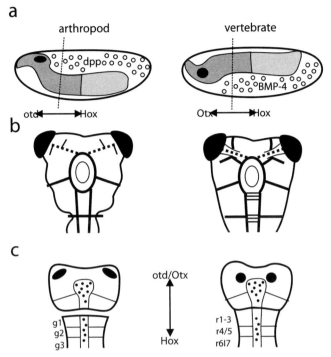

Figure 13.2. "Homology" of the head of arthropods and vertebrates. (*a*) Shift in the dorsoventral orientation of the body in deuterostomes. (*b*) Identical pattern, in both groups, of the pathways of neurons (axonal scaffold) that is required formation of the brain proper. The neural ring surrounding the stomodeum (alimentary tract) has, in deuterostomes, its counterpart in the foundation of infundibulum; Arendt and Nübler-Jung (1996, 1999) therefore locate here the original orifice of the mouth. (*c*) Homology of the ontogeny; *g* and *r* represent the first somites coded by the homeotic code, flanked by head structures, which in turn use in both cases the so-called *Otx* module. Adapted from Arendt and Nübler-Jung (1996, 1999).

On Homologies

In the contemporary view of the evolution of multicellular organisms as parallel, mutually independent lineages, homology is usually taken as a result of divergence from a common ancestor already endowed with the trait. The assumption of *historical homology*, however, is derived: before Darwin, homology was understood as a relation to an archetypal plan or form (see, e.g., Wagner, 1989).[6] Only biological structuralists today hold such views; most

---

6. Wagner (1989) extends the concept of homology by adding the notion of homonomy, that is, homology within the same organism: "Structures from two individuals or from the same individual are homologous if they share a set of developmental constraints, caused by locally acting self-regulatory mechanisms of organ differentiation. These structures are thus developmentally individualized parts of the phenotype" (p. 62)

biologists suppose that the only true homologies can be found at the level of replicators only. After all, "homologies" at the level of morphology, function, and behavior do not share any "common origin" in the strict sense: they must be built *de novo* in each individual. They can even develop by using nonhomologous genetic machinery or through nonhomologous intermediary structures.

Strangely enough, no one seriously questions most historical homologies at the level of the phenotype, as described long before the rise of molecular biology, even if incompatibilities between different levels of description might be observed. What, then, should be understood by the concept of historical continuity in the realm of epigenetically modeled structures, which by definition lack any continuity? Dickinson (1995) states that homology at the macroscopic level is an understanding reached by biologists by comparative studies and, of course, by consensus with their peers. Perhaps similarity should be a priori considered homology, if there is no phylogenetic proof against it. Moreover, Salthe (1991) stressed the necessity of considering only a single level of description.

Consider the "objective" homology in sequences of nucleic acids. Even here we cannot avoid paradoxes. First, as with macroscopic traits, aligning and judging the statistical weights of differences are *also* matters of deeper understanding of contexts. Second, the method is based on measuring *differences* (digital strings can be either identical or different), but homology was initially an estimate of *similarity*, which should be *seen*, because it is sometimes even difficult to define objectively.

Differences between homologous sequences (of DNA or proteins) may be random, or they may bear an adaptive significance for their carrier. A high degree of sequence identity in specimens from evolutionarily distant organisms can be explained in different ways. It may simply be an optimal solution of a given problem; that is, any further search in the sequence space would only decrease the fitness of the organism. Or it can be a vestige of an evolutionary entrenchment that cannot be escaped. Processes leading to convergence may also play a role, whereas that of the necessity for horizontal communication may be decisive (see above and chapter 14). In the last case, homology may be simply a list of different dialects of the same communication language, from syntax to semantics (see, e.g., Syvanen, 1985).

Another comparative structure can be seen in a shared gene expression during development, the *Hox* system being an example of this. A developmental biologist studying evolution will stress, however, that homology should be applied to structures only, not to shared "genetic statements" (Abouheif, 1997; Abouheif et al., 1997; Bolker and Raff, 1996). It is impossible to assign a clear-cut function to 90% of the genes in a cell, because they are part of a complicated network of regulatory modules. Moreover, even the modules need not be in any direct correlation with morphology. The heritability of traits is thus hidden under a deposit of complicated epistatic inter-actions, and the very *process* of form building remains no less hidden than it was at the beginnings of genetics (especially in multicellular organisms). It should, then, be much safer to discuss homology only at the level of morpho-logical traits and of processes leading to the buildup of such traits. Tabin et al. (1999), in relation to the appendages of arthropods and vertebrates, stated:

> There has been no continuity of any structure from which the insect and vertebrate appendages could be derived, i.e., they are not homologous structures. However, there is abundant evidence for continuity in the ge-netic information for building body wall outgrowths and/or appendages in several phyla that must date at least to the common, potential appendage-bearing pre-Cambrian ancestor of most protostomes and deuterostomes. (Tabin et al., 1999, p. 650)

As in the case of the genetic code, metabolic pathways, cell types, and, indeed, morphogenetic regulatory pathways, we discover a conserved universality of tools that does not allow the reconstruction of the morphology without some knowledge of the historical context. What we need, in addition, to be able to recognize homology, is the semblance, *eidos* (in Neubauer's sense; see part II), which enables the same to be self-defined as the same. From the point of view of genidentity, as I have shown, the fact that there is a flow-through of mat-ter and energy in organisms is ancillary (or, in other words, at the level of matter and energy, organisms do not show genidentity). Similarly, it may also emerge that there is an informational flow-through of a particular quality. From the point of eidetic biology, it is self-definition (or self-consciousness) that is at stake in living beings, and this process may, to a considerable extent, be emancipated from both the material background and the information in-scribed in DNA.

Tradition as a Medium for *Eidos*

Living beings understand their situation in the world through meaning, and this is enacted in the process of interpretation. We need to determine whether this interpretation is indeed a hermeneutic achievement or simply a result of complicated but strictly causal relations that cannot be changed.

The causal explanation is well known, and I do not discuss it here (see, e.g., Carroll et al., 2001; Davidson, 2001); rather, I will to trace the alternative un-derstanding of life as culture (spread across many scales of space and time). The unique character of an individual, population, species, and so forth, is an expression of self-understanding, self-explanation of what is at its disposal in the form of (genetic) texts—an explanation mediated by tradition, previous experience, and buffering of unexpected occurrences. As shown above, a signal, a piece of information, can have different meanings in different contexts, in individuals, species, and communities: there is no legitimate meaning that would be binding for all the participants of a discourse or reading of a text. This does not mean that *any* interpretation would do! As Heelan (1998) states, cultural interpretation in humans comes from tradition, from outcomes preferred in the past, from outcomes dependent on the linguistic, historical, religious—in short, cultural—background of the community. My goal is to show that living beings apply the same life-supporting strategy.

Why Roses Are Roses

Such an assumption requires the existence of a morphogenetic field that, for simplicity, can be understood as a body. This demand would not be in any way strange if it were not for the fact that bodies are mortal. Most biologists therefore focus their attention on the genetic texts that pass from one organism to another "unchanged."[7] If this were really the case, then no room would be left for cultural interpretation, and the only way in which a new individual could appear would be strict epigenetic rules, as E. O. Wilson understands them. The only alternative to this would be wild experiments leading to random developmental trajectories, which is obviously not the case in ontogeny. But the morphogenetic field *has* continuity—it is the body of the cell (e.g., a zygote). Because of this, the genetic text can be *read* in such a way that it *becomes* information. Ruyer's affirmation that "we have never been dead" is the most poignant expression of the situation.

Harold (1995) states that, despite a common conviction to the contrary, we do not know the answer to the question of "why roses and rabbits, yeast and *Escherichia coli* display the same forms, generation after generation, within a narrow range of variations" (p. 2765; see also Harold, 1990). The answer, he says, should be sought in the organized complexity presented by the cell. He says of those who take the genome as an architect of morphology (note that he speaks of cells, not of multicellular beings): "What never ceases to amaze me is how many scientists believe, or profess to believe, that genetic information is not only necessary but also *sufficient* to determine cellular morphology" (p. 2774). In Harold's opinion, morphogenesis at whatever level cannot be orchestrated by the genome, because it epitomizes an order of a different category, which corresponds to the size and organization of the scales of a cell or a multicellular body. This points again to the species-specific inter-

---

7. I put "unchanged" in quotes because crossing-over, sex, and similar processes take such notions somewhat out of focus.

pretation of form, an introspection of the meaning of both text and external cues. All of this is based on the historical experience of the cell, cell line, species. . . . A fertilized egg will manipulate the genetic text, observing the *habits* within its species, habits constituted by an endless chain of its forbears. These habits and rules are essential to constitute the particular species-specific morphology. For these reasons, I feel it is appropriate to compare the species to a culture. A new species can thus originate either by mutation of DNA or by changing the habits of reading. A new trait, that is, habit in the tradition, can be subsequently incorporated into the genetic text (i.e., by genetic assimilation), verbally to become a "written tradition."

A species, in the sense of culture, is characterized by the set of individuals living at a given moment. They belong there because they share (1) the genetic text in the form of more or less identical genomes ("more or less" owing to possible slight differences, e.g., between sexes, or to allele variability); (2) the tradition of explication of such texts, that is, the technology for extracting meaning from the text; and (3) codified short-term behavior that can help to overcome crises and misunderstandings if the tradition becomes incompatible with the situation. Such behavior (more or less improvised) includes reactions ranging from reflexes through regeneration in an individual, up to reaction norm reactions that can become spread over several generations (as epimutations or memes). Several examples below serve to illustrate this.

Chimeras

The study of chimeric embryos, that is, embryos gained by the fusion of two embryos belonging to nonrelated individuals or even species, may be a classic example of mixed species as intercultural communication. As basic regulatory modules are shared by all vertebrates, the chimera, if it survives, must find a compromise between two different interpretations of signals coming from such modules. Mouse–chicken chimeras developing into a viable morphology are a good example of such trends in research (Fontaine-Pérus et al., 1997).

Chaperones

An article by Rutherford and Lindquist (1998), reporting on the role of the chaperone protein Hsp90 in morphological evolution, looks very Waddingtonian. The protein (one of the most abundant in cytoplasm) does not function by assisting the conformation shaping of native proteins, as other chaperones do, but controls the conformation of "adult," that is, functional, proteins (see, e.g., Mayer and Bukau, 1999). By binding to them, it stabilizes their structure and increases their susceptibility to interactions, for example, with their regulatory ligand. Many regulatory proteins in fact can work only as complexes with Hsp90. The chaperone, moreover, helps in restituting the conformations of these and many other proteins, if they are damaged by stress factors (temperature, heavy metals, etc.). This second function implies that Hsp90 is even able to bring *mutated* proteins into a required—that is, functional—conformation. It thus enables an effective buffering against both epigenetic and genetic stresses. The population can harbor many different alleles, but these will cause no changes in phenotype: because of the Hsp90 assistance they will attain the required "wild-type" conformation anyway.

Owing to the pleiotrophic engagement of Hsp90 protein, its homozygotic mutation is lethal; heterozygotic lineages survive, albeit with high frequency (up to 5%) of malformations in a variety of body structures (limbs, wings, and eyes). Such an effect could be due, first, to the lowered buffering capacity of the chaperone present (note that only one allele is functional), especially in cases when developing embryos experienced some stress. Second, DNA replication and repair might become impaired for the same reason (some of the proteins involved require Hsp90 assistance), which would result in higher mutagenicity. The third possibility would be that some latent genetic variation was revealed because of improper buffering by Hsp90. After many control experiments, Rutherford and Lindquist (1998) opt for the third possibility (in support of such a conclusion, see also Gibson and Hogness, 1996).

The selection for new phenotypes in Hsp90 heterozygotes was even more exciting. It turned out that, after several generations, the phenotypic change became fixed in 80% of individuals. What is more important is that by this time the mutant Hsp90 had disappeared from the population because of outcrossing. As for the presence of Hsp90, the population was normal again; that is, there was no lack of Hsp90 function in individuals despite their new phenotypes. The results suggest that within a few generations of instability the new phenotype became independent of the mutation of the chaperone; that is, the trait became genetically assimilated. What is important here is the finding that no mutation in the direction of the new trait was required: latent morphological variability is present in advance, and a transient lowering of the Hsp90 capacity will enable its appearance. After this occurs, a rapid and effective selection toward new phenotypes is possible.

However, why is there no reversal of phenotypes after the return of the chaperone product to the norm? Genetically, this can be explained by the shift in frequencies of particular alleles during the period of chaperone "anarchy." All the traits studied were polygenic. Suppose that a change in the phenotype, which can no longer be buffered by the chaperone, requires an accumulation of mutations in 70% of the alleles involved. If, say, 65% of variation was already present before the crisis in the latent form, only a small number of mutations must be accumulated during the crisis, thus making the change irreversible. In this way, Hsp90 chaperones function as "capacitors" of morphological evolution: mutant alleles can be slowly accumulated for generations, to become "discharged" in a new phenotype following some environmental crisis.

In terms of the language metaphor, particular utterances produced by the set of proteins are all interpreted by the semantic field of Hsp90, which focuses them into a very narrow area of possible phenotypic "interpretations." In crises, the secondary meanings of utterances will surface. The "discourse" becomes richer after it finally becomes fixed again in a different setup.

Redundancy

As in a spoken language, redundancy is a characteristic feature of the language of proteins. The majority of important developmental processes are often safeguarded by two or more parallel regulatory pathways. If some of these pathways break down (for genetic or epigenetic reasons), the required phenotype can still be attained; that is, there are different ways of "saying the same thing." Even in a relatively small genome, as in yeast, about 30% of genes are "redundant" (Brookfield, 1997a,b; Nasmyth et al., 1991). Similarly, Cooke et al. (1997) reported 22 *null* mutants in *Drosophila* that bore no recognizable phenotypic effects. Of course, such mutations can never affect housekeeping genes, where the effect would be apparent immediately. All of the mutations described, however, affected genes believed to be crucial in development. In mice, for example, a null mutation of tenascin, an extracellular matrix protein believed to be indispensable in embryonic development, also had no apparent phenotype trait (Saga et al., 1992). Redundancy does not simply mean duplication: seemingly redundant pathways may, under normal circumstances, function in different contexts. After the elimination of one of them, however, the rest will rescue the meaning of the original message. Here apparently lies the explanation of why regulatory and developmental pathways are redundant whereas most metabolic pathways are not (Nasmyth et al., 1991). Metabolic enzymes are usually present in a single paralogue, even in vertebrates that, in the course of their evolution, underwent double (hetero)diploidization of their genomes (Bailey et al., 1997). This means that there should theoretically be four paralogues of each gene present in a haploid set.[8] This indeed holds very often for regulatory genes, whereas housekeeping genes become reduced again to a single copy. The explanation may reside in the fact that metabolic enzymes were optimized long ago, and so one

---

8. But not all authors stick to the tetraploidization theory in vertebrates; see, for example, West et al. (1999).

form of the enzyme (in several alleles present in the population) is sufficient for the required task, and redundant copies became eliminated.[9] In contrast to what occurs in ontogeny, compromises between the demands of the genome, individual, population, environment, and so forth, must be negotiated again and again (a hermeneutic task); in such cases the redundancy of regulatory pathways cannot but increase the fitness of an individual.

Evolution of Ontogenies

Some developmental biologists, in the wake of Schmalhausen and Waddington, are pushing for the inclusion of ontogeny as a legitimate part of evolutionary theory. The question is not to rehabilitate, for example, the recapitulation teaching of Ernst Haeckel. However, after a century of independent development of developmental and evolutionary biology, it is high time to coordinate the attitudes, vocabulary, and goals. Raff (1996), for example, emphasizes the question of how new ontogenetic trajectories might arise in ontogeny. Animal phyla have been genetically isolated for at least half a billion years and probably even two or three times as long. A comparative analysis of regulatory systems in ontogeny would therefore be an invaluable source of information for reconstructing evolution. It would not be an easy task because of the great variability in both gene expression and epigenetic processes. As a result, very similar morphologies can appear owing to the plethora of different ontogenetic processes. The goal—specific morphology—remains constant, but the processes leading to it may differ. This holds even for closely related species, including those that provide viable and fertile crosses:

> We are faced with a paradox. Body plans are clearly stable over long evolutionary spans. If they were not, we would not recognize persistent higher taxonomic categories such as phyla and classes. Yet basic elements of body plans are attained by different developmental pathways. They have been extensively modified by additions, and in the evolution of direct developing species, losses and remodeling of larval body plans. Adult body plans have also been remodeled. Since shared body plans can be attained by different pathways, why should they be so stable and channel development through evolutionarily conserved phylotypic stages? (p. 197)

Raff states that, in a phylum, the single stage that cannot be circumvented is that of the phylotype, which represents the essence of the phyletic body plan. He sees the explanation for this in the modularity of development: in stages other than phylotypic, whole modules (regulated strictly and in minute de-

---

9. Nothing can be absolutized in biology: two functional paralogues exist, for example, for the gene coding for lactate dehydrogenase.

tail) can often be left out without any consequence to the viability of an individual, because other modules can "reconstruct" the whole through mutual interaction.

It should be said, however, that even the definition of the phylotypic stage is by no means easy. Richardson et al. (1997) state that it is practically impossible to find a structure that binds together, for example, all vertebrates. Haeckel's well-known and *ad nauseam* reproduced icon showing the identity of early developmental stages is now seen as an inadmissible idealization. Raff himself shows that even the phylotypic stage can be left out in some cases. A good example of this is provided by sea urchins: several pairs of closely related species can be found where one member of the pair develops through the phylotypic larva (pluteus), whereas the second has a direct development from bigger eggs rich in yolk. The progeny of interspecies crosses is viable, with development depending on which species is the donor of the egg. What is even more surprising is that if the surplus yolk is removed from large eggs before fertilization, a new kind of development is observed, producing a larva resembling dipleurula—a hypothetical larval stage of early (now extinct) deuterostomes (Raff et al., 1999). Similar results with direct and indirect development were obtained in ascidia (Jeffery, 1994; Satoh and Jeffery, 1995) and in frogs (Hanken et al., 1997).

"Cambrian Explosion"

The Cambrian fossil record is distinguished by a short time window (10 million years) during which multicellular animals appeared, in all known body plans, extant or extinct (Gould, 1989; Conway Morris, 1993). In Precambrian layers, multicellular animals can be found only sporadically (though burrows and fecal pellets often occur), and their systematic position is not clear.

The interpretation of the fossil record offered by gradualists is based on the notion that the whole explosion is only illusive. Precambrian animals may have been very small (in the order of millimeters) and without shells or skeletons, and so left no fossils. The explosion may simply indicate the appearance of predators followed by the development of hard skeletons in all groups, hence the enrichment of the record. Global climatic changes could also have occurred, enabling massive adaptive radiation into new biotopes. The numbers of animals increased greatly, and so did their fossilized remnants. The gradualist explanation is also supported by comparative analysis of DNA in extant phyla: the reconstruction of phylogenetic trees placed the time of the divergence of protostomes and deuterostomes at least 1200 million years before the present (e.g., Wray et al., 1996). Cladistic analyses also provide support for this interpretation.

A speculative explanation of the explosion is offered by Davidson et al. (1995), who suppose that animal forms are rooted in microscopic organisms similar to contemporary primary larvae present in particular groups. They call attention to the fact that the metamorphosis of a larva into an adult starts from so-called "set-aside cells," which have nothing in common with larval structure and can be distinguished as an amorphous conglomerate of cells. The scenario supposes that these surplus cells appeared in the Precambrian period and gave rise to the entire kaleidoscope of bizarre morphologies that can be found in the record. Such wild experiments, however, did not endanger the survival of the lineage, because reproduction was still secured by the microscopic stages and had been accomplished *before* the individual started "experimenting." Only later did some successful forms take over the reproduction, accompanied by the stabilization of their form in much narrower reaction norm limits, thereby establishing the extant phyla. Metagenesis (alternation of sexual and asexual generations), as present in extant plants and many animal phyla, may serve as inspiration for the reconstruction of such early events of evolution.

Some authors, however, maintain that the explosion in the fossil records depicts the real state of events in the evolution of animals (e.g., Erwin 1999; Valentine et al., 1999; Conway Morris, 1997). They place the common ancestor of protostomes and deuterostomes to 670 million years ago (and even reinterpret the above-mentioned calculations of Wray et al. [1996] in this light). According to these views, the "point" of emergence of bilateralians is 570 million years ago, and deuterostomes appeared only 544 million years before now.

Developmental Psychobiology

Developmental psychobiology may have a valuable contribution to make. Psychomotor ontogeny can be interpreted from two angles. One is that genetic and inherited elementary reflexes are being sought to explain the development of structure; the second sees the process as an unceasing interaction between the developing fetus (or newborn), its environment, and its genetic thesaurus. In the latter case, the result is a product of hermeneutic work (see, e.g., Michel and Moore, 1995). If this view prevails in the future, it will provide an excellent support for the species-as-culture thesis.

This list of examples of species as culture is obviously incomplete, and items mentioned are treated only briefly. The whole area will undoubtedly see great development in the near future.

14

ONTOGENY OF THE
PLANETARY ORGANISM

Messieurs, it is microbes who will have the last word!
Louis Pasteur

Gene flux between bacterial replicons and their hosts is likely
to be the rule rather than the exception and appears to
respond quickly to environmental changes.
Julian Davies

From the very beginning, life partakes *directly* in the *history* of our planet. As
"interpretation machines" living beings process and filter formidable amounts
of information coming both from their environment and from endogenous
resources. In the course of this interpretation, they activate a wide range of
mechanical subroutines, and they project their own future, form their own
ontogeny. Ontogeny is a development of a living being in time and is dependent on the interpretation of spatial and temporal cues. These come as genetic
and/or epigenetic memory, as the history of the lineage, and as individual experience. I consider ontogeny a key factor of life: if an entity such as the planetary superorganism exists, we should prove that it is capable of ontogeny
(see also Markoš, 1995, 1999).

Is Gaia an Organism?

The starting point of my analysis is multicellular organisms. The existence of
multicellular bodies requires three types of structuring agents:

205

1. A shared gene pool: multicellular organisms share essentially the same genomes, and often (in clonal organisms) also identical, or nearly identical, genotypes.
2. The body's communication systems: a plethora of optical, electrical, and diffusible signals (morphogens, growth factors, etc.) constitute the means of communication and signaling between the cells in the body. The quality, intensity, time course, or gradient of the signal can constitute the message.
3. The body: this is a dynamical spatiotemporal network built by cells and an extracellular matrix (ECM). The network of the ECM is a collective product of the cells that are present. It consists of many types of very complicated organic molecules, and often also minerals. The network provides the cells with crucial information about their situation (position) in the space and time of the organism.

These three types of agent may not be sufficient preconditions for ontogeny (e.g., energy metabolism must also function), but in any case they should be considered as necessary. Moreover, the ontogeny of a planetary organism would be unparalleled not only in its size, but also because it would become identical to its evolution.

The dynamics of the planetary biome has been determined mainly by the behavior of prokaryotes—bacteria and archaea. If this is the case, then the properties discussed above should be distinguishable in systems ("bodies") constituted by prokaryotes. These had appeared on the planet relatively soon after its formation, and they have inhabited and molded it ever since. Eukaryotic organisms are latecomers and themselves are products of prokaryotic symbioses (or mergers).[1] Could Gaia's body, if it exists, be constituted by the prokaryotic world?

The Gene Pool as a Shared Record

The cooperation of cells in a multicellular body (in frames of the neo-Darwinian paradigm; see, e.g., Dawkins, 1982) is explained as a consequence of a shared genotype: cooperation will increase the chance of transferring the genes to the next generation. Behavior, morphology, and ontogeny appear as epiphenomena of the existence of replicators manipulating their own transfer into the next generation. The genome may bear a capacity (i.e., genetic programs) to code for many different phenotypes, and the environment is a trigger to select among these subroutines. Ecosystems are usually taken as a result of interactions between selfish, genetically isolated individuals that enforce their fitness in their biotopes.

---

1. See, for example, Cavalier-Smith (1997), Margulis (1996), and Margulis et al. (1996).

Such a dual view breaks down in prokaryotes, which are not individuals in the above sense. It is well documented that in the prokaryotic world, the intercellular flux of genetic material is very effective. Prokaryotes can absorb, disseminate, and exchange strings of DNA, while not necessarily being limited by the taxonomic status of the donor and acceptor of the genetic material (Amábile-Cuevas and Chicurel, 1992; Salyers and Shoemaker, 1996). Theoretically, any bacterium on the planet has access to any gene present in the biosphere. Thus, a single global "genome" is shared by all prokaryotes. In addition, individual cells are able to manipulate the content of their own share of the genome by rearrangement, changing the frequency of mutation, and possibly even by directed mutations.

Gene Transfer Superhighway

This expression by Salyers and Shoemaker (1996) points to the fact that gene transfers between cells can be accomplished quite easily: by conjugation, as virus transfection or as the mobilization of plasmids, transposons, and integrons. The mobile transposons may themselves—like a kind of Russian doll—be host to a very fluid system of cassettes of insertion sequences coding for a plethora of phenotypic effects (figure 14.1a,b).[2] Gene transfer mechanisms are best understood in cases of antibiotic resistance, but the phenomenon is only the tip of an iceberg in the system of genetic communication among prokaryotes: "Surprisingly, many of the resistant organisms have very effective plasmid-borne mutator genes. The plasmids seem to have been constructed with the functions necessary to help in the evolution of the resistance gene, for example, to edit for its functional expression in a heterologous host" (Davies, 1997, p. 28). Absorption of (often hypermutated) "naked" DNA directly from the environment is also very common, especially in slowly growing or quiescent prokaryotes. Stationary cells can even kill their still-growing neighbors and extract their DNA.[3] A high intensity of horizontal transfers can also be inferred from the high mosaicism of evolutionary trees, as revealed both at the level of large sectors of genomes and that of individual genes or their parts (e.g., respiratory enzymes).[4]

Thanks to gene transfer, the genealogy of prokaryotes is a mosaic rather than a "tree" with branches of diverging clones. The two systems of variation

---

2. See, for example, Sonea and Panisset (1983), Amábile-Cuevas and Chicurel (1992), Salyers and Shoemaker (1996), Hall et al. (1996), Lenski (1998), Tschäpe (1994), Lan and Reeves (1996), and Matic et al. (1995).

3. See, for example, Lewis and Gattie (1991), Costerton et al. (1994, 1995), Dreiseikelmann (1994), Lorenz and Wackernagel (1994), and Higgins (1992).

4. See, for example, Amábile-Cuevas (1996), Arber (1995), Arber et al. (1994), Maynard Smith et al. (1991, 1993), Maynard Smith (1992), Sikorski et al. (1990), and Burger et al. (1996).

a

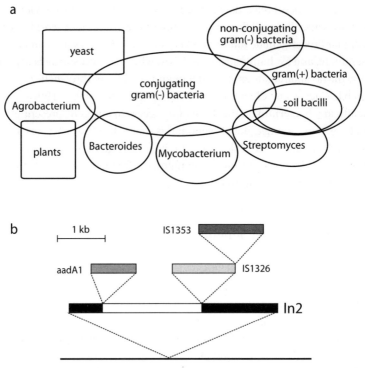

b

Figure 14.1. Horizontal transfer of genetic information. (*a*) Cases of proven flow of plasmids between different groups of organisms. Adapted from Amábile-Cuevas and Chicurel (1992). (*b*) Transfer in the form of gene cassettes. The *lower thick line* is the transposon DNA ensuring insertions or removal of the entire cassette into and from the host genome. The transposon bears an integron labeled *In2*, which in its turn has other inserts. The transposon, a mobile unit itself, can be inserted into a phage genome and propagate as part of that phage genome. "Pathogenicity islands" present an even more sophisticated version of such a "genetic Russian doll," as the entire set can be from 30 to several hundred kilobases long. Adapted from Hall et al. (1996) and Hacker et al. (1997).

generators—DNA exchange and induced mutations—may work hand in hand. Mutagenesis induced in a dying cell may solve the survival problems of a neighbor, who will ingest the mutated string.

One very powerful means of transferring a whole set of genes—tools necessary for survival in some environments—are cassettes of transposons and integrons, which can efficiently pass on the genes necessary, for example, for antibiotic resistance or a certain type of infection in the host. In the second case, these elements are termed "pathogenicity islands" (figure 14.1): they can transform a benign commensal bacterium (*Escherichia, Vibrio*) into a dangerous pathogen.[5]

5. See, for example, Slauch et al. (1997), Hacker et al. (1997), Ochman and Groisman (1995), Stephens and Shapiro (1996), Groisman and Ochman (1996), Mel and Mekalanos (1996), and Suarez and Russmann (1999).

Manipulating the Sequences of Strings

Interspecies gene transfers, however, are not purely accidental. Their frequency apparently depends on the activity of two control systems. The first is the system of mismatch repair, which hinders recombination with nonhomologous DNA. Its counterpart is the so-called SOS system, enabling increased mutagenesis in cases of emergency. During nonproblematic growth, the first system prevails and the gene transfer is practically nil; in crises the second may take over (Matic et al., 1995).

In adaptive evolution, a very important function is played by a group of mutator genes whose production may raise the frequency of mutations by two to three orders. In this way, a large asexual population can increase its rate of adaptation in a new environment, with a mutator gene frequency as low as 10^{-5} (Taddei et al., 1997). In freshly taken prokaryotic isolates, up to 1% of cells carry the mutator gene (Matic et al., 1995, 1997). It has therefore been assumed that a temporary increase in the frequency of mutator genes takes place whenever the population encounters an environmental challenge.

So-called induced (or Cairnsian) mutations[6] also deserve attention, as they suggest the possibility of goal-oriented adaptive modifications of DNA. Whereas the systems of mutagenesis discussed above are random, these are aimed at a particular section of DNA whose mutational reconstruction may bring relief for the cell in a given precarious situation. If the scenario is to appear true, the bacterium should be able to choose and adjust, from the internal or external supply of DNA, a string that would be relevant to solving a momentary problem.

The two systems of creating variability—DNA exchange and induced mutagenesis—should not, however, be considered separately. Extensive mutagenesis in dying cells, followed by dissemination of DNA after their death, can represent a solution for living recipients of such DNA.

Thus, the prokaryotic biosphere has various means of sharing a common thesaurus of the gene pool and creating new entries to it. The question remains as to whether opportunities to perform gene exchange are sufficiently frequent to play the supposed role of a unifying agent. The answer seems to be yes. First, cells of different species can exchange parts of their genetic thesaurus. Second, the environment presents a plentiful reservoir of DNA. Free DNA tends to become adsorbed and concentrated on the surface of water-dispersed particles, and cells have tools that can "graze" it therefrom (Lewis and Gattie, 1991; Gallori et al., 1994; Paget and Simonet, 1994; Hermansson and Linberg, 1994).

---

6. See, for example, Foster and Cairns (1992), Hall (1990), Cairns et al. (1988), Symonds (1994), Sniegowski (1995), and various contributions in Amábile-Cuevas (1996).

The possibility of DNA transfer by viral particles should not be neglected, either. In oceans, for example, their titers may be as high as 10^6–10^{10} per mL (Sikorski et al., 1990; Davies, 1994; Cochlan et al., 1993; Fuhrman, 1999). Nothing is known about their hosts (apparently all organisms present at the spot), their role in the control of the populations of hosts, or their turnover. It is estimated, however, that 2–5% of the prokaryotes present in the pelagic marine system will undergo, during their lifetime, the incorporation of foreign DNA (Frischer et al., 1994; Goodman et al., 1994; Hermansson and Linberg, 1994). To sum up: "Gene flux between bacterial replicons and their hosts is likely to be the rule rather than the exception and appears to respond quickly to environmental changes. . . . [T]he appearance of the resistance genes is a recent event—that is, the multiresistance plasmids found in pathogens must have been created in the past five decades" (Davies, 1994, p. 378). "We are incapable of defining any environment in microbial terms. . . . We know nothing of the gene traffic in natural environments such as soil and the gastrointestinal tract, which comprise mixtures of a large number of bacterial genera and species" (p. 380).

Diffusible Signals

As in the case of cells in a multicellular body, prokaryotes communicate by means of signals released into the environment and effective over a variety of distances and lengths of time. Signaling systems serve to control the population density, or the accessibility and quality of resources.[7] Consortia, complicated space and time structures resembling "ecosystems" or even "tissues," and including many prokaryotic species, are fascinating examples of elaborate methods of communication in prokaryotes (see, e.g., articles in Guerrero and Pedrós-Alio, 1993). However, all examples studied so far concern short-range signals in situations that can be easily analyzed. We can only guess whether such signaling also exists on the "Gaian" scale. It is, however, known that the prokaryotic products described in the above-mentioned cases are common constituents of various environments—soils, waters, atmosphere, and aerosols.

The spectrum of signaling compounds synthesized by prokaryotes varies from cyclic nucleotides, through derivatives of homoserine lacton, phenolics and antibiotics, to oligopeptides and proteins.[8] Of course, similar communication by diffusible signals has also been described in eukaryotes, especially

---

7. See, for example, Shapiro (1995), Shapiro and Dworkin (1997), Kaiser and Losick (1993), Russo et al. (1992), and Beppu (1992).

8. Kaiser and Losick (1993), Huisman and Kolter (1994), Demaster (1999), Maplestone et al. (1992), and Davies (1994).

fungi (Beppu, 1992), and plants; in biotopes shared with prokaryotes (e.g., soils), the communication proceeds indeed across all phyla.

The synthesis of some "secondary metabolites" (as they are called) often requires a pathway of 10–30 steps — in other words, a considerable expenditure of enzymes and energy (Maplestone et al., 1992). It is not always apparent what function such compounds have to justify such a use of cellular resources. Moreover, all the necessary genes are often colocalized in a single locus in the genome, suggesting an easy way of mobilization and transfer. Great heterogeneity and often very low concentrations and short lifetimes of signals have so far prevented more systematic study, and the cases described so far are more or less anecdotal.

Antibiotics in very low concentrations (much lower than would be toxic for bacteria) might, according to some authors (e.g., Davies, 1994, 1997), represent a class of pheromones. In organisms with a resistance to the antibiotic in question, they would mobilize a rapid horizontal spread of a plasmid bearing the resistance (with the frequency of transmission increasing hundreds of times). The resistance can also be evoked by quorum-sensing signals (Kaiser and Losick, 1993; Swift et al., 1996; Amábile-Cuevas and Cardenas-Garcia, 1996) or, as described in human enteric prokaryotes, by such seemingly nonspecific and inadequate cues as, for example, traces of mercury (coming from tooth amalgams) or disinfectants (Salyers and Shoemaker, 1996; Amábile-Cuevas and Cardenas-Garcia, 1996). Such resistance is "physiological" and, as Lenski (1998) notes, does no harm to its bearers (compared to experimental situations where resistance is induced in "naive" strains that have never experienced a given antibiotic and are therefore forced to "improvise" to a great extent).

If global signals really exist to influence the behavior of prokaryotic ecosystems, then the question of the medium ensuring the coherence of the Gaian "body" will become important. It is, of course, the atmosphere that is able to dissipate a signal round the globe within days. Marine currents work with greater delay, but, as Amon and Benner (1994) have noted, oceans contain a bewildering heterogeneity of organic compounds with a high turnover that may also play other roles than simply that of banal nutrients. It is regrettable that in contemporary nutrient- and pollutant-oriented environmental research, only marginal attention is devoted to the enormous heterogeneity and turnover of organic matter in the environment, and to the possible role of these compounds in prokaryotic communication.

The Body: Cells and the Extracellular Matrix

The study of the organization of the assumed "body" of the planetary superorganism is again hampered by scarce information. Prokaryotes constitute the greatest part of the planetary biomass, but there is little available information about its structure and dynamics. As many as 99% of prokaryotes resist cultivation in the laboratory (Davies, 1998), and our knowledge of the quality, quantitative representation, physiology, life strategies, and cooperation of cells in various consortia ("tissues") is far from complete. The biodiversity of communities is estimated from the diversity of DNA extracted from environmental samples, by which criterion it is very high. Otherwise, only macroscopic phenomena, such as the "metabolism" or "morphogenesis" of sediments, soils, coatings, and so forth, are available for direct observation. There is a prevailing consensus that the complexity of prokaryotic colonies and consortia (in soil, sediments, biofilms, colonies, floating particles, alimentary tracts, rhizosphere, etc.) is comparable to that of tissue in eukaryotic multicellular organisms.[9]

If our knowledge of cells and the structures built by the cells in the "tissues" is limited, even less is known about the second component—the extracellular matrix. As in "true" multicellular organisms, this is built from organic macromolecules (cell walls, exudates, foams, coatings, depositions), biominerals, and sedimentary rocks.[10] In the case of a planetary superorganism, the lithosphere, hydrosphere, and atmosphere, to a great extent products of living cells, also fulfill the definition of ECM. Humus and kerogen in the rocks may also act as an information storage medium. Such epigenetic information from the past may be available for recent prokaryotes and control their behavior. First, of course, it must be proved that microorganisms are able to recognize such information and behave accordingly. So far, positive answers have only been gained from short-term laboratory experiments with organic ECM secreted by the extant prokaryotic population (Behmlander and Dworkin, 1994a,b; Dalton et al., 1994). As far as I know, however, only Krumbein (1996) speaks about the ECM of the planetary organism.

Ecosystems and Gaia

Current views assign only one type of memory to ecosystems, that of DNA replicators; epigenetic information tends to be underestimated or ignored. Ecology, then, is understood as a science of the flows of matter and energy in a community, ecosystem, or planet, or as a science of dynamics and biodiver-

---

9. For illustration, in 1 g of soil, there are 10^6 to 10^8 bacterial cells, 10^6 to 10^7 actinomycetes, 10^5 to 10^6 protists, 10^4 to 10^6 fungi, and about 10^4 algae. The consortia are relatively stable, and it is not easy for a new species to gain a foothold (Maplestone et al., 1992; Wostemeyer et al., 1997; Costerton et al., 1994, 1995; Guerrero and Pedrós-Alio, 1993; Shapiro and Dworkin, 1997; Sonea and Panisset, 1983).

10. See, for example, Dalton et al. (1994), Costerton et al. (1994, 1995), Gold (1999), Behmlander and Dworkin (1994a,b), and contributions to Guerrero and Pedrós-Alio (1993).

sity of communities, as catalyzers of such flows.[11] This is why Gaia, as presented by Lovelock, emerges as an "organism" described in terms of energy balances, and her homeostasis is a question of thermodynamic equilibria. This is why Daisyworld does not need to remember its previous states, and the existence of genes determining colors is sufficient for the automatic maintenance of its thermostability. I tried to show in chapter 10 that for a planet to be a genuine superorganism, such a definition is highly unsatisfactory, even if the question of the daisies' origin is put aside. In chapter 12 I mentioned the development in the realm of cell biology, starting from simple equilibria and metabolic cycles to a deeper understanding of the structural dynamics of the cell. Ecology and geophysiology are, I believe, at the start of a similar path, especially concerning prokaryotic communities. Further research should lead to testable hypotheses of a global community conceived as a dynamic, highly structured, mutually interconnected network of signaling molecules, genes, and structures, maintaining the knowledge of a single totality. It is also a challenge for conservation biology. Until now, the focus has been on pollution by nutrients and metabolic poisons that endanger biodiversity. In the background, however, trace amounts of signal molecules and their analogs may be in circulation, threatening to disrupt the integrity of the communities by interfering with the syntax and semantics of signals. The overuse of antibiotics may be an example. For these purely practical reasons, it is highly desirable to develop a theory of information processing in Gaia's body.

Ontogeny-That-Is-Phylogeny

If the planetary superorganism is a real entity—a body—then how can we explain its evolution, which would have no parallel on other time scales and is identical to both ontogeny and phylogeny? When speaking of ontogeny in multicellular organisms, we accept that cells have active access to their genetic thesaurus, choosing and interpreting the genetic message in continuous confrontation with their internal space–time and with the external environment. In my opinion, such constant interpretation, a hermeneutic circle from structure to genes and back, is the cornerstone of ontogenetic processes. The medium for this process of "extracting the meaning" may be nucleic acids, concentration gradients, a dynamic network of macromolecules (cytoskeleton, nucleoskeleton, ECM), and structures of a higher order and longer lifetime. This "ontogenetic field"—the essence of the whole evolutionary experience—will decide and lay out the ontogenetic trajectory. In this sense, the whole process is teleological: the future is outlined in the present.

---

11. It should be recalled, however, that this view will usually encompass only multicellular eukaryotes.

In the case of the planetary superorganism, I have suggested (Markoš, 1995, 1999) the notion of ontogeny-that-is-phylogeny. At this highest (planetary) and at the same time lowest (prokaryotic) level of space and time scales, the distinction between the two processes disappears. They are complementary faces of evolution as a self-structuration, based on the memory and experience of the past that can be molded, reshaped, reinterpreted, ignored, overwritten, and deleted. Seen in this light, Lovelock's Gaia is a necessary precondition for a true planetary superorganism to live and evolve. At this level of description, the entire global community of organisms can be seen as a coherent, dynamic, highly structured, interconnected network of signaling molecules, genes, and structures. The absence of reproduction and variable offspring becomes irrelevant.

The common denominator of both processes may be history, which is, by definition, contingent and nonteleological. Yet beings with history remember past experience. They continuously reshape and reinterpret this memory; they exaggerate, recall, forget, and so on, and as a result of this work of interpretation they *decide* and project their future. A contingency modulated by past experience gives, *ex post*, an impression of a controlled teleological process. We easily accept the notion of history as an evolutionary process. Ontogeny, however, is not simply a blind execution of a program. It is a process shaped by the past experience of the species, an outcome of the interpretation of the world by members of the species, an interpretation that is valid here and now. In this view, there is some element of teleology even in evolution, and the development of Gaia could then be understood *also* as ontogeny on a different time scale. It is known that a prokaryotic population recognizes the danger of a coming limitation long before the actual limitation takes place and takes corresponding measures to confront the challenge. For example, Gaia might, on the basis of past experience, be able to sense an approaching glacial period at a time when no parameter of the planet would suggest such a development. Similarly, a directed ability to heal the consequences of common catastrophes may become apparent. Her organism might, on the other hand, be upset by uncommon situations, such as a rise in the concentration of CO_2 in a situation when other cues suggest the approach of a glacial period, or the extinction of rainforests in a regime that should maintain them and that may even require their presence. Bananas eaten in temperate climate mean the composition of humus modified by banana skins. Might this be a signal of climate warming for local bacteria? Maybe we could find less absurd examples if we looked for them.

Thus, producing variable progeny may not be the essential condition for defining an organism. Gaia can rightly be considered an organism because it has a history, which is its ontogeny. It has a genidentity, or, if you wish, it is a Ruyerian tree of life, connecting all living beings on the planet into a single coherent entity.

EPILOGUE

We bitterly realize the relativity of our judgments, and in
spite of this we must be able to decide exactly and
unequivocally what science is and what it is not. The only
objective and relatively exact criterion to do so is the quality
of our method, of the art of working with the sources. . . .
We, however, refuse to stick to such a criterion when we are
after science as we would like it to be and as we try to
cultivate it when working through nights. That is, not science
whose cart we push and pull in our daily toil. We know
without any doubt that to stick to craftsmanship means to
produce books which will be formally correct, but hopelessly
meaningless, provincial, without any appeal to anybody.
Regretfully we express such ideas from time to time. Of
course, our peers take them as a provocation, uninvited
disturbance. As an arrogant negation of accustomed and,
above all, tacitly agreed rules. It would be enough for them
to simply ignore such disturbances, but somehow it does not
work. For the infallible factographers, the "postmodernist"
function as a red rag to a bull, as guilty conscience. But
that is not our problem but theirs.

Dušan Třeštík

I am deeply convinced that a single, objective and noncontradictory view of
the world is impossible, and that for this reason we cannot limit ourselves to a
single preferred image of the world. By "we" I mean all cognizant beings—
not only humans with their culture and history, but all living beings. We all

learn, on short time scales, to breathe in this world, into which we were thrown as the smallest branches of the tree of life, which has lasted for four billion years. Our "thrownness" is based on the fact that our predecessors left at our disposal a digital text—the inscription of experience—that is to be confronted with the world *we* belong to. They also left behind their experience, embodied as our nature, our bodies—or rather, the knowledge of how to build them. The environment, the frame for our thoughts and behavior, ideas about what is adequate (equity, *epieikeia*, decorum), belong to another class of legacy. Because of these two kinds of tradition, we feel at home in our world. But "being at home" is not an obvious and automatic state—it requires a high degree of hermeneutic effort. The common world in which we all participate often requires a radical change in our system of values. Nothing is "made" forever, "so that": cultures that relied on the constancy of the world collapsed in the first breeze that came from an unexpected direction. The same holds for species, which in this book I have compared to cultures. We do not live in a gradualist world lasting for millions of years, which has brought about a perfection of forms and physiology, tending toward perfect harmony! The game is still going on here and now, with all the equipment at hand. Species—cultures that cannot revalue their being according to the demand of time—must yield to other, more flexible outlines. The past and the future serve as prompts. The sociobiologists (sorry: evolutionary ethologists) are right in that we carry with us all sorts of ballast that—*once, and in certain contexts*—appeared to be useful. But the Golden Age with a constant environment never existed—in the past, as now, hypotheses about the world were in mutual conflict, and to be able to decide between them was, and is, a hermeneutic task (or art). We carry past layouts, and in the context of the present instant we reappraise, modify, recall or forget, pick up or throw them away, sometimes with fatal consequences, sometimes with an aspiration to reach the stars.

The hermeneutic endeavor is very demanding of intellect, time, and resources. We willingly abandon it whenever we can rely on automatism. It is not worth wasting time and resources on the banalities of everyday life.

Some chapters of this book (especially part II) focus on certain selected world layouts. I include those chapters as illustrations, reminders that there may be many different projections of the world besides the "best" one that is acknowledged today. They also help me to highlight my own view of life as a hermeneutic category. Most of the schemes presented in those chapters insist on the *scientific* character of the particular ideas. Even if they do not say so explicitly, we can always feel in the background: We all agree in what is represented by natural science, scientific theory, inductive method, testing. The problem is that our learned (or less learned) opponents neglect (unwillingly, for lack of data, or because of sheer naiveté) these or those aspects and their view is therefore distorted. The distortion has become even more profound, because they have allowed their thoughts to become inundated with some (metaphysical, pseudo-scientific, mythical) aspects of that area of knowledge that do not represent any knowledge at all. They have been ruminating over the same truths for more than two thousand years! But, eureka, we finally arrived at the correct, truly scientific knowledge.

In the course of the book I also show that views of the subject of biology itself have changed many times. I have tried to demonstrate that, in its quest to become an exact science, biology has, willingly or unwillingly, developed methods that are excellently suited for the study of machinelike, repetitive, foreseeable behavior suppressing uniqueness. Its focus lies in the realm of automatisms.

Not only our equipment, but also the organisms studied are constructs (lines, clones, transgenes) prepared in such a way as to minimize variability and self-reference, that is, constructed as machines. This approach is, of course, fully legitimate, especially in areas where living beings themselves have delegated some of their expressions to the realm of algorithm-controlled mechanisms (e.g., basic biochemical and physiological reactions, instincts). It is only the extrapolation of such models to the whole realm of life that lacks legitimacy.

Anyone who has read up to this point may well comment: "Well, the author has offered me a volume containing a mix of well-known data and curiosities, and he demands that I change my view of living beings, which would one day change biology itself. If we biologists accept the opinion that living beings are hermeneutic in nature, we must break the confines of objectivist science and seek a broader perspective. But what direction should we take?"

Some of the older conceptions I have illustrated here could possibly provide some inspiration, but they can hardly satisfy our needs. We must accept that living beings *cannot* be totally reduced to a set of simple and understandable principles, however persuasive neo-Darwinism, structuralism, or the theory of biological field (Gurwitsch) may look. On the other hand, we cannot be content with biology as an ever-growing list of particularities endlessly compiled into newer and newer volumes. I suggest we let ourselves be inspired by hermeneutics, which should bring our search to a single "principle": everything is being enacted, negotiated here and now, again and again. Cell differentiation, ontogeny, the "collapse" of the phenotype from the field bearing potentialities of the reaction norm, the ecology of proteins, cells, or organisms: all this is a never-ending process of seeking and employing possibilities, potentialities, past experience and projects, and layouts of the future at which the struggle is aimed. On what, then, should we focus our attention?

(1) There is an urgent need to explain the role—and advantage—of redundancies, genetic or epigenetic. Is it a move to lessen the genetic or epigenetic load (Nasmyth et al., 1991, Brookfield, 1997a,b) or a means of effecting

flexible, context-imposed shifts within the reaction norm? So far, we have only isolated data, but there has been at least one effort to build a concise database (Kanehisa, 2000) encompassing sequences of genes, proteins and their place in metabolism, and the metabolites involved. It is possible to know whether a given species has the gene for a particular protein, and in what context it would be expressed. Apparently, it is only question of time as the database grows quantitatively (including new and new species) and qualitatively—by encompassing much more complicated networks of regulatory proteins and signaling molecules. This would enable us to search for regularities in cellular "utterances" and/or to foresee them. And maybe one day such a database will correlate its data with the morphology of organisms. All such activities will move our focus from "address book entries" (i.e., gene sequences) to the structures and meanings of genetic statements. I would predict that such a development will bring about a substantial deviation from the genocentric view of life in force today, with replicators that have no properties other than mere occurrence (onticity).

(2) The comparison of phenotypes built on identical or only slightly differing genomes could be very inspiring. It is commonly accepted that identical genomes can give rise to different phenotypes, for example, in cases of seasonal polypheny in insects (two different-looking generations each year), in the hormonal determination of sex, in neotenic and "fully developed" salamanders, and in parasites within different hosts. Such forms will undoubtedly differ in gene expression: according to accepted views, they will differ primarily in the set of proteins expressed and secondarily in morphology. But are such views corroborated? Do the proteomes in the cells of corresponding tissues differ in genetically identical but phenotypically different individuals? (The proteome is the set of all proteins present *at a given time* in the cell.) And if the answer is yes, which ones: all, some, or only those in embryonic cells? Certainly, in the instance of the decision making we may be able to detect a particular regulatory protein with a characteristically ephemeral period of appearance. But how does this regulation correspond with the morphology observed?

If we compare two digits on an appendage, they will differ in the homeogenes expressed and, of course, in their morphology. Can we, however, differentiate between the cells on the two digits by criteria other than homeotic gene expression? Will there be a difference in the expression of other genes? Or will there be no difference in gene expression, but plenty of differences at the post-transcriptional or post-translational levels, or in quantitative representations of different proteins (e.g., because different half-lives have been set), and will all this *somehow* cause a different morphology? All these represent epigenetic regulations; it may still be that the regulatory trigger (external or internal) present at the beginning would confer a cue as to how to start with assembling origami. A cue addressed to *what*? To a mechanism that will react in a particular and predestined way when the button is pushed, or to a structure that *understands* what has been demanded? If there is almost no difference in gene expression, and despite this we find different morphologies, we should suppose a change in the dynamics of genes (e.g., the spatial structure of protein networks). An analysis of proteomes in selected cells and in short consecutive intervals may provide an answer. But at an adequate level of description, such a question may not be solvable.

(3) One very difficult part of genetics deserves extra attention—the research into suppressor mutations. They are hard to investigate, and results are by no means unequivocal. One of the interpretations of suppressor mutation is a notion that the organism uses whatever is at hand to evade difficulties. A less traditional, but truly hermeneutic interpretation would be that "an organism can arrange whatever it needs." Such a starting point would lead directly to accepting genetic assimilation.

(4) New insights could be gained from the comparative analysis of cognate species differing in morphology or life style, for example, of one species with larval development and another with direct development, with and without metagenesis, or a parasite and a cognate free-living species. The well-known parallel between humans and bonobos also comes to mind. Universal genetic regulatory networks are a good prototype to start with: what is the link between the universal homeotic code and the endless choice of morphologies?

(5) Excellent material for study is offered by natural "speciation laboratories." This is the case of differentiation of fish in isolated waters—of cichlids in East African lakes (Johnson et al., 1996; Parker and Kornfield, 1997; Stiassny and Meyer, 1999) and sticklebacks in Canadian lakes (e.g., Braithwaite and Odling-Smee, 1999). The diversification of cichlids apparently started from a single pair of fish, and after several thousands of years it ended in tens of species. A thorough comparison of genomes should reveal whether the speciation event is based in mutation or alteration of the genome, or whether the whole event is epigenetic.

(6) Another hotspot of research may be the study of chimeras of multicellular organisms, which has a long tradition in plant research. Recently, it has become possible to prepare animal chimeras, even interspecific ones: such models can form the basis for experimental hermeneutics. Embryonic stem cells, which can be easily cultivated in a cell culture, offer an even simpler model. If transferred into an adult organism, they cause carcinomas, but when inserted into an early embryo they are able to understand the context in which they find themselves and participate organically in building the body. Only special labels can reveal the fact that the resulting organism is a chimera. Even ordinary cell cultures present an interesting challenge—do they belong to the reaction norm of the species? Many of them underwent genetic assimilation and are no longer able to build the original organism. In given conditions, they are, however, fully viable. A new species? Experiments

with the transplantation of nuclei or pronuclei into enucleated oocytes fall into the same category.

(7) Epigenetic inheritance free of the remains of misunderstandings and Lamarckist or anti-Lamarckist rhetoric should become a major theme for the coming century.

(8) Evolutionary biology, I believe, will soon move into an area that it has tried to avoid so far: the analysis of trends and the extrapolation of such trends into the future, that is, the generation of forecasts.

(9) Finally, both branches of prokaryotic organisms should become an equal part of the landscape—not only as kind of appendix to eukaryotes. In chapter 14 I developed a vision of a planetary organism whose body is constituted of prokaryotes. It is not a question of arguing for or against this vision: I wish only to call attention to the little-acknowledged possibility of a horizontal transfer of genetic information on the scale of the whole planet. It is not only genetic information that plays a role here—I have tried to show that the whole planetary body might possess a well-developed system of communication and of control of its own ontogeny. If we understand Gaia from this angle, we will become less interested in the circulation of nutrients and energy, however important they may be, and start looking for signals that until now we have not been able to distinguish from the background. We will pay attention not only to potential carcinogens in the environment, but also to compounds that appear harmless from our anthropocentric point of view but that may be able to disrupt the information processing of the Gaian prokaryotic body. Through such an understanding, a new ecology should emerge that knows many more ways of cooperation among organisms than short-term *tit for tat*: ecology based on identification and reflecting the context and reacting according to experience and tradition. The first step toward understanding such huge systems is, of course, the study of prokaryotic communities.

(10) Is it possible to draw inferences for a phenotype from a known genotype? The answer is yes only for banal traits such as albinism or the fragile X syndrome. The question of why this, and not another genome (or its genotype versions), allows these species-specific phenotypes, and not others, remains unanswered. It would be worth trying to assign phenotypes to a known genotype and to predict genomic characteristics from the phenotype. If such predictions seem to be impossible, this will be a strong argument for taking into account the history and tradition, the hermeneutic experience of a given line of organisms, an experience transmitted as a *pattern* (or, if you want, *eidos*). As with the gene, a pattern is also bound to a material medium, but is not identical to it. In the case of the gene, the accusation that science is studying something immaterial can be avoided in two ways: the gene was declared to be either a string of nucleotides (i.e., a material body) or a piece of information. For information, as a mathematical concept, immaterial existence can

be tolerated. We then pretend that there is no dualism of principle versus embodiment. *Pattern* (semblance, *eidos,* entelechy) is not in common use and therefore arouses more irritation than does the gene. It may be that this second, nongenetic biological principle would be allowed to enter biology through memes. Hermeneutics could become a method of studying it, based on certain experimental models, as listed above.

But what kind of creature is hidden under the notion of "hermeneutic biologists"? What do their working hours look like? Well, you will not recognize them by their doings—they are busy performing standard biology like anyone else. Maybe in the introductions and discussions of their papers you will recognize slightly different accents and suggestions (see, e.g., the slight wording modifications illustrated in the introduction to part III) opening new realms within the framework of the current paradigm—no revolutionary zealots changing current paradigms! They know that plurality of view is the most precious gem in the quest for wisdom.

I strongly believe that an organism cannot be defined solely in terms of thermodynamic, biochemical, and information magnitudes. If we want to understand the difference between living beings and machines (however complicated), then meaning (i.e., an internal interpretation of the situation, not forced on us from outside) should become the central focus of our interest. It is here that, in my opinion, the border between the living and nonliving lies. I know that it means becoming a proponent of vitalism, but what is biology without vitalism—without the viewpoint that living beings are irreducible to some "lower" levels of description? It should be the goal of every biologist to elaborate a modern version of vitalistic teaching devoid of the ballast of long-forgotten past quarrels. Understanding the hermeneutic situation present in us, in all living beings, is one of the first steps on our long path in such a direction.

REFERENCES

Abouheif, E. (1997). Developmental genetics and homology: a hierarchical approach. *Trends Genet. 13*, 405–408.

Abouheif, E., et al. (1997). Homology and developmental genes. *Trends Genet. 13*, 432–433.

Abram, D. (1996). The mechanical and the organic: Epistemological consequences of the Gaia hypothesis. In: *Gaia in Action: Science of the Living Earth*, P. Bunyard, ed. (Edinburgh, U.K.: Floris), 234–247.

Akam, M. (1998). *Hox* genes: From master genes to micromanagers. *Curr. Biol. 8*, R676–R678.

Alix, J.-H. and Hayes, D. (1983). Why are macromolecules modified post-synthetically? *Biol. Cell 47*, 139–160.

Amábile-Cuevas, C. F., ed. (1996). *Antibiotic Resistance: From Molecular Basics to Therapeutic Options* (Austin: Landes).

Amábile-Cuevas, C. F. and Cardenas-Garcia, M. (1996). Antibiotic resistance: Merely the tip of the iceberg of the plasmid driven evolution. In: *Antibiotic Resistance: From Molecular Basics to Therapeutic Options*, C. F. Amábile-Cuevas, ed. (Austin: Landes), 35–56.

Amábile-Cuevas, C. F. and Chicurel, M. E. (1992). Bacterial plasmids and gene flux. *Cell 70*, 189–199.

Amon, R. M. W. and Benner, R. (1994). Rapid cycling of high-molecular-weight dissolved organic matter in the ocean. *Nature 369*, 549–552.

Anderson, P. W. (1972). More is different. Broken symmetry and the nature of the hierarchical structure of science. *Science 177*, 393–396.

Arber, W. (1995). The generation of variation in bacterial genomes. *J. Mol. Evol. 40*, 7–12.

Arber, W., et al. (1994). Generation of genetic diversity by DNA rearrangements in resting bacteria. *FEMS Microbiol. Ecol. 15*, 5–13.

Arendt, D. and Nübler-Jung, K. (1996). Common ground plans in early brain development in mice and flies. *BioEssays 18*, 255–259.

Arendt, D. and Nübler-Jung, K. (1999). Dorsal or ventral: Similarities in fate maps and gastrulation patterns in annelids, arthropods and chordates. *Mech. Dev. 61*, 7–21.

Atkins, P. (1992). Will science ever fail? *New Scientist*, 8 Aug, 32–35.

Atlan, H. and Koppel, M. (1990). The cellular computer DNA: Program or data? *Bull. Math. Biol. 52*, 335–348.

Bailey, W. J., et al. (1997). Phylogenetic reconstruction of vertebrate Hox cluster duplications. *Mol. Biol. Evol. 14*, 843–853.

Baldwin, J. M. (1896). A new factor in evolution. *Am. Nat. 30*, 441–451, 536–553.

Bally-Cuif, L. and Wassef, M. (1995). Determination events in the nervous system of the vertebrate embryo. *Curr. Opin. Genet. Dev. 5*, 450–458.

Barnier, J. V. et al. (1995). The mouse B-raf gene encodes multiple protein isoforms with tissue-specific expression. *J. Biol. Chem. 270*, 23381–23389.

Bateson, G. (1988). *Mind and Nature. A Necessary Unity* (Toronto: Bantam).

Behmlander, R. M. and Dworkin, M. (1994a). Biochemical and structural analyses of the extracellular matrix fibrils of *Myxococcus xanthus. J. Bacteriol. 176*, 6295–6303.

Behmlander, R. M. and Dworkin, M. (1994b). Integral proteins of the extracellular matrix fibrils of *Myxococcus xanthus. J. Bacteriol. 176*, 6304–6311.

Beppu, T. (1992). Secondary metabolites as chemical signals for cellular differentiation. *Gene 115*, 159–165.

Berg, L. S. (1922). *Nomogenez, ili Evoljucia na Osnove Zakonomernostjej* [Nomogenesis, or Evolution Based on Rules]. (Peterburg: Gosudarstvennoje Izdatel'stvo).

Bertalanffy, L. von (1932). *Theoretische Biologie. Erster Band: Allgenmeine Theorie, Physikochemie, Aufbau und Entwicklung des Organismus.* (Berlin: Gebr. Bontraeger).

Bertalanffy, L. von (1960). *Problems of life. An evaluation of modern biological and scientific thought.* (New York: Harper & Brothers).

Bodnar, J. W., et al. (1997). Deciphering the language of the genome. *J. Theor. Biol. 189*, 183–193.

Bohr, J., et al. (1996). The formation of protein structure. *Europhys. News 27*, 50–54.

Bolker, J. and Raff, R. A. (1996). Developmental genetics and traditional homology. *BioEssays 18*, 489–494.

Bonhoeffer, S., et al. (1996). No signs of hidden language in noncoding DNA. *Phys. Rev. Lett. 76*, 1977.

Braithwaite, V. A. and Odling-Smee, L. (1999). The paradox of the stickleback: Different yet the same. *Trends Ecol. Evol. 14*, 460–461.

Brakefield, P. M., et al. (1996). Development, plasticity and evolution of butterfly eyespot patterns. *Nature 384*, 236–242.

Bray, D. (1995). Protein molecules as computational elements in living cells. *Nature 376*, 307–312.

Brookfield, J. F. Y. (1997a). Genetic redundancy. *Adv. Genet. 36*, 137–155.

Brookfield, J. F. Y. (1997b). Genetic redundancy: Screening for selection in yeast. *Curr. Biol. 7*, R366–R368

Brown, C. J. and Rosenzweig, R. F. (1998). Multiple duplications of yeast hexose transport genes in response to selection in a glucose-limited environment. *Mol. Biol. Evol.* 15, 931–942.

Bryngelson, J. D., et al. (1995). Funnels, pathways, and the energy landscape of protein folding: A synthesis. *Proteins Struct. Func. Genet.* 21, 167–195.

Burger, G., et al. (1996). Genes encoding the same three subunits of respiratory complex II are present in the mitochondrial DNA of two phylogenetically distant eukaryotes. *Proc. Natl. Acad. Sci. USA* 93, 2328–2332.

Cairns, J., et al. (1988). The origin of mutants. *Nature* 335, 142–145.

Cairns-Smith, A. G. (1985). *Seven Clues to the Origin of Life* (Cambridge: Cambridge University Press).

Cambridge Dictionary of Science and Technology (1992). (Cambridge: Cambridge University Press).

Carroll, S. B., Grenier, J. K., and Weatherbee, S. D. (2001). *From DNA to Diversity: Molecular Genetics and the Evolution of Animal Design.* (Malden, Mass.: Blackwell).

Cavalier-Smith, T. (1997). Cell and genome coevolution: Facultative anaerobiosis, glycosomes and kinetoplastan RNA editing. *Trends Genet.* 13, 6–8.

Chang, J. J., et al., eds. (1998). *Biophotons* (Dodrecht, The Netherlands: Kluwer).

Clegg, J. S. (1992). Cellular infrastructure and metabolic organization. *Curr. Topics Cell. Reg.* 33, 3–14.

Cochlan, W. P., et al. (1993). Spatial distribution of viruses, bacteria and chlorophyll a in neritic, oceanic and estuarine environments. *Mar. Ecol. Prog. Ser.* 92, 77–87.

Conway Morris, S. (1993). The fossil record and the early evolution of the Metazoa. *Nature* 361, 219–225.

Conway Morris, S. (1997). Molecular clocks: Defusing the Cambrian "explosion"? *Curr. Biol.* 7, R71–R74

Cooke, J., et al. (1997). Evolutionary origins and maintenance of redundant gene expression during metazoan development. *Trends Genet.* 13, 360–364.

Costerton, J. W., et al. (1995). Microbial biofilms. *Annu. Rev. Microbiol.* 49, 711–745.

Costerton, J. W., et al. (1994). Biofilms, the customized microniche. *J. Bacteriol.* 176, 2137–2142.

Couly, G. F., et al. (1993). The triple origin of skull in higher vertebrates. A study in quail-chick chimeras. *Development* 117, 409–429.

Dalton, H. M., et al. (1994). Substratum-induced morphological changes in a marine bacterium and their relevance to biofilm structure. *J. Bacteriol.* 176, 6900–6906.

d'Arcy Thompson, W. (1917). *On Growth and Form* (Cambridge: Cambridge University Press).

Davidson, E. H. (2001). *Genomic Regulatory Systems: Development and Evolution* (San Diego: Academic Press).

Davidson, E. H., et al. (1995). Origin of bilaterian body plans: Evolution of developmental regulatory mechanisms. *Science* 270, 1319–1325.

Davies, J. (1994). Inactivation of antibiotics and the dissemination of resistance genes. *Science* 264, 375–382.

Davies, J. (1998). The renaissance of microbiology. *Int. Microbiol. 1*, 255–258.

Davies, J. E. (1997). Origins, acquisition and dissemination of antibiotic resistance determinants. In: *CIBA Foundation Symposium 207: Antibiotic Resistance: Origin, Evolution, Selection and Spread* (Chichester, U.K.: Wiley), 15–35.

Dawkins, R. (1982). *The Extended Phenotype* (Oxford, England: Freeman).

Dawkins, R. (1987). *The Blind Watchmaker* (Harlow, U. K.: Longman).

Dawkins, R. (1989). *The Selfish Gene*, 2nd ed. (Oxford: Oxford University Press).

Dawkins, R. (1995). *River Out of Eden* (London: Weidenfeld and Nicolson).

de Beer, G. (1962). *Embryos and Ancestors*, 3rd ed. (Oxford, England: Clarendon).

Deely, J. (2001). Umwelt. *Semiotica 136*, 125–135.

De Keeper, P., et al. (1991). Turing-type chemical patterns in the chlorite-iodide-malonic acid reaction. *Physica D 49*, 161–169.

Delbrück, M. (1949). A physicist looks at biology. *Trans. Conn. Acad. Arts Sci. 38*, 173–190.

Demaster, D. J. (1999). Induction of microbial secondary metabolism. *Int. Microbiol. 1*, 259–264.

Dickinson, W. J. (1995). Molecules and morphology: Where is the homology? *Trends Genet. 11*, 119–121.

Dobzhansky, T., et al. (1977). *Evolution* (San Francisco: Freeman).

Drake, S. (1992). *Galileo* (Oxford: Oxford University Press).

Dreiseikelmann, B. (1994). Translocation of DNA across bacterial membranes. *Microbiol. Rev. 58*, 293–316.

Driesch, H. (1905). *Der Vitalismus als Geschichte und als Lehre* (Leipzig, Germany: Barth).

Driesch, H. (1914). *The History and Theory of Vitalism* (London: Macmillan).

Driesch, H. (1929). *The Science and Philosophy of the Organism. The Gifford Lectures Delivered before the University of Aberdeen in the Year 1907* (London: Adam and Charles Black).

Duboule, D. (1995). Vertebrate Hox genes and proliferation: An alternative pathway to homeosis? *Curr. Opin. Genet. Dev. 5*, 525–528.

Eco, U. (1964). *Apocalittici e integrati* (Milano, Italy: Bompiani). Partial translation into English: *Apocalypse Postponed* (Bloomington: Indiana University Press), 1994.

Edelman, G. M., et al., eds. (1990). *Morphoregulatory Molecules* (New York: Wiley).

Eden, K. (1997). *Hermeneutics and the Rhetorical Tradition* (New Haven, Conn.: Yale University Press).

Ehrlich, H. L. (1996). *Geomicrobiology* (New York: Dekker).

Eigen, M. and Winkler-Oswatitsch, R. (1992). *Steps towards Life. A Perspective on Evolution* (Oxford: Oxford University Press).

Emmeche, C. (1997). The biosemiotics of emergent properties in a pluralist ontology. In: *Semiosis. Evolution. Energy: Towards a Reconceptualization of the Sign*, E. Taborsky, ed. (Aachen, Germany: Shaker Verlag), 89–108.

Encyclopaedia Britannica (1995). (Chicago: Encycolpaedia Britannica, Inc.).

Engels, F. (1972). *Dialectics of Nature* (Moscow: Progress Publishers). Compiled from manuscript written from 1873–1882.

Erwin, D. H. (1999). The origin of bodyplans. *Am. Zool. 39*, 617–629.

Feynman, R. P., Leighton, R. B., and Sands, M. (1963). *The Feynman Lectures on Physics* (Reading, Mass.: Addison/Wesley).

Fiala, J. (1991). Biologické základy poznání (H. Maturana) [Biological fundamentals of knowledge (H. Maturana)]. *Scientia et Philosophia 1*, 35–55.

Figdor, M. C. and Stern, C. D. (1993). Segmental organization of embryonic diencephalon. *Nature 363*, 630–634.

Finkelstein, R. and Boncinelli, E. (1994). From fly head to mammalian forebrain: The story of *otd* and *Otx*. *Trends Genet. 10*, 310–315.

Finkelstein, R. and Perrimon, N. (1991). The molecular genetics of head development in *Drosophila melanogaster*. *Development 112*, 899–912.

Flegr, J. (1998). On the "origin" of natural selection by means of speciation. *Riv. Biol./Biol. Forum 91*, 291–304.

Fontaine-Pérus, J., et al. (1997). Mouse-chick chimera: A developmental model of murine neurogenic cells. *Development 124*, 3025–3036.

Foster, P. L. and Cairns, J. (1992). Mechanisms of directed mutation. *Genetics 131*, 783–789.

Foulkes, N. S. and Sassone-Corsi, P. (1996). CREM: A bZip transcription factor central to the cAMP nuclear response. In: *Eukaryotic Gene Transcription*, S. Goodbourn, ed. (Oxford: Oxford University Press), 59–101.

Fox, J. L. (1991). Microheterogeneity of biological macromolecules. *ASM News 57*, 310–316.

Frischer, M. E., et al. (1994). Plasmid transfer to indigenous marine bacterial populations by natural transformation. *FEMS Microbiol. Ecol. 15*, 127–135.

Fuhrman, J. A. (1999). Marine viruses and their biogeochemical and ecological effects. *Nature 399*, 541–548.

Gadamer, H.-G. (1985). *Griechische Philosophie II* (Tübingen, Germany: Mohr), 3–8.

Gadamer, H.-G. (1996). *Truth and Method,* 2nd rev. ed. (London: Sheed and Ward). Originally published 1960.

Galleni, L. (1994). Teilhard de Chardin's search for laws in evolutive orientation: A philosophical and/or scientific challenge. In: *Studies in Science and Technology*, G. V. Coyne and K. Schmitz-Moormann, eds. (Geneva: Labor et Fides), 121–126.

Galleni, L. (1995). How does the Teihlardian vision of evolution compare with contemporary theories? *Zygon 30*, 25–45.

Gallori, E., et al. (1994). Transformation of *Bacillus subtilis* by DNA bound on clay in non-sterile soil. *FEMS Microbiol. Ecol. 15*, 119–126.

Gans, C. and Northcutt, R. G. (1983). Neural crest and the origin of vertebrates: A new head. *Science 220*, 268–274.

Garcia Fernandez, J. and Holland, P. W. H. (1994). Archetypal organization of the amphioxus Hox gene cluster. *Nature 370*, 563–566.

Gibson, G. (1999). Insect evolution: Redesigning the fruitfly. *Curr. Biol. 9*, R86–R89.

Gibson, G. and Hogness, D. S. (1996). Effect of polymorphism in the *Drosophila* regulatory gene Ultrabithorax on homeotic stability. *Science 271*, 200–203.

Gilbert, S. F. (1994). *Developmental Biology* (Sunderland, Mass.: Sinauer).

Gilbert, S. F. and Sarkar, S. (2000). Embracing complexity: Organicism for the 21st century. *Dev. Dynam. 219*, 1–9.

Gilbert, S. F., et al. (1996). Resynthesizing evolutionary and developmental biology. *Dev. Biol. 173*, 357–372.

Gillespie, J. H. (1991). *The Causes of Molecular Evolution* (New York: Oxford University Press).

Gold, T. (1999). *The Deep Hot Biosphere* (New York: Copernicus/Springer).

Goodman, A. E., et al. (1994). Gene transfer among bacteria under conditions of nutrient depletion in simulated and natural aquatic environments. *FEMS Microbiol. Ecol. 15*, 55–60.

Goodsell, D. S. (1991). Inside a living cell. *Trends Biochem. Sci. 16*, 203–206.

Goodwin, B. C. (1982). Development and evolution. *J. Theor. Biol. 97*, 43–55.

Goodwin, B. C. (1993). Development as a robust natural process. In: *SFI Studies in the Sciences of Complexity*, Vol. III, *Thinking about Biology*, W. D. Stein and F. J. Varela, eds. (Reading, Mass.: Addison-Wesley), 123–148.

Goody, R. (1995). *Principles of Atmospheric Physics and Chemistry* (New York: Oxford University Press).

Gorczynski, R. M. and Steele, E. J. (1980). Inheritance of acquired immunological tolerance to foreign histocompatibility antigens in mice. *Proc. Natl. Acad. Sci. USA 77*, 2871–2875.

Gordon, J. I., et al. (1991). Protein N-myristoylation. *J. Biol. Chem. 266*, 8647–8650.

Gorlich, D. and Mattaj, I. W. (1996). Nucleocytoplasmic transport. *Science 271*, 1513–1518.

Gould, S. J. (1977). *Ontogeny and Phylogeny* (Cambridge, Mass.: Harvard University Press).

Gould, S. J. (1989). *Wonderful Life* (New York: Norton).

Gould, S. J. (1991). Kropotkin was no crackpot. In: *Bully for Brontosaurus*, S. J. Gould, ed. (New York: Norton), 325–339.

Gould, S. J. (1996). *The Mismeasure of Man.* (New York: Norton).

Grassé, P.-P. (1973). *L'Évolution du Vivant. Matériaux pour Une Nouvelle Théorie Transformiste* (Paris: Albin Michel). English version: *Evolution of Living Organisms. Evidence for a New Theory of Transformation* (New York: Academic Press), 1977.

Graves, J. E. and Somero, G. (1982). Electrophoretic and functional enzymic evolution in four species of eastern Pacific barracudas from different thermal environments. *Evolution 36*, 97–106.

Graves, J. E., et al. (1983). Kinetic and electrophoretic differentiation of lactate dehydrogenases of teleost species from the Atlantic and Pacific coasts of Panama. *Evolution 37*, 30–37.

Groisman, E. A. and Ochman, H. (1996). Pathogenicity islands: Bacterial evolution in quantum leaps. *Cell 87*, 791–794.

Grondin, J. (1994). *Introduction to Philosophical Hermeneutics* (New Haven, Conn.: Yale University Press).

Guerrero, R. and Pedrós-Alio, C., eds. (1993). *Trends in Microbial Ecology: Proceedings of the Sixth International Symposium on Microbial Ecology* (Barcelona: Spanish Society for Microbiology).

Gurwitsch, A. G. (1930). *Die histologischen Grundlagen der Biologie* [The Histological Basis of Biology] (Jena, Germany: Fischer).

Gurwitsch, A. G. (1944). *Teorija Biologicheskovo Polja* [The Theory of Biological Field] (Moscow: Sovetskaja Nauka).

Hacker, J., et al. (1997). Pathogenicity islands of virulent bacteria: Structure, function and impact on microbial evolution. *Mol. Microbiol. 23*, 1089–1097.

Hall, B. G. (1990). Spontaneous point mutations that occur more often when advantageous than when neutral. *Genetics 126*, 5–16.

Hall, R. M., et al. (1996). Gene cassettes and integrons: Moving antibiotic resistance genes in Gram-negative bacteria. In: *Antibiotic Resistance: From Molecular Basics to Therapeutic Options*, C. F. Amábile-Cuevas, ed. (Austin: Landes), 19–34.

Hameroff, S. R. (1994). Quantum coherence in microtubules: A neural basis for emergent consciousness? *J. Consciousness Stud. 1*, 91–118.

Hamilton, W. D. and Lenton, T. M. (1998). Spora and Gaia: How microbes fly with their clouds. *Ethol. Ecol. Evol. 10*, 1–16.

Hanken, J., et al. (1997). Mechanistic basis of life-history evolution in anuran amphibians: Direct development. *Am. Zool. 37*, 160–171.

Harold, F. M. (1990). To shape a cell: An inquiry into the causes of morphogenesis of microorganisms. *Microbiol. Rev. 54*, 381–431.

Harold, F. M. (1995). From morphogens to morphogenesis. *Microbiology 141*, 2765–2778.

Hartwell, L. H., et al. (1999). From molecular to modular biology. *Nature 402*, C47–C52.

Havel, I. M. (1996). Scale dimensions on nature. *Int. J. Gen. Syst. 24*, 295–324.

Heelan, P. A. (1998). The scope of hermeneutics in natural science. *Stud. Hist. Philos. Sci. 29*, 273–278.

Heidegger, M. (1996). *Being and Time.* (Albany: SUNY Press). Originally published 1927.

Heisenberg, W. (1959). *Physics and Philosophy. The Revolution in Modern Science* (St. Leonards, Australia: Allen and Unwin).

Held, L. E., Jr. (1992). *Models for Embryonic Periodicity* (Basel, Switzerland: Karger).

Helmholtz, H. (1896). *Vorträge und Reden II*, 4th ed. (Braunschweig, Germany: Vieweg und Sohn). Originally published 1875.

Helmhotz, H. (1982). *Über die Erhaltung der Kraft* (Berlin: Akademie-Verlag). Originally published 1847.

Henderson's Dictionary of Biological Terms (1989). (London: Longman).

Herault, Y., et al. (1999). *Hox* gene expression in limbs: Colinearity by opposite regulatory controls. *Dev. Biol. 208*, 257–165.

Hermansson, M. and Linberg, C. (1994). Gene transfer in the marine environment. *FEMS Microbiol. Ecol. 15*, 47–54.

Hess, B. and Mikhailov, A. (1995). Microscopic self-organization in living cells: A study of time matching. *J. Theor. Biol. 176*, 181–184.

Hess, B. and Mikhailov, A. (1996). Transition from molecular chaos to coherent spiking of enzymic reactions in small spatial volumes. *Biophys. Chem.* 58, 365–368.

Higgins, N. P. (1992). Death and transfiguration in bacteria. *Trends Biochem. Sci.* 17, 207–211.

Ho, M. W. (1988). On not holding nature still: Evolution by process, not by consequence. In: *Evolutionary Processes and Metaphors*, M. W. Ho and S. W. Fox, eds. (Chichester, U.K.: Wiley), 117–144.

Ho, M. W. (1993). *The Rainbow and the Worm* (Singapore: World Scientific).

Ho, M. W. (1994). What is (Schrödinger's) negentropy? In: *What Is Controlling Life?* E. Gnaiger et al., eds. (Innsbruck, Austria: Innsbruck University Press), 50–61.

Ho, M. W., ed. (1995). *Living Processes*, Book 2, *Bioenergetics* (Milton Keynes, U. K.: Open University).

Hoffmeyer, J. (1996). *Signs of Meaning in the Universe* (Bloomington: Indiana University Press).

Hoffmeyer, J. (1997). The global semiosphere. In: *Semiotics around the World: Proceedings of the Fifth Congress of the International Association for Semiotic Studies*, I. Rauch and G. F. Carr, eds. (Berlin,: Mouton de Gruyter), 933–936.

Hoffmeyer, J. (1998). The unfolding semiosphere. In: *Evolutionary Systems. Biological and Epistemiological Perspectives on Selection and Self-organization*, G. Van de Vijver et al., eds. (Dordrecht, The Netherlands: Kluwer), 281–293.

Hofstadter, D. R. (1979). *Gödel, Escher, Bach: An Eternal Golden Braid* (New York: Vintage).

Huisman, G. W. and Kolter, R. (1994). Sensing starvation: A homoserine lactone-dependent signaling pathway in *Escherichia coli*. *Science* 265, 537–539.

Huttner, W. (1987). Protein tyrosine sulfation. *Trends Biochem. Sci.* 12, 361–363.

Israeloff, N. E. et al. (1996). Can Zipf distinguish language from noise in noncoding DNA? *Phys. Rev. Lett.* 76, 1976

Jablonka, E. and Lamb, M. J. (1995). *Epigenetic Inheritance and Evolution. The Lamarckian Dimension* (Oxford: Oxford University Press).

Jacob, F. (1974). *The Logic of Living Systems* (London: Allen Laine).

Jacob, F. (1977). Evolution and tinkering. *Science* 196, 1161–1166.

Jantsch, E. (1979). *The Self-organizing Universe* (Oxford, England: Pergamon).

Jeffery, W. R. (1994). A model of ascidian development and developmental modifications during evolution. *J. Mar. Biol. Assn. UK* 74, 35–48.

Johnson, T. C., et al. (1996). Late Pleistocene desiccation of Lake Victoria and rapid evolution of cichlid fishes. *Science* 273, 1091–1093.

Kaiser, D. and Losick, R. (1993). How and why bacteria talk to each other. *Cell* 73, 873–885.

Kanehisa, M. (2000). *Post-genome Informatics* (Oxford: Oxford University Press).

Kant, I. (1988). *The Critique of Pure Reason, the Critique of Practical Reason and Other Ethical Treatises, The Critique of Judgement*, 30th ed. (Chicago: Encyclopaedia Britannica, Inc.).

Kauffman, S. A. (1993). *The Origins of Order. Self-organization and Selection in Evolution* (New York: Oxford University Press).

Kauffman, S. A. (2000). *Investigations* (Oxford: Oxford University Press).

Kobata, A. (1992). Structures and functions of the sugar chains of glycoproteins. *Eur. J. Biochem. 209*, 483–501.

Kornblihtt, et al. (1996). The fibronectin gene as a model for splicing and transcription studies. *FASEB J. 10*, 248–257.

Kováč, L. (1999/2000). Potreba syntézy prírodných a kultúrnych vied I-IV. [A need for unification of the natural and cultural sciences, pts. 1–4]. *Vesmír 78*, 644–649, 697–700; *79*, 46–49, 105–109.

Kratochvíl, Z. (1994). *Filozofie živé přírody*. [A philosophy of living nature] (Prague: Herrmann and Synové).

Kropotkin, P. (1902). *Mutual Aid: A Factor of Evolution* (New York: McClure Phillips).

Krumbein, W. E. (1996). Geophysiology and parahistology of the interactions of organisms with the environment. *Mar. Ecol. 17*, 1–21.

Kull, K. (1998). Organism as a self-reading text: Anticipation and semiosis. *Int. J. Comput. Anticip. Syst. 1*, 93–104.

Kull, K. (2000). Copy *versus* translate, meme *versus* sign: development of biological textuality. *Eur. J. Semiotic Stud. 12*, 101–120.

Lan, R. T. and Reeves, P. R. (1996). Gene transfer is a major factor in bacterial evolution. *Mol. Biol. Evol. 13*, 47–55.

Lenski, R. E. (1998). Bacterial evolution and the cost of antibiotic resistance. *Int. Microbiol. 1*, 265–270.

Lenton, T. M. (1998). Gaia and natural selection. *Nature 394*, 439–446.

Lewis, D. L. and Gattie, G. T. (1991). The ecology of quiescent microbes. *ASM News 57*, 27–32.

Lewin, K. (1922). *Der Begriff der Genese in Physik, Biologie und Entwicklungsgeschichte* [The Concept of Genesis in Physics, Biology, and Evolution] (Berlin: Springler).

Li, W.-H. (1997). *Molecular Evolution* (Sunderland, Mass.: Sinauer).

Lipshitz, H. D. (1996). "Resynthesis or revisionism?" [letter to editor]. *Dev. Biol. 177*, 616–619.

Lis, H. and Sharon, N. (1993). Protein glycosylation. Structural and functional aspects. *Eur. J. Biochem. 218*, 1–27.

Lodish, H., et al. (1995). *Molecular Cell Biology* (New York: Scientific American).

Lorenz, M. G. and Wackernagel, W. (1994). Bacterial gene transfer by natural genetic transformation in the environment. *Microbiol. Rev. 58*, 563–602.

Lovelock, J. E. (1975). *Gaia. A New Look at Life on Earth* (Oxford: Oxford University Press).

Lovelock, J. E. (1990). *The Ages of Gaia* (New York: Bantam).

Lovelock, J. E. (1996). The Gaia hypothesis. In: *Gaia in Action. Science of the Living Earth*, P. Bunyard, ed. (Edinburgh, U. K.: Floris), 15–33.

Lovelock, J. E. (1997). A geophysiologist's thoughts on the natural sulfur cycle. *Philos. Trans. R. Soc. Lond. [Biol.] 352*, 143–147.

Lovelock, J. E. and Kump, L. R. (1994). Failure of climate regulation in a geophysiological model. *Nature 369*, 732–734.

Lumsden, A. and Krumlauf, R. (1996). Patterning the vertebrate neuraxis. *Science 274*, 1109–1115.

Lutz, B., et al. (1996). Rescue of *Drosophila* labial null mutant by the chicken ortholog Hoxb-1 demonstrates that the function of Hox genes is phylogenetically conserved. *Gene Dev. 10*, 176–184.

Lysenko, T. D. (1952). O polozhenii v biologicheskoi nauke. Doklad na sessii Akademii selskokhoziaistvennykh nauk V. I. Lenina, 31. 7. 1948 [On the situation in biology. A presentation read at the session of the Lenin All-Union Academy of Agricultural Sciences, July 31, 1948]. In: *Agrobiologia* (Moscow: Gosudarstvennoe Izdatelstvo Selskokhoziaistvennoi Literatury), 546–581.

Lysenko, T. D. (1958). O biologicheskom vide i vidoobrazovanii. [About biological species and speciation] In: *Izbrannyie Sochinjenia II.* (Moscow: Gosudarstvennoe Izdatelstvo Selskokhoziaistvennoi Literatury), 273–303.

Mahner, M. and Bunge, M. (1997). *Foundations of Biophilosophy* (Berlin: Springer).

Malá československá encyklopedie (1987). [Sort Czechoslovak Encyclopedia]. (Prague: Academia).

Mantegna, R. N., et al. (1994). Systematic analysis of coding and noncoding DNA sequences using methods of statistical linguistics. *Phys. Rev. Lett. 73*, 3169–3172.

Maplestone, R. A., et al. (1992). The evolutionary role of secondary metabolites—a review. *Gene 115*, 151–157.

Margulis, L. (1996). Archaeal–eubacterial mergers in the origin of Eukarya: Phylogenetic classification of life. *Proc. Natl. Acad. Sci. USA 93*, 1071–1076.

Margulis, L., et al. (1996). We are all symbionts. In: *Gaia in Action. Science of the Living Earth,* P. Bunyard, ed. (Edinburgh, U. K.: Floris), 167–185.

Markoš, A. (1995). The ontogeny of Gaia: The role of microorganisms in planetary information network. *J. Theor. Biol. 176*, 175–180.

Markoš, A. (1999). Planetary superorganism and symbiogenesis. In: *Endocytobiology,* Vol. 2,*From Symbiosis to Eukaryotes,* E. Wagner et al., eds. (Geneva: Geneva University Press), 719–740

Markoš, A. (2000). *Tajemství hladiny. Hermeneutika živého* [the Czech version of this book]. (Prague, Czech Rep.: Vesmír).

Mathews, C. K. (1993). The cell—bag of enzymes or network of channels? *J. Bacteriol. 175*, 6377–6381.

Matic, I., et al. (1995). Interspecies gene exchange in bacteria: The role of SOS and mismatch repair systems in evolution of species. *Cell 80*, 507–515.

Matic, I., et al. (1997). Highly variable mutation rates in commensal and pathogenic *Escherichia coli. Science 277*, 1833–1834.

Matsuo, I., et al. (1995). Mouse Otx2 functions in the formation and patterning of rostral head. *Gene Dev. 9*, 2646–2658.

Matthews, E. S. and White, S. (1993). Electron transfer proteins—enzymes. *Curr. Opin. Struct. Biol. 3*, 902–911.

Mayer, M. and Bukau, B. (1999). Molecular chaperones: The busy life of Hsp90. *Curr. Biol. 9*, R322–R325

Maynard Smith, J. (1990). Models of a dual inheritance system. *J. Theor. Biol. 143*, 41–53.

Maynard Smith, J. (1991). The evolution of bacteria: does sex matter? In: *The Unity of Evolutionary Biology: Proceedings of the Fourth International Congress on Systematics and Evolutionary Biology*, E. C. Dudley, ed. (Portland, Or.: Dioscorides), 417–423.

Maynard Smith, J. (1992). Analyzing mosaic structure of genes. *J. Mol. Evol. 34*, 126–129.

Maynard Smith, J. (1996). *Evolutionary Genetics* (Oxford: Oxford University Press).

Maynard Smith, J. and Szathmáry, E. (1995). *The Major Transitions in Evolution* (Oxford, England: Freeman).

Maynard Smith, J., et al. (1991). Localized sex in bacteria. *Nature 349*, 29–31.

Maynard Smith, J., et al. (1993). How clonal are bacteria? *Proc. Natl. Acad. Sci. USA 90*, 4384–4388.

Mcadams, H. H. and Shapiro, L. (1995). Circuit simulation of genetic networks. *Science 269*, 650–656.

McClare, C. W. F. (1971). Chemical machines, Maxwell's demon and living organisms. *J. Theor. Biol. 30*, 1–34.

McClare, C. W. F. (1972). A "molecular energy" muscle model. *J. Theor. Biol. 35*, 569–595.

McClintock, B. (1984). The significance of responses of the genome to challenge. *Science 226*, 792–801.

Medvedev, Z. A. (1969). *The Rise and Fall of T. D. Lysenko* (New York: Columbia University Press).

Mel, S. F. and Mekalanos, J. J. (1996). Modulation of horizontal gene transfer in pathogenic bacteria by in vivo signals. *Cell 87*, 795–798.

Merriam Webster's Collegiate Dictionary. (1993). 10th ed. (Springfield, Mass.: Merriam-Webster).

Michel, G. F. and Moore, C. L. (1995). *Developmental Psychobiology, an Interdisciplinary Science* (Cambridge, Mass.: MIT Press).

Monod, J. (1979). *Chance and Necessity* (London: Collins/Fount).

Müller, W. A. (1996). *Developmental Biology* (Heidelberg, Germany: Springer).

Nasmyth, K., et al. (1991). Some facts and thoughts on cell cycle control in yeast. *Cold Spring Harb. Symp. Quant. Biol. 56*, 9–16.

Neubauer, Z. (1990). Za kreacionismus a vitalismus [For creationism and vitalism]. In: *Hledání Společného Jazyka* I. Šetlík, ed. (Prague, Czech Rep.: Czechoslovak Academy of Sciences Institute of Physiology), 138–147.

Neubauer, Z. (1996). Mimo dobro a zlo: Nietszchova biologická ontologie [Beyond good and evil: Biological ontology of Nietzsche]. *Kritický Sborník 16*, 15–22.

Neubauer, Z. (1997). Esse obiectivum—esse intentionale. Cestou k fenomenologické biologii.[Esse obiectivum—esse intentionale. Towards phenomenological biology]. *Sci. Philos. 8*, 113–160.

Neubauer, Z. (2001). Biomoc. život jako vůle k moci. [Biopower. Life as a will toward power.]. Available at: http://www.vhled.cz, accessed May 2001.

Neubauer, Z., et al. (1989). *Geometrie Živého.* [Geometry of the Living.] (Prague, Czech Rep.: Czechoslovak Academy of Sciences, Institute of Physiology), 191–234.

Nietzsche, F. (1984). *Beyond Good and Evil. Prelude to a Philosophy of the Future* (New York: Random House).

Nietzsche, F. (1997). *Untimely Meditations* (Cambridge: Cambridge University Press).

Nowak, M. A., et al. (1997). Evolution of genetic redundancy. *Nature 388*, 167–171.

Ochman, H. and Groisman, E. A. (1995). The evolution of invasion by enteric bacteria. *Can. J. Microbiol. 41*, 555–561.

Ovádi, J. (1995). *Cell Architecture and Metabolite Channeling* (Heidelberg, Germany: Springer).

Paget, E. and Simonet, P. (1994). On the track of natural transformation in soil. *FEMS Microbiol. Ecol. 15*, 109–117.

Panganiban, G., et al. (1997). The origin and evolution of animal appendages. *Proc. Natl. Acad. Sci. USA 94*, 5162–5166.

Parker, A. and Kornfield, I. (1997). Evolution of the mitochondrial DNA control region in the mbuna (Cichlidae) species flock of Lake Malawi, East Africa. *J. Mol. Evol. 45*, 70–83.

Patthy, L. (1995). *Protein Evolution by Exon-Shuffling* (New York: Springer).

Pawson, T. and Scott, J. D. (1997). Signaling through scaffold, anchoring, and adapter proteins. *Science 278*, 2075–2080.

Penrose, R. (1997). *The Large, the Small and the Human Mind* (Cambridge: Cambridge University Press).

Pfanner, N. (1998). Mitochondrial import: Crossing the aqueous intermembrane space. *Curr. Biol. 8*, R262–R265

Pfanner, N., et al. (1997). Mitochondrial preprotein translocase. *Annu. Rev. Cell Dev. Biol. 13*, 25–51.

Piaget, J. (1971). *Structuralism* (London: Routlege and Kegan Paul).

Pigliucci, M. (1997). Butterflies in the spotlight. *BioEssays 19*, 285–286.

Pokorný, J., ed. (1995). *Biophysical Aspects of Coherence. Neural Network World* [Special Issue] 5(5).

Pokorný, J. and Wu, T.-M. (1998). *Biophysical Aspects of Coherence and Biological Order* (Prague: Academia).

Popov, O., et al. (1996). Linguistic complexity of protein sequences as compared to texts of human languages. *BioSystems 38*, 65–74.

Porter, K. R., et al. (1983). The cytoplasmic matrix. *Mod. Cell Biol. 2*, 259–302.

Prigogine, I. (1980). *From Being to Becoming. Time and Complexity in the Physical Sciences* (San Francisco: Freeman).

Prigogine, I. and Stengers, I. (1977). The new alliance. *Scientia 112*, 320–332, 643–652.

Prigogine, I. and Stengers, I. (1985). *Order Out of Chaos* (London: Flamingo).

Prusinkiewicz, P. and Lindenmeyer, A. (1990). *The Algorithmic Beauty of Plants* (New York: Springer).

Prusinkiewicz, P. (1999) Paradigms of pattern formation: Towards a computational theory of morphogenesis. In: *Pattern Formation in Biology, Vision and Dynamics*, A. Carbone, M. Gromov, and P. Prusinkiewicz, eds. (Singapore: World Scientific), 3–23.

Ptashne, M. (1987). *A Genetic Switch* (Palo Alto, Calif.: Blackwell).

Ptashne, M. and Gann, A. (1998). Imposing specificity by localization: Mechanism and evolvability. *Curr. Biol. 8*, R812–R822

Rádl, E. (1909). *Dějiny Vývojových Theorií v Biologii XIX. Století* [History of Evolutionary Theories in the 19th Century] (Prague: Leichter).

Raff, E. C., et al. (1999). A novel ontogenetic pathway in hybrid embryos between species with different modes of development. *Development 129*, 1937–1945.

Raff, R. A. (1996). *The Shape of Life. Genes, Development, and the Evolution of Animal Form* (Chicago: University of Chicago Press).

Random House Webster's College Dictionary (1990). Glencoe ed. (New York: Random House, Inc.)

Richardson, et al. (1997). There is no highly conserved embryonic stage in the vertebrates: Implications for current theories of evolution and development. *Anat. Embryol. 196*, 91–106.

Ricoeur, P. (1974). *The Conflict of Interpretations: Essays in Hermeneutics.* (Evanston, Ill.: Northwestern University Press).

Ricoeur, P. (1976). *Interpretation Theory: Discourse and the Surplus of Meaning* (Fort Worth: Texas Christian University Press).

Ridley, M. (1994). *The Red Queen. Sex and the Evolution of Human Nature* (New York: Penguin).

Rogers, B. T. and Kaufman, T. C. (1997). Structure of the insect head in ontogeny and phylogeny: A view from *Drosophila. Int. Rev. Cytol. 174*, 1–84.

Roll-Hansen, N. (1985). New perspectives on Lysenko? *Ann. Sci. 42*, 261–278.

Ruddon, R. W. and Bedows, E. (1997). Assisted protein folding. *J. Biol. Chem. 272*, 3125–3128.

Russo, V. E. A., et al., eds. (1992). *Development. The Molecular Genetic Approach* (Berlin: Springer).

Russo, V. E. A., et al., eds. (1996). *Epigenetic Mechanisms of Gene Regulation* (Plainview, N.Y.: Cold Spring Harbor Laboratory Press).

Rutherford, S. L. and Lindquist, S. (1998). Hsp90 as a capacitor for morphological evolution. *Nature 396*, 336–342.

Ruyer, R. (1974). *La Gnose de Princeton* [The Princeton Gnosis]. (Paris: Fayard).

Saga, Y., et al. (1992). Mice develop normally without tenascin. *Gene Dev. 6*, 1821–1831.

Salthe, S. N. (1991). Two forms of hierarchy theory in Western discourses. *Int. J. Gen. Syst. 18*, 251–264.

Salyers, A. A. and Shoemaker, N. B. (1996). More than just plasmids: Newly discovered gene transfer agents and their implications for controlling the spread of resistance. In: *Antibiotic resistance: From Molecular Basics to Therapeutic Options,* C. F. Amábile-Cuevas, ed. (Austin: Landes) 1–18.

Satoh, N. and Jeffery, W. R. (1995). Chasing tails in ascidians: Developmental insights into the origin and evolution of chordates. *Trends Genet. 11*, 354–359.

Saussure, F. (1959). *Course in General Linguistics* (New York: Philosophical Library). Originally published 1916.

Schaff, J., et al. (1997). A general computational framework for modeling cellular structure and function. *Biophys. J. 73*, 1135–1146.

Schlichtling, C. D. and Pigliucci, M. (1998). *Phenotypic Evolution. A Reaction Norm Perspective* (Sunderland, Mass.: Sinauer).

Schmalhausen, I. I. (1986). *Factors of Evolution. The Theory of Stabilizing Selection* (Chicago: University of Chicago Press). Originally published 1946.

Schweber, S. S. (1993). Physics, community and the crisis in physical theory. *Phys. Today* November, 34–40.

Searls, D. B. (1992). The linguistics of DNA. *Am. Sci. 80*, 579–591.

Sebeok, T. A., and Umiker-Sebeok, J., eds. (1992). *Biosemiotics. The Semiotic Web 1991* (Berlin: Mouton de Gruyter).

Sermonti, G. (1987). Structure biology at Osaka [editorial]. *Riv. Biol./Biol. Forum 80*, 159–160.

Shapiro, J. A. (1995). The significances of bacterial colony patterns. *BioEssays 17*, 597–607.

Shapiro, J. A. and Dworkin, M., eds. (1997). *Bacteria as Multicellular Organisms* (New York: Oxford University Press).

Shapiro, L. and Losick, R. (1997). Protein localization and cell fate in bacteria. *Science 276*, 712–718.

Sharman, A. C. and Brand, M. (1998). Evolution and homology of the nervous system: Cross-phylum rescues of *otd/Otx* genes. *Trends Genet. 14*, 211–214.

Shimamura, K., et al. (1995). Longitudinal organization of the anterior neural plate and neural tube. *Development 121*, 3923–3933.

Shorter Oxford English Dictionary on Historical Principles (1990). 3rd ed. (New York: Oxford University Press).

Sibatani, A. (1987a). An attempt to structuralize biology. *Riv. Biol./Biol. Forum 80*, 178–182.

Sibatani, A. (1987b). On structuralist biology. *Riv. Biol./Biol. Forum 80*, 558–564.

Sikorski, R. S., et al. (1990). Trans-kingdom promiscuity. *Nature 345*, 581–582.

Slack, J. M. W., et al. (1990). The zootype and the phylotypic stage. *Nature 361*, 490–492.

Slauch, J., et al. (1997). Survival in a cruel world: How *Vibrio cholerae* and *Salmonella* respond to an unwilling host. *Gene Dev. 11*, 1761–1774.

Sniegowski, P. D. (1995). The origin of adaptive mutants: Random or nonrandom? *J. Mol. Evol. 40*, 94–101.

Sonea, S. and Panisset, M. (1983). *A New Bacteriology* (Boston, Mass.: Jones and Bartlett).

Sonneborn, T. M. (1950). Heredity, environment, and politics. *Science 111*, 529–539.

Srere, P. A. (1990). Citric acid cycle redux. *Trends Biochem. Sci. 15*, 411–412.

Stent, G. S. (1972). Prematurity and uniqueness of scientific discovery. *Sci. Am. 227* 84–93.

Stephens, C. and Shapiro, L. (1996). Bacterial pathogenesis: Delivering the payload. *Curr. Biol. 6*, 927–930.

Stiassny, M. L. J. and Meyer, A. (1999). Cichlids of the rift lakes. *Sci. Am. 280*, 44–49.

Stubblefield, E. (1986). A theory of developmental control by a program encoded in the genome. *J. Theor. Biol. 118*, 129–143.

Suarez, M. and Russmann, H. (1999). Molecular mechanisms of *Salmonella* invasion: The type III secretion system of the pathogenicity island 1. *Int. Microbiol. 1*, 197–204.

Swift, S., et al. (1996). Quorum sensing: A population-density component in the determination of bacterial phenotype. *Trends Biochem. Sci. 21*, 214–219.

Symonds, N. (1994). Directed mutation: A current perspective. *J. Theor. Biol. 169*, 317–322.

Syvanen, M. (1985). Cross-species gene transfer: Implications for a new theory of evolution. *J. Theor. Biol. 112*, 333–343.

Tabin, C. J., et al. (1999). Out on a limb: Parallels in vertebrate and invertebrate limb patterning and the origin of appendages. *Am. Zool. 39*, 650–663.

Taddei, F., et al. (1997). Role of mutator alleles in adaptive evolution. *Nature 387*, 700–702.

Teilhard de Chardin, P. (1956). *La Place de l'Homme dans la Nature. Le Groupe Zoologique Humain* (Paris: Seuil).

Tschäpe, H. (1994). The spread of plasmids as a function of bacterial adaptability. *FEMS Microbiol. Ecol. 15*, 23–31.

Tsonis, A. A., et al. (1997). Is DNA a language? *J. Theor. Biol. 184*, 25–29.

Umesono, Y., et al. (1999). Distinct structural domains in the planarian brain defined by the expression of evolutionary conserved homeobox genes. *Dev. Genes Evol. 209*, 31–39.

Valentine, J. W., et al. (1999). Fossils, molecules and embryos: New perspectives on the Cambrian explosion. *Development 126*, 851–859.

Voss, R. F. (1996). Comment on "linguistic" features of noncoding DNA sequences. *Phys. Rev. Lett. 76*, 1978.

Waddington, C. H. (1975). *The Evolution of an Evolutionist* (Edinburgh: Edinburgh University Press). Originally published 1941–1961.

Wagner, G. P. (1989). The biological homology concept. *Annu. Rev. Ecol. Syst. 20*, 51–69.

Wallis, G. A. (1995). The importance of being sulfated. *Curr. Biol. 5*, 225–227.

Warren, R. W., et al. (1994). Evolution of homeotic gene regulation and function in flies and butterflies. *Nature 372*, 458–461.

Watson, J. D., et al. (1987). *Molecular Biology of the Gene,* 4th ed. (Menlo Park, Calif.: Benjamin/Cummings).

Watt, W. B. (1977). Adaptations at specific loci. I. Natural selection on phosphoglucose isomerase of *Colias* butterflies: Biochemical and population aspects. *Genetics 87*, 177–194.

Watt, W. B. (1983). Adaptation at specific loci. II. Demographic and biochemical elements in the maintenance of the *Colias* PGI polymorphism. *Genetics 103*, 691–724.

Webster, G. (1984). The relations of natural forms. In: *Beyond Neo-Darwinism. An Introduction to the New Evolutionary Paradigm,* M. W. Ho and P. T. Saunders, eds. (London: Academic Press), 193–217.

Webster, G. (1987). The nature and scope of structuralist analysis in biology. *Riv. Biol./Biol. Forum 80*, 173–177.

Webster, G. and Goodwin, B. C. (1982). The origin of species: A structuralist approach. *J. Soc. Biol. Str.. 5*, 15–47.

Webster, G. and Goodwin, B. C. (1996). *Form and Transformation. Generative and Relational Principles in Biology* (Cambridge: Cambridge University Press).

Welch, G. R. and Easterby, J. S. (1994). Metabolic channeling versus diffusion: Transition-time analysis. *Trends Biochem. Sci. 19*, 193–197.

West, G. B., et al. (1999). The fourth dimension of life: Fractal geometry and allometric scaling of organisms. *Science 284*, 1677–1699.

Westerhoff, H. V. and Welch, G. R. (1992). Enzyme organization and the direction of metabolic flow—physicochemical considerations. *Curr. Topics Cell. Reg. 33*, 361–390.

Williams, G. R. (1997). *The Molecular Biology of Gaia* (New York: Columbia University Press).

Wilson, D. S. and Sober, E. (1989). Reviving the superorganism. *J. Theor. Biol. 136*, 337–356.

Wilson, E. O. (1978). *On Human Nature* (Cambridge: Harvard University Press).

Wilson, E. O. (1998). *Consilience. The Unity of Knowledge* (New York: Knopf).

Wolpert, L. (1991). *The Triumph of the Embryo* (Oxford: Oxford University Press).

Wolpert, L. (1992). *The Unnatural Nature of Science* (London: Faber).

Wolpert, L., et al. (1998). *Principles of Development* (London: Current Biology).

Wostemeyer, J., et al. (1997). Horizontal gene transfer in the rhizosphere: A curiosity or a driving force in evolution? *Adv. Bot. Res. 24*, 399–429.

Wray, G. A., et al. (1996). Molecular evidence for deep Precambrian divergences among metazoan phyla. *Science 274*, 568–573.

Zimmermann, R. (1998). The role of molecular chaperones in protein transport into the mammalian endoplasmic reticulum. *Biol. Chem. 379*, 275–282.

INDEX